A Cartoon Collection
by Mark Heath

Andrews McMeel
Publishing

Kansas City · Sydney · London

Andrews McMeel Publishing, LLC
an Andrews McMeel Universal company
1130 Walnut Street, Kansas City, Missouri 64106

www.andrewsmcmeel.com

ISBN: 978-0-7407-5685-6

Library of Congress Catalog Control Number: 2005933866

www.spotthefrog.net

ATTENTION: SCHOOLS AND BUSINESSES

Andrews McMeel books are available at quantity discounts with bulk purchase for educational, business, or sales promotional use. For information, please e-mail the Andrews McMeel Publishing Special Sales Department: specialsales@amuniversal.com.

For Mary, my Karl.

Preface

Frogs and I have something in common. They're often out of sight and out of mind, until you spot one or two and realize they've been watching you. I like to imagine they're taking notes on the human condition, scribbling punch lines underwater. Bug-eyed cartoonists.

But drawing a strip about frogs didn't occur to me until I met Mary.

She found my listing at an online dating service. I went with my strengths and described myself as lazy and bald and a freelance cartoonist. "I love cartoons," she wrote back, proving that love is selectively blind.

That's the trick to getting along. Seeing the good. Winking at the bad.

Whatever Spot does, Karl forgives it. He understands that Spot is a frog, just as Mary understands that I'm a cartoonist. I fret. I obsess. I'll have Mary read six versions of a strip and ask which is funniest (though jokes, like frogs, rarely shine when dissected). I talk about Spot and Buddy and Lumpy as if they live with us—vexing relatives or lively companions, depending on how the writing goes. If you've seen *Harvey* with Jimmy Stewart, that's my life. With more Harveys. It's the sort of thing that could lead to a boot out the door. But it hasn't happened. Spot and Karl and the guy who draws them are still welcome.

For me, that's the essential tone of *Spot the Frog*. Everyone is welcome, even the flies (if you're a frog, especially the flies). I hear from readers who appreciate the sweetness and good nature of the strip. I can't take credit for it. It's not intentional. When I write, I'm focused on punch lines, story lines, pen lines. The cordiality is simply the fruit you pick when you allow characters—and cartoonists—to be accepted for themselves.

The strip is inspired by my life, but I'm not Spot. He leaps and smiles, I sit and frown. He loves people and adventure. I'm antsy in checkout lines. I'm more like Lumpy, the antisocial toad. Or Buddy, who's full of bravado (I'm writing an introduction about me) but privately feels much smaller (will anyone read it?) I try to be like Karl, but so far I've only mastered the hairline and paunch.

In another way, however, I am like Spot, because I live with someone who accepts me.

Everything springs from that.

Introduction

Magic happens in the funniest places. You're ambling through your e-mail one day and instead of tossing an advertisement, you impulsively read it and discover that a new comic strip is debuting—a strip about a little frog who's renting an aquarium from an old guy. And the author does the sort of interview that makes you realize he isn't attempting the seven-thousandth strip of urban-edgy-smartmouth-cool, but something fresh. Hopeful but wary, you take a peek.

And thus you stumble into the pastoral, courageous, and heartfelt wonder that is *Spot the Frog*.

At least, that's how I found Spot.

Spot—small and green, daring and innocent, with an unnerving method of swallowing—stands beside no less than A. A. Milne's Winnie-the-Pooh as a character who is wise without knowing, triumphant without struggling, honest and open and yet undevoured in a world that attempts to devour everything. Spot leaps on faith, crashes more frequently than not, and yet emerges idealistic, upbeat, and undeterred. He's my kind of guy.

Mark Heath has created an oasis of the mind with Spot, Buddy, Lumpy, Karl, and a wonderful supporting cast of quirky irregulars—from a cat whose feet never touch the ground to a madly smiling kite to various birds unwilling to share either their birdbath or the Zen of what it is to be birds.

Or maybe "oasis" isn't the right word. Perhaps Mark has given us a small green patch of unmowed grass, suitable for meditation, welcoming to frogs (and quiet humans) who desire a place in which they can transcend the daily grind and simply be.

If you are just discovering Spot, I envy you this first journey. If you are one of the faithful returning to a well-loved home, you are not alone.

—Holly Lisle,

fantasy/science fiction author and *Spot the Frog* fan

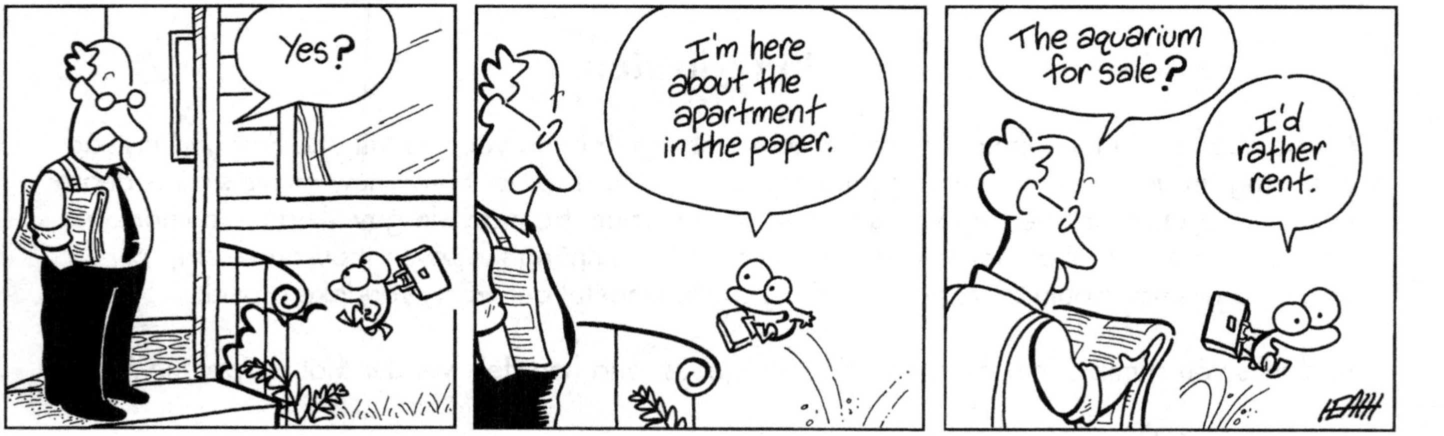
Yes?
I'm here about the apartment in the paper.
The aquarium for sale?
I'd rather rent.

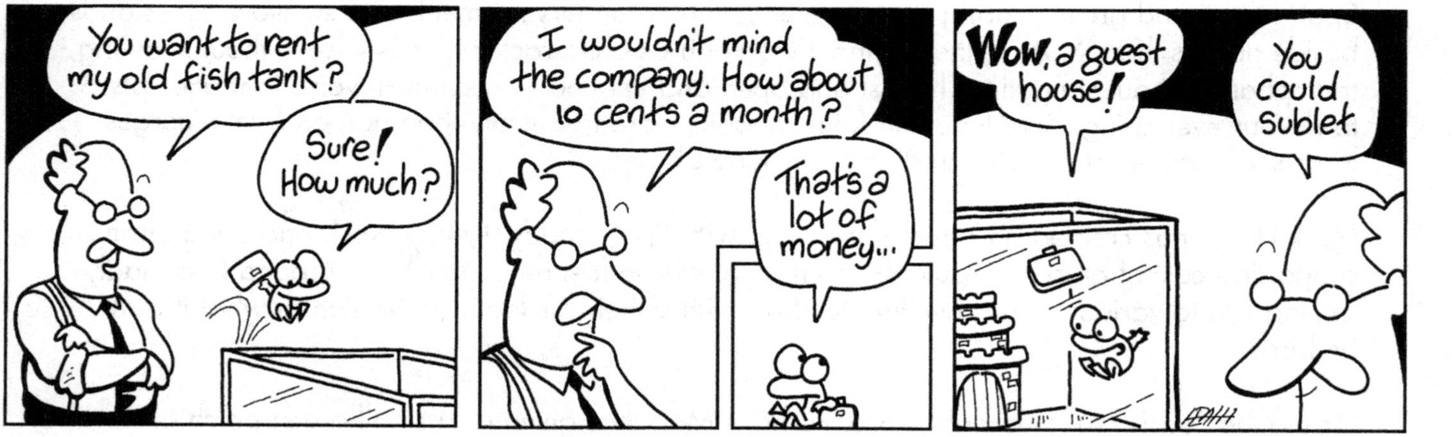
You want to rent my old fish tank?
Sure! How much?
I wouldn't mind the company. How about 10 cents a month?
That's a lot of money...
WOW, a guest house!
You could sublet.

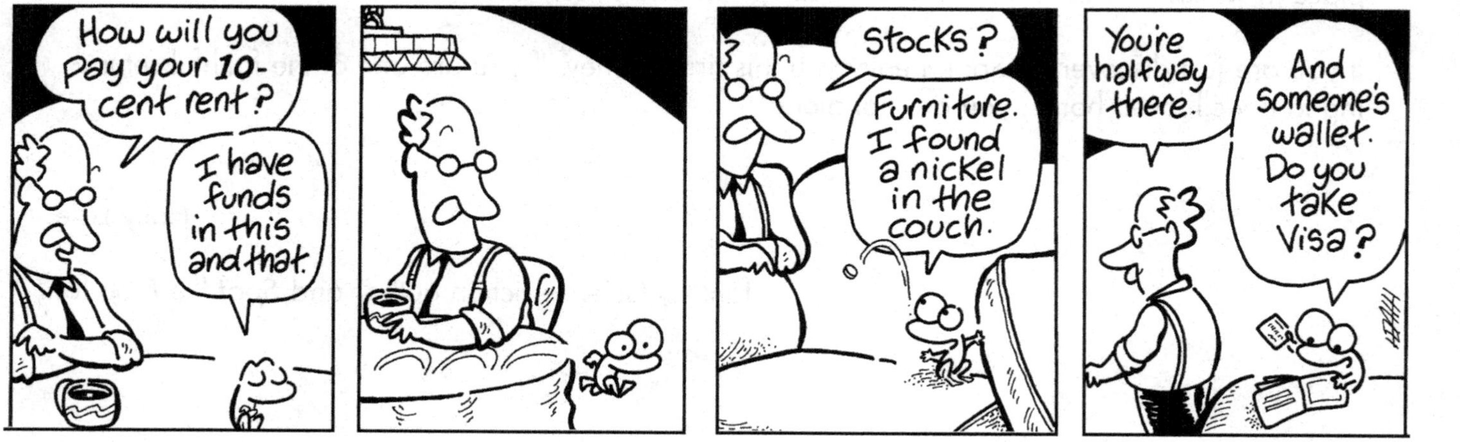
How will you pay your 10-cent rent?
I have funds in this and that.
Stocks?
Furniture. I found a nickel in the couch.
You're halfway there.
And someone's wallet. Do you take Visa?

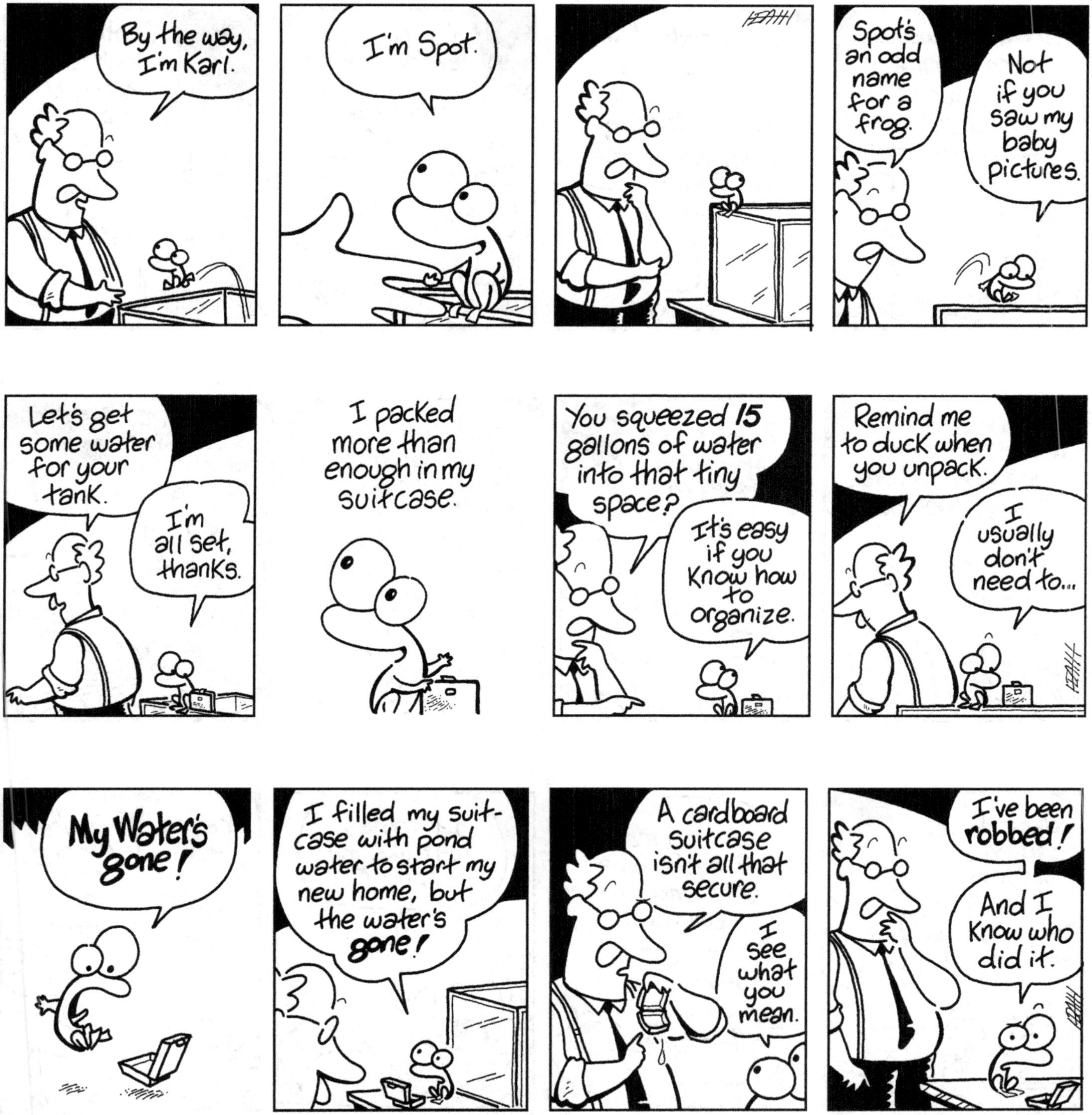
By the way, I'm Karl.
I'm Spot.
Spot's an odd name for a frog.
Not if you saw my baby pictures.
Let's get some water for your tank.
I'm all set, thanks.
I packed more than enough in my suitcase.
You squeezed 15 gallons of water into that tiny space?
It's easy if you know how to organize.
Remind me to duck when you unpack.
I usually don't need to...
My Water's gone!
I filled my suit-case with pond water to start my new home, but the water's gone!
A cardboard suitcase isn't all that secure.
I see what you mean.
I've been robbed!
And I know who did it.

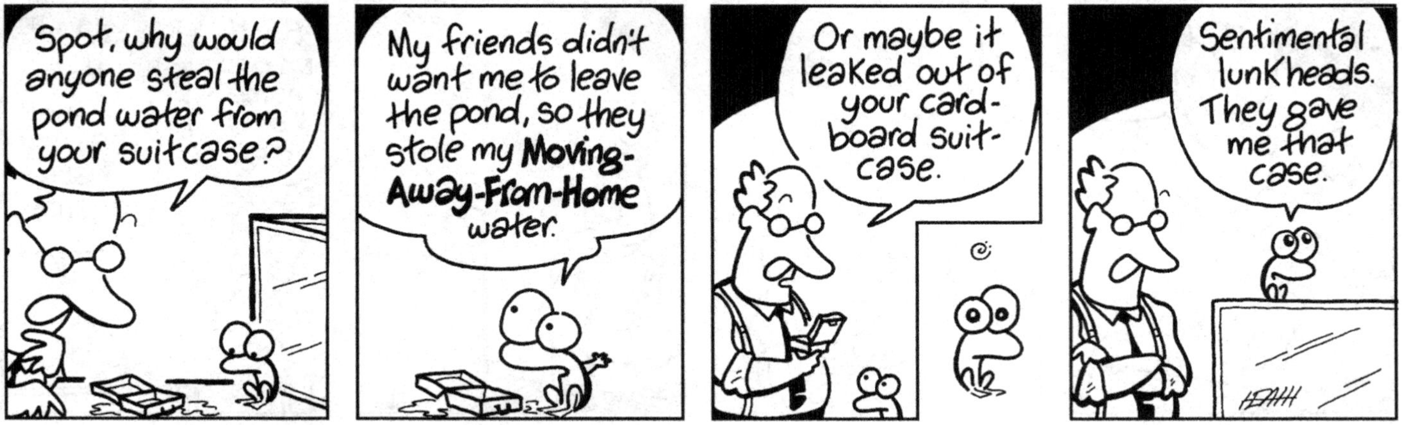
Spot, why would anyone steal the pond water from your suitcase?
My friends didn't want me to leave the pond, so they stole my **Moving-Away-From-Home** water.
Or maybe it leaked out of your card-board suit-case.
Sentimental lunkheads. They gave me that case.

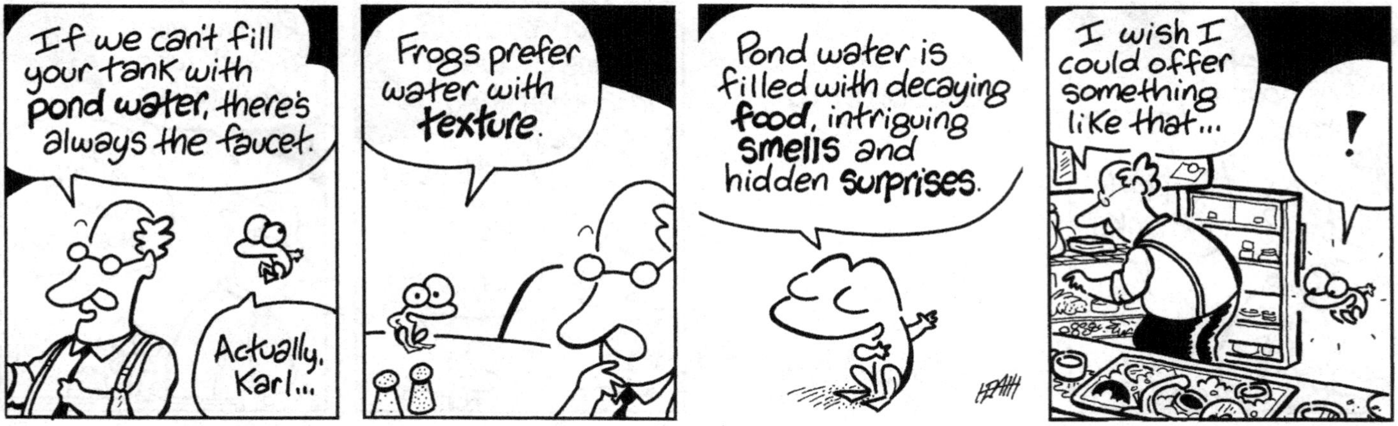
If we can't fill your tank with **pond water**, there's always the faucet.
Actually, Karl...
Frogs prefer water with **texture**.
Pond water is filled with decaying **food**, intriguing **smells** and hidden **surprises**.
I wish I could offer something like that...
!

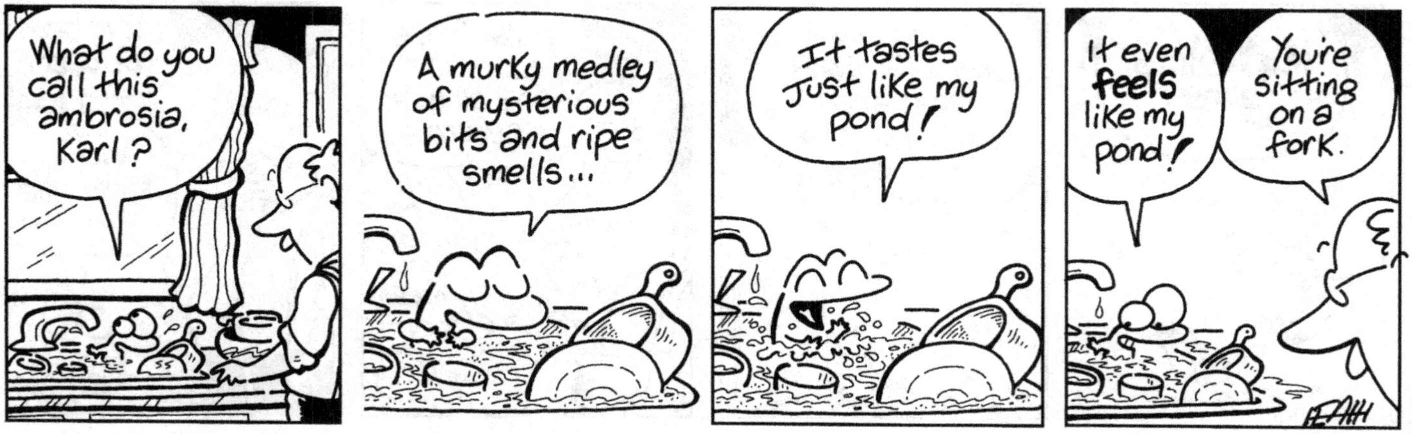
What do you call this ambrosia, Karl?
A murky medley of mysterious bits and ripe smells...
It tastes just like my pond!
It even **feels** like my pond!
You're sitting on a fork.

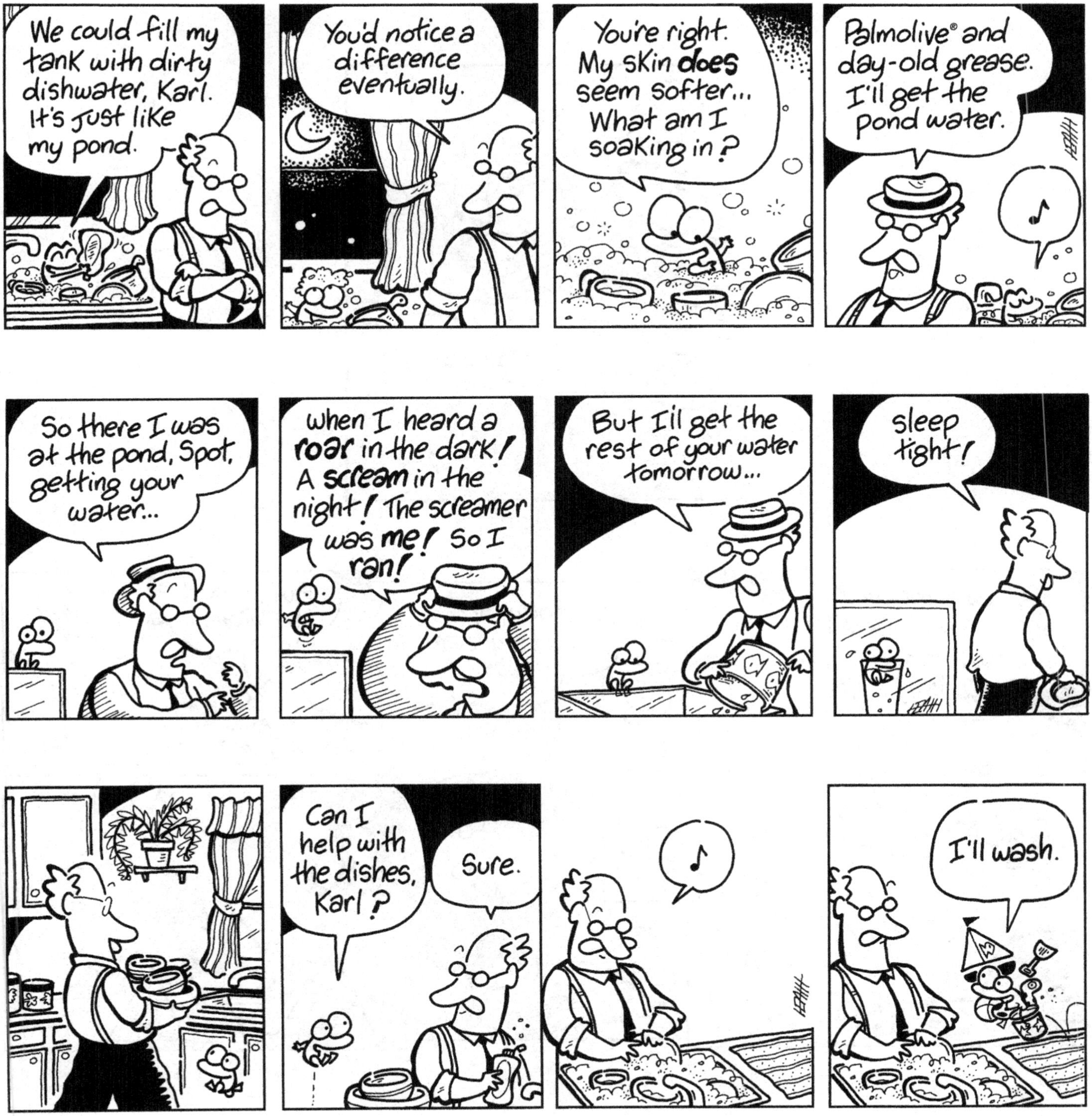
We could fill my tank with dirty dishwater, Karl. It's just like my pond.
You'd notice a difference eventually.
You're right. My skin **does** seem softer... What am I soaking in?
Palmolive® and day-old grease. I'll get the pond water.
♪
So there I was at the pond, Spot, getting your water...
when I heard a **roar** in the dark! A **scream** in the night! The screamer was **me**! So I **ran**!
But I'll get the rest of your water tomorrow...
sleep tight!
Can I help with the dishes, Karl?
Sure.
♪
I'll wash.

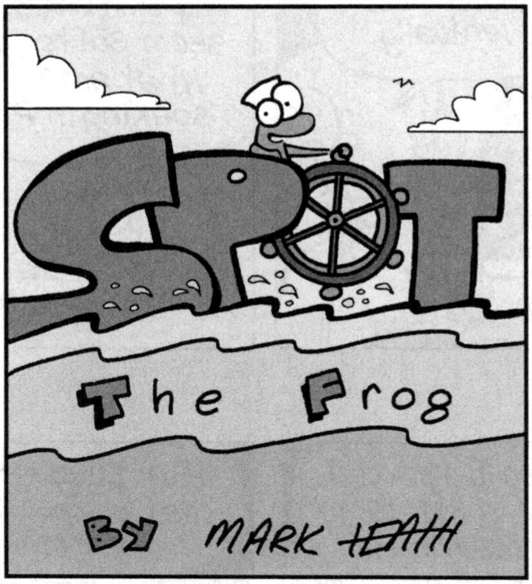
SPOT
The Frog
BY MARK HEATH

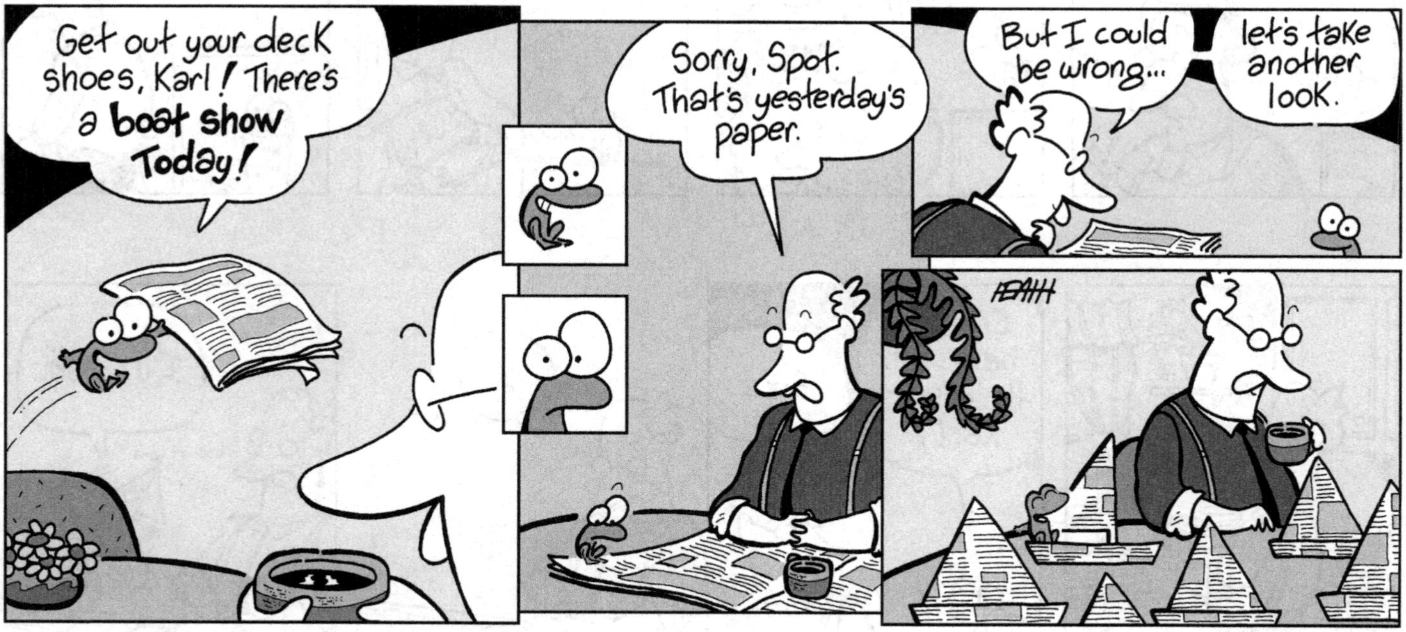
Get out your deck shoes, Karl! There's a **boat show Today!**
Sorry, Spot. That's yesterday's paper.
But I could be wrong...
let's take another look.
HEATH

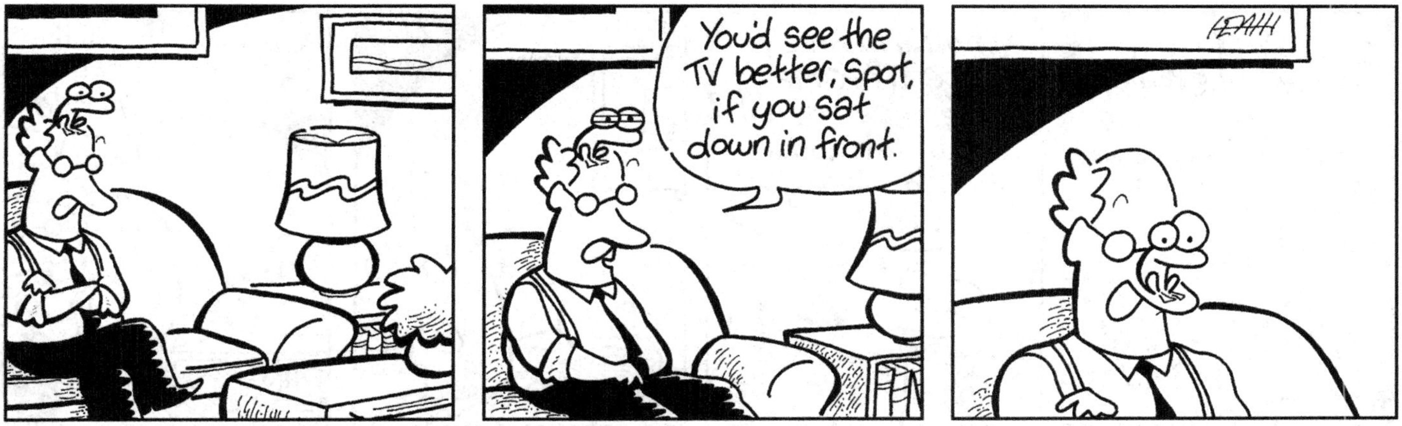
You'd see the TV better, Spot, if you sat down in front.

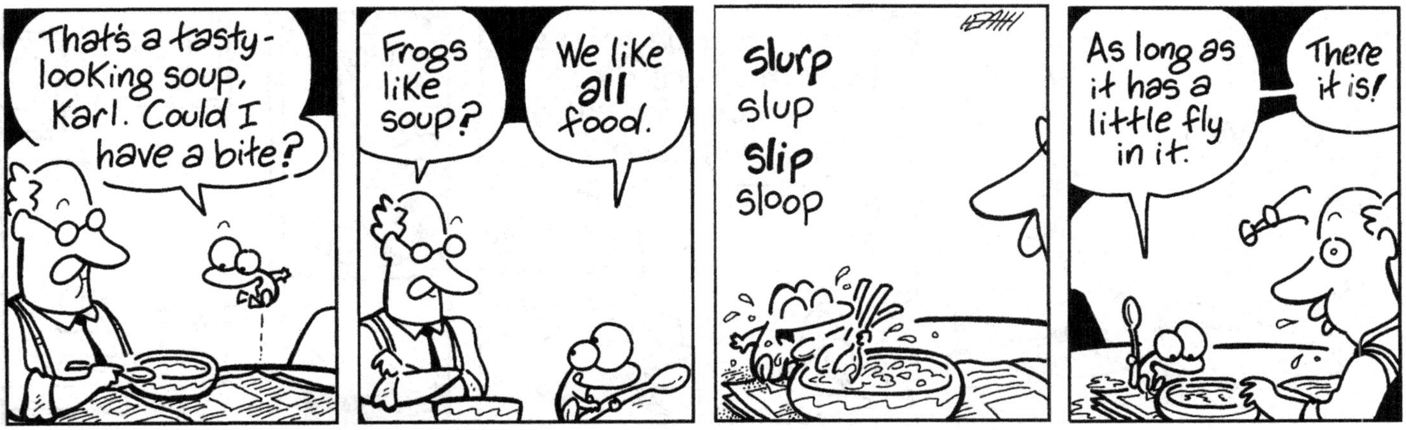
That's a tasty-looking soup, Karl. Could I have a bite?
Frogs like soup?
We like **all** food.
Slurp
slup
Slip
sloop
As long as it has a little fly in it.
There it is!

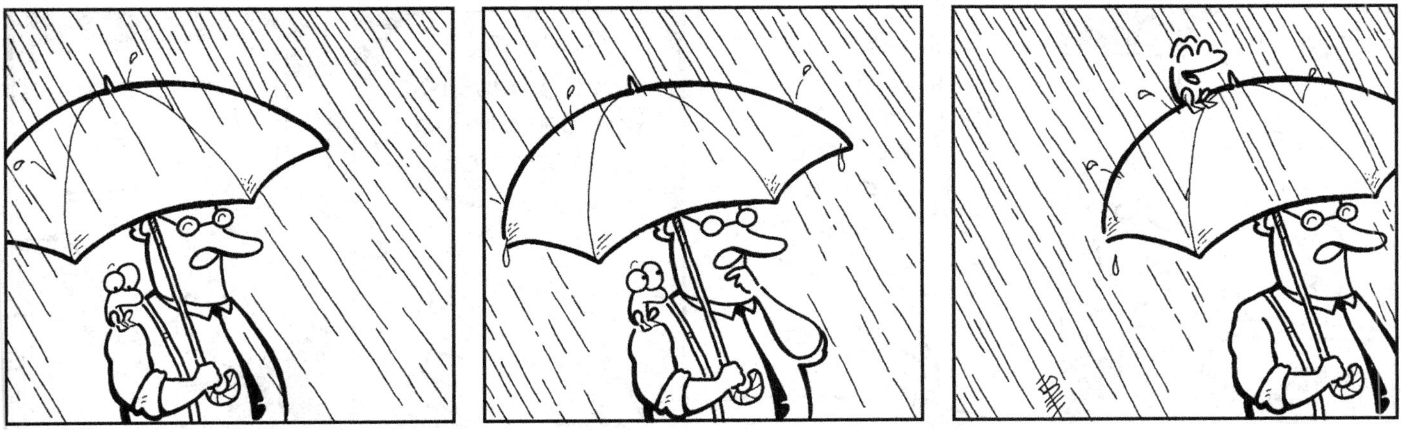

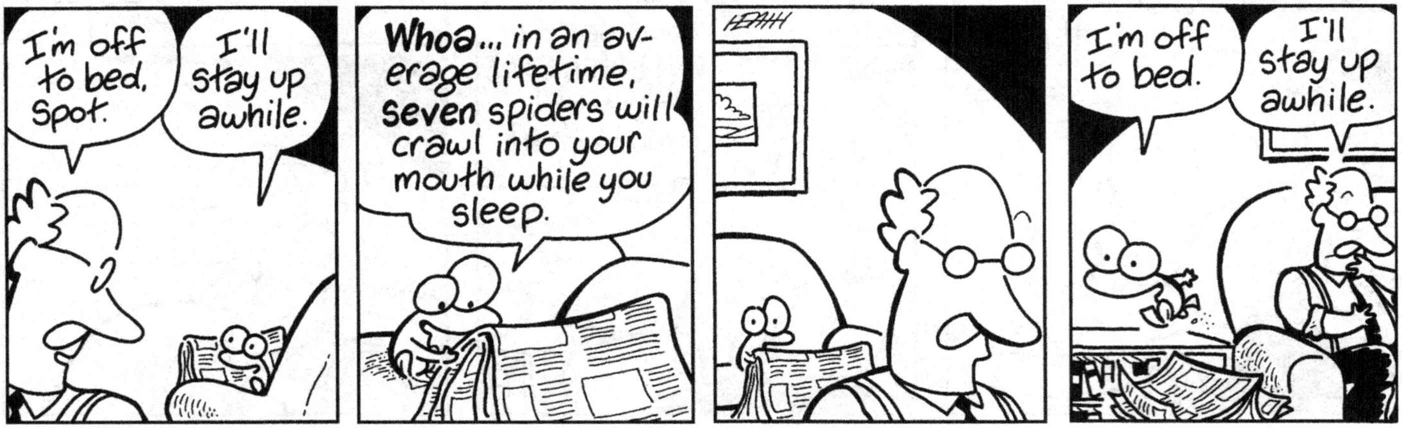
I'm off to bed, Spot.
I'll stay up awhile.
Whoa... in an average lifetime, seven spiders will crawl into your mouth while you sleep.
I'm off to bed.
I'll stay up awhile.

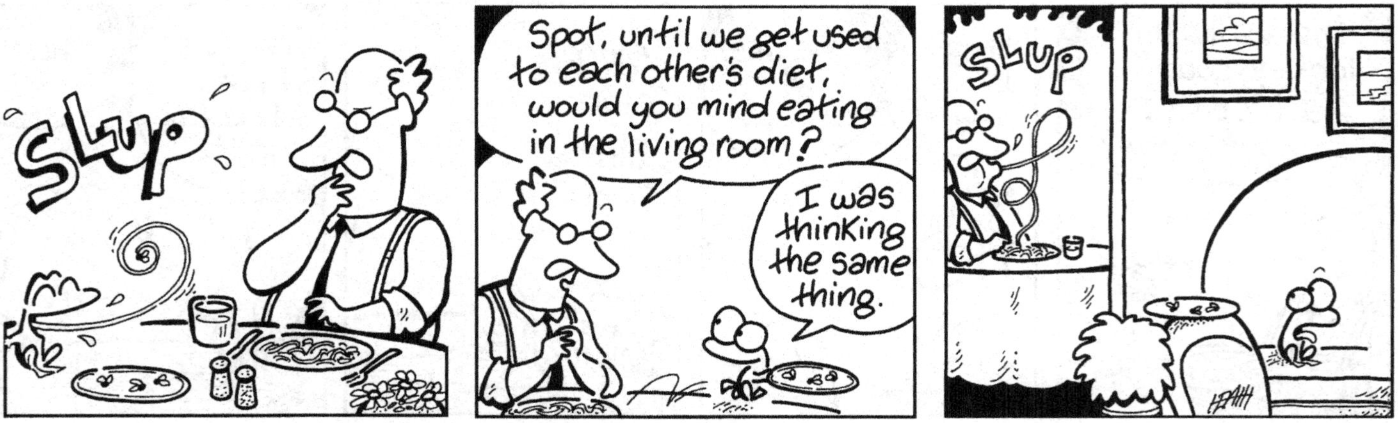
SLUP
Spot, until we get used to each other's diet, would you mind eating in the living room?
I was thinking the same thing.
SLUP

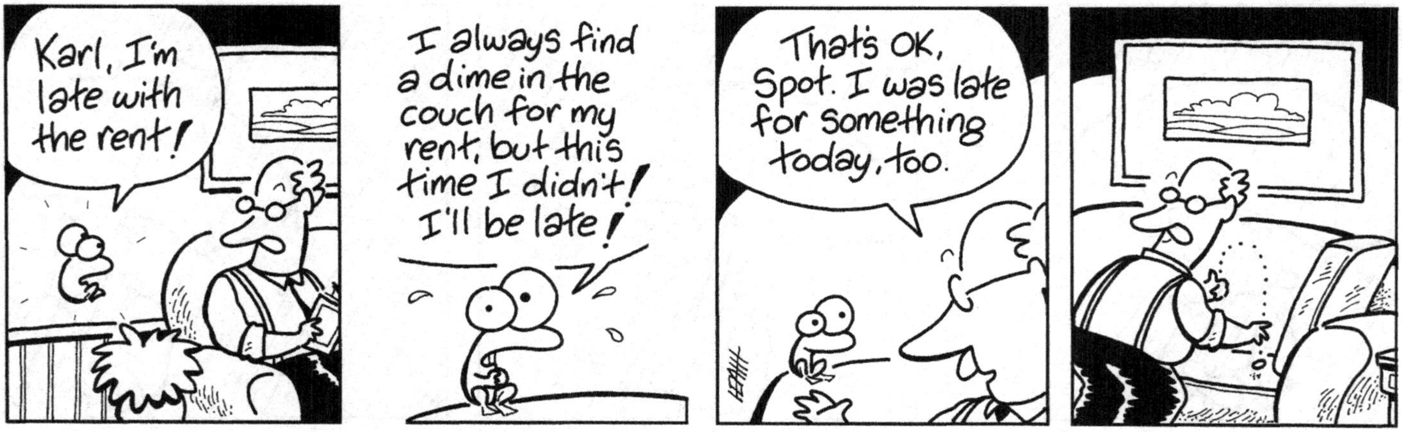
Karl, I'm late with the rent!
I always find a dime in the couch for my rent, but this time I didn't! I'll be late!
That's OK, Spot. I was late for something today, too.

The Frog
BY M HEATH

Karl, I'm in the middle of a magazine and my lamp burned out!
Watcha need? 75 watt?
Better make it 100.
HEATH

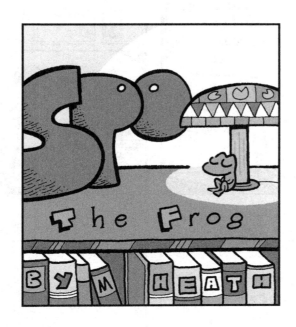

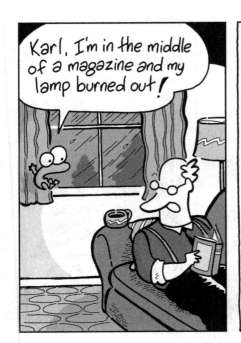

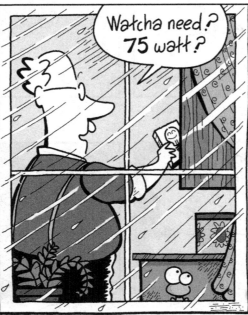

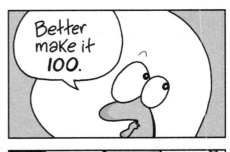

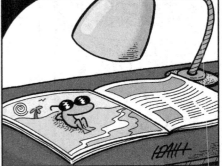

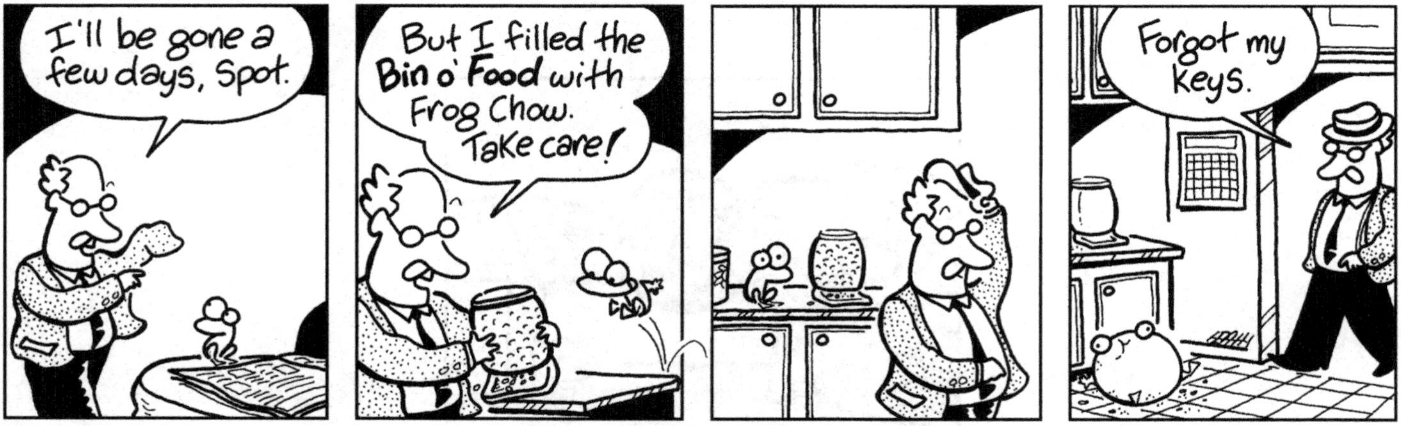

I'll be gone a few days, Spot.
But I filled the **Bin o' Food** with Frog Chow. Take care!
Forgot my keys.

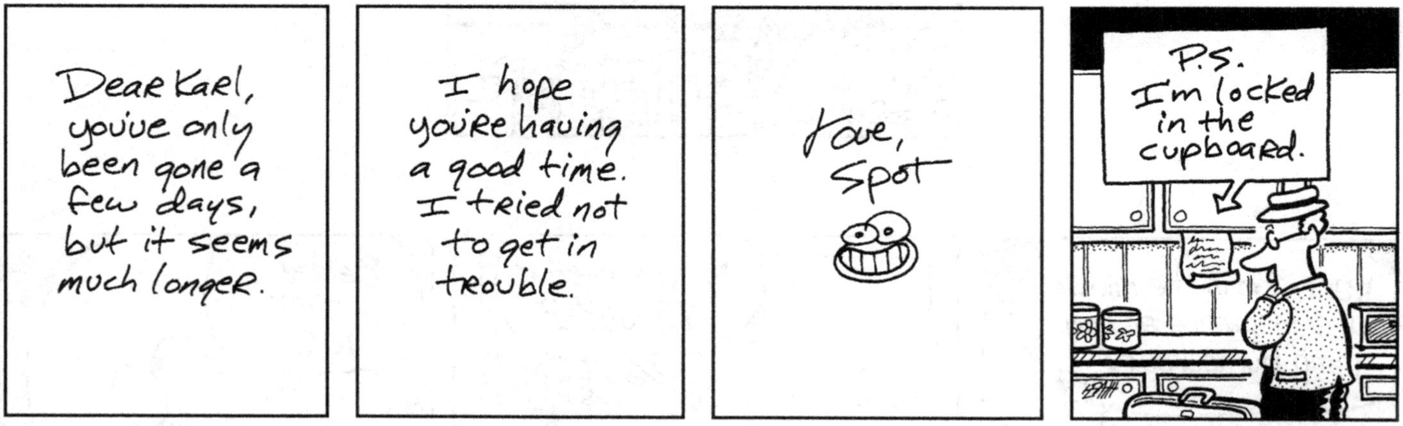

Dear Karl, you've only been gone a few days, but it seems much longer.
I hope you're having a good time. I tried not to get in trouble.
Love, Spot
P.S. I'm locked in the cupboard.

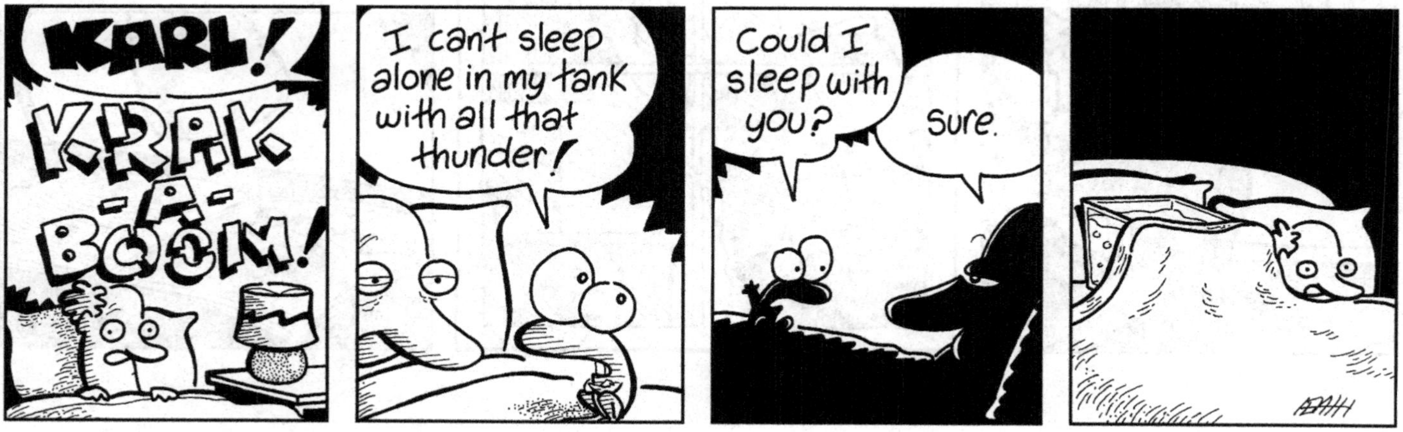

KARL!
K-RAK -A- BOOM!
I can't sleep alone in my tank with all that thunder!
Could I sleep with you?
Sure.

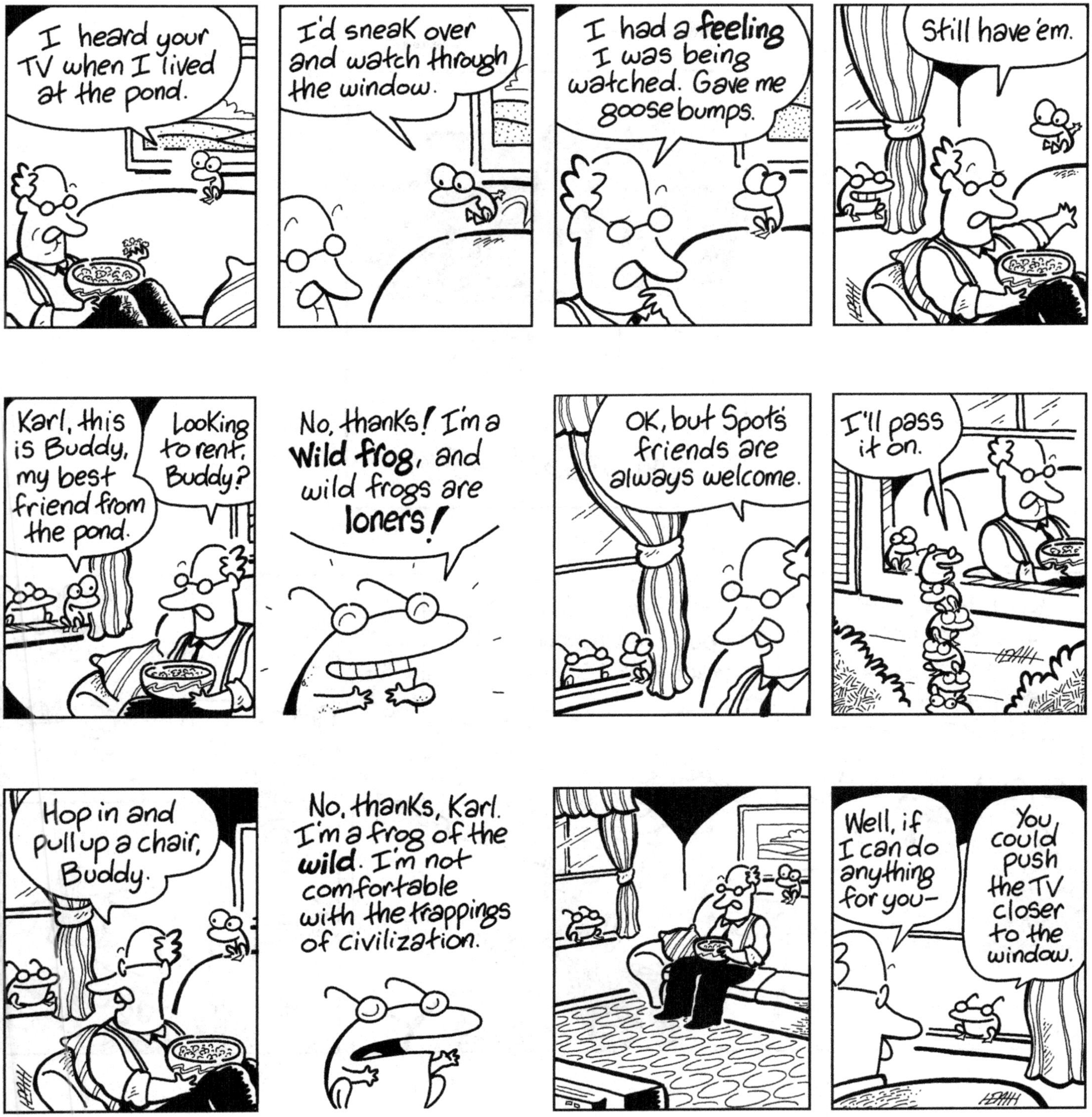

I heard your TV when I lived at the pond.
I'd sneak over and watch through the window.
I had a feeling I was being watched. Gave me goose bumps.
Still have 'em.
Karl, this is Buddy, my best friend from the pond.
Looking to rent, Buddy?
No, thanks! I'm a wild frog, and wild frogs are loners!
OK, but Spot's friends are always welcome.
I'll pass it on.
Hop in and pull up a chair, Buddy.
No, thanks, Karl. I'm a frog of the wild. I'm not comfortable with the trappings of civilization.
Well, if I can do anything for you-
You could push the TV closer to the window.

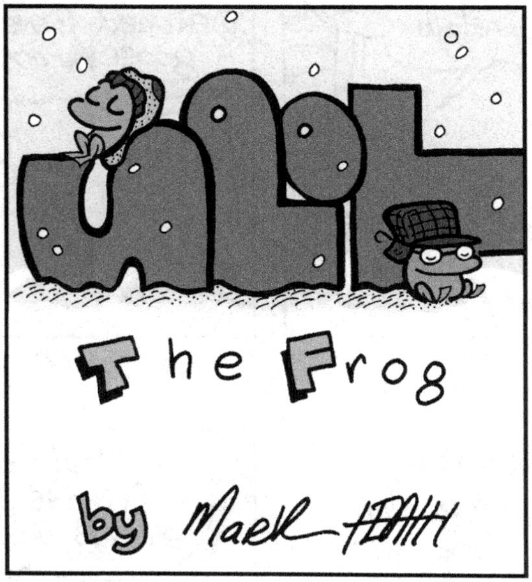

The Frog
by Mark Heath

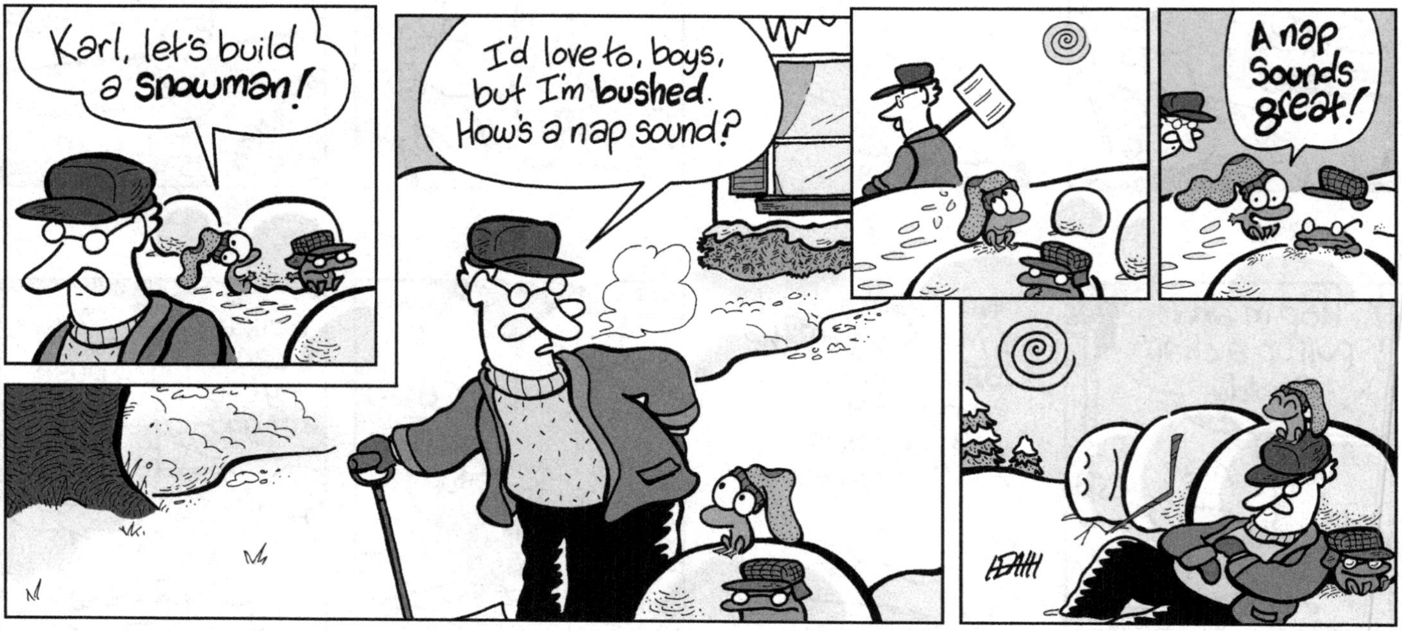

Karl, let's build a **snowman**!
I'd love to, boys, but I'm **bushed**. How's a nap sound?
A nap sounds great!
HEATH

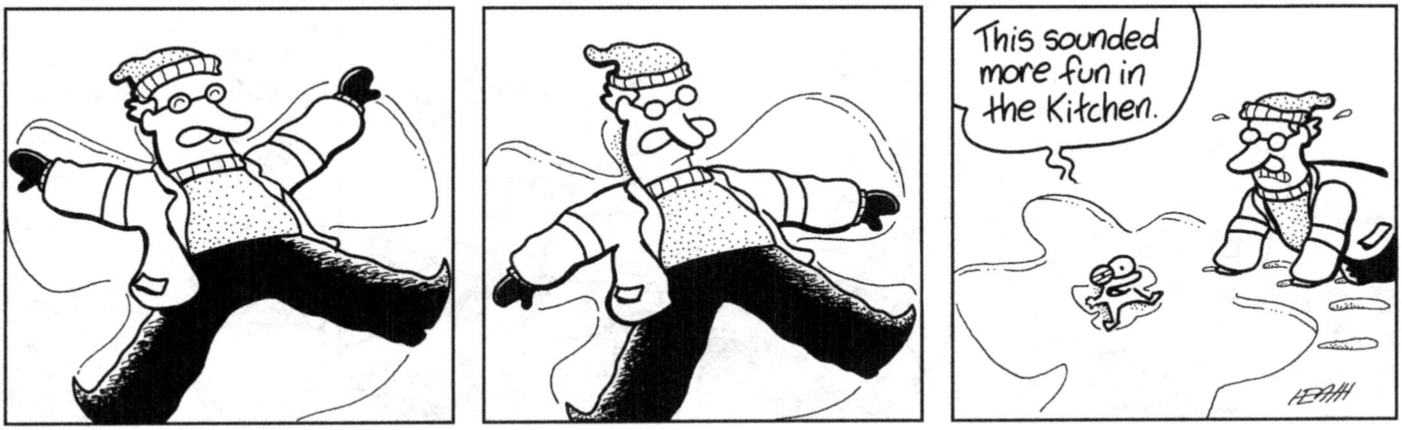
This sounded more fun in the Kitchen.

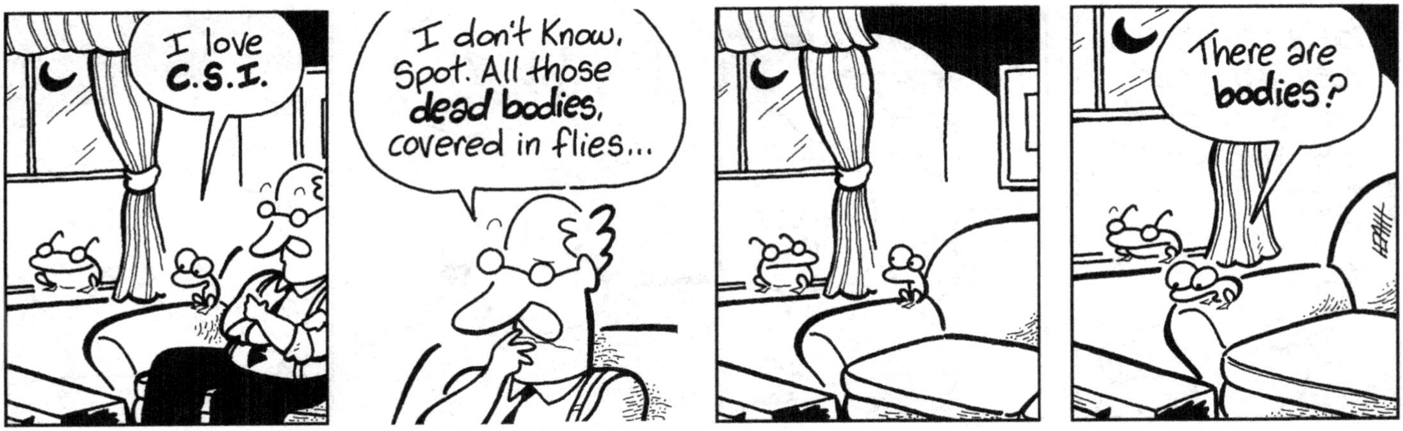
I love C.S.I.
I don't Know, Spot. All those dead bodies, covered in flies...
There are bodies?

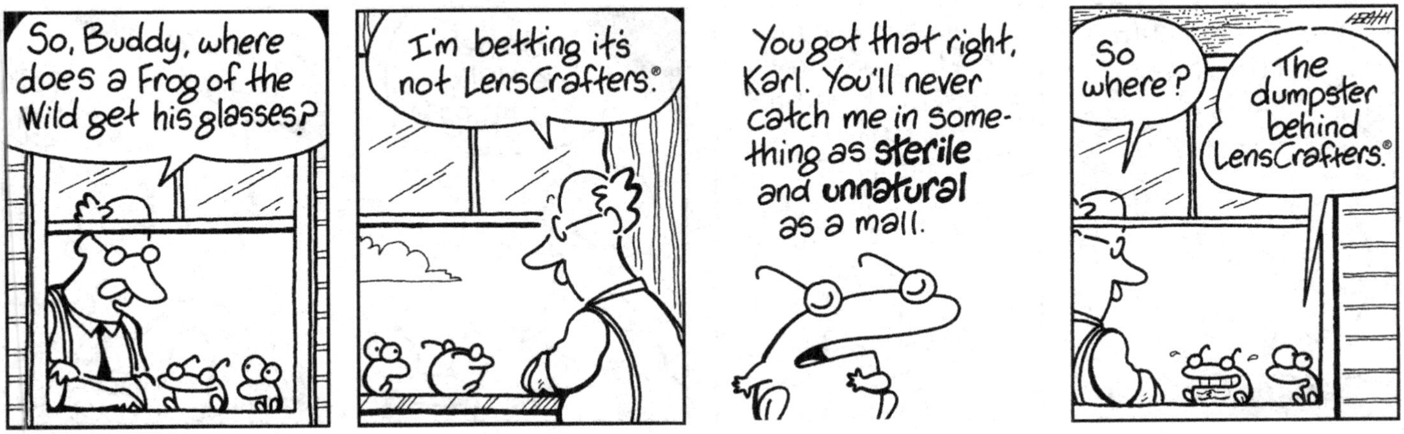
So, Buddy, where does a Frog of the Wild get his glasses?
I'm betting it's not LensCrafters.®
You got that right, Karl. You'll never catch me in something as sterile and unnatural as a mall.
So where?
The dumpster behind LensCrafters.®

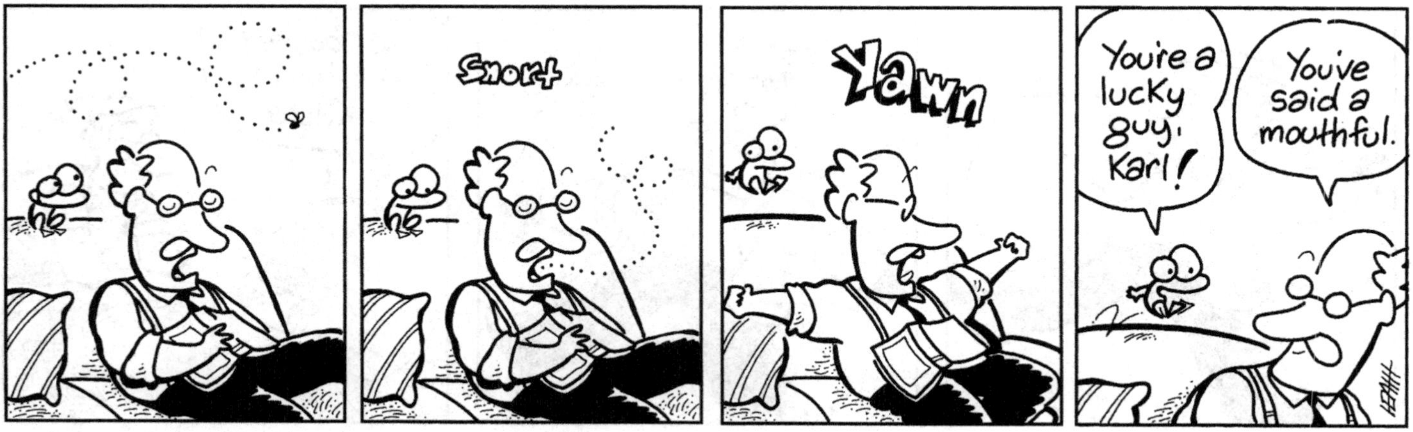
Snort
Yawn
You're a lucky guy, Karl!
You've said a mouthful.

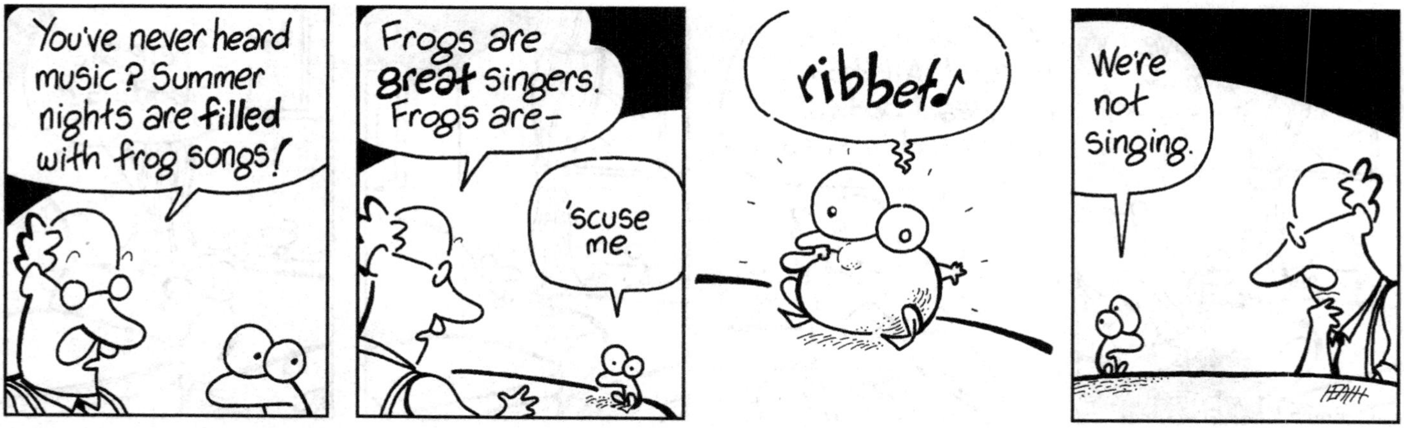
You've never heard music? Summer nights are filled with frog songs!
Frogs are great singers. Frogs are–
'scuse me.
ribbet♪
We're not singing.

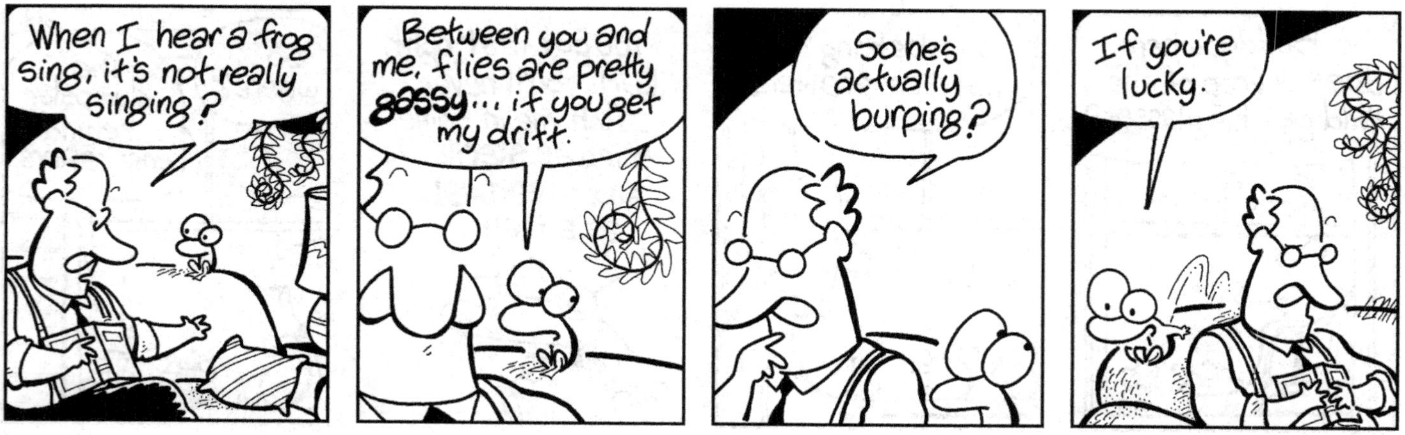
When I hear a frog sing, it's not really singing?
Between you and me, flies are pretty gassy... if you get my drift.
So he's actually burping?
If you're lucky.

SPOT
The Frog
by MARK HEATH

How can you guys stay warm with just **hats**?
Frogs are **tough**!

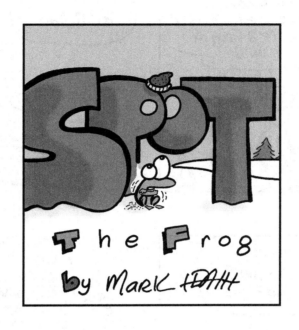

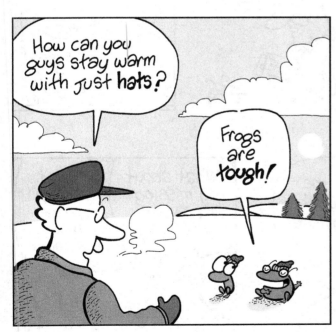

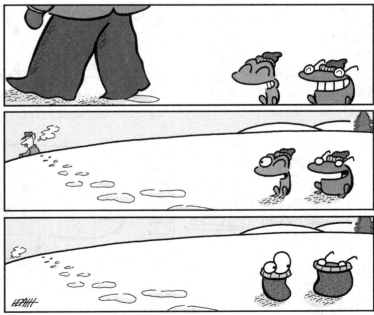

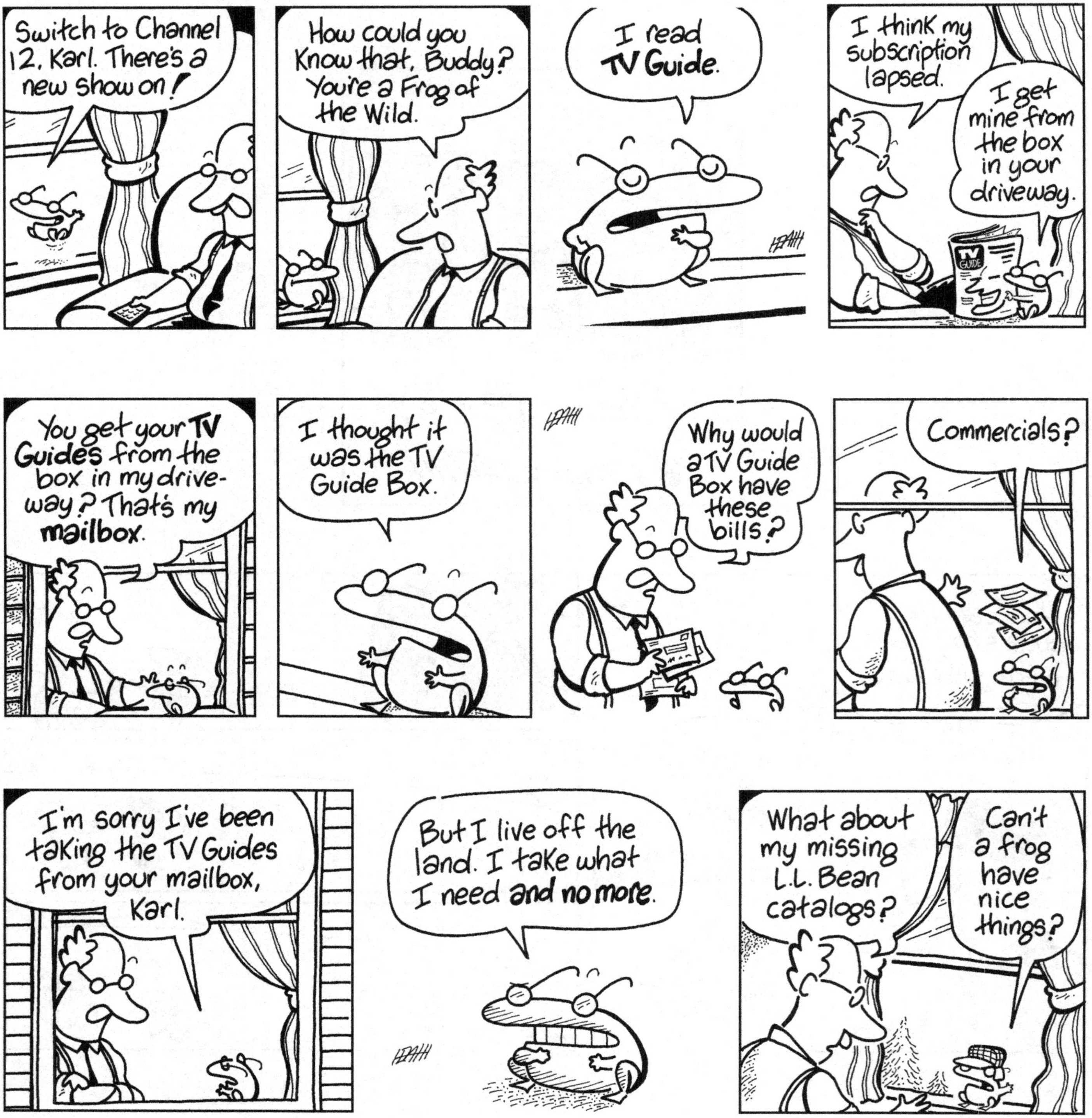

Switch to Channel 12, Karl. There's a new show on!
How could you know that, Buddy? You're a Frog of the Wild.
I read **TV Guide**.
I think my subscription lapsed.
I get mine from the box in your driveway.
TV GUIDE
You get your **TV Guides** from the box in my driveway? That's my **mailbox**.
I thought it was the TV Guide Box.
Why would a TV Guide Box have these bills?
Commercials?
I'm sorry I've been taking the TV Guides from your mailbox, Karl.
But I live off the land. I take what I need **and no more**.
What about my missing L.L. Bean catalogs?
Can't a frog have nice things?

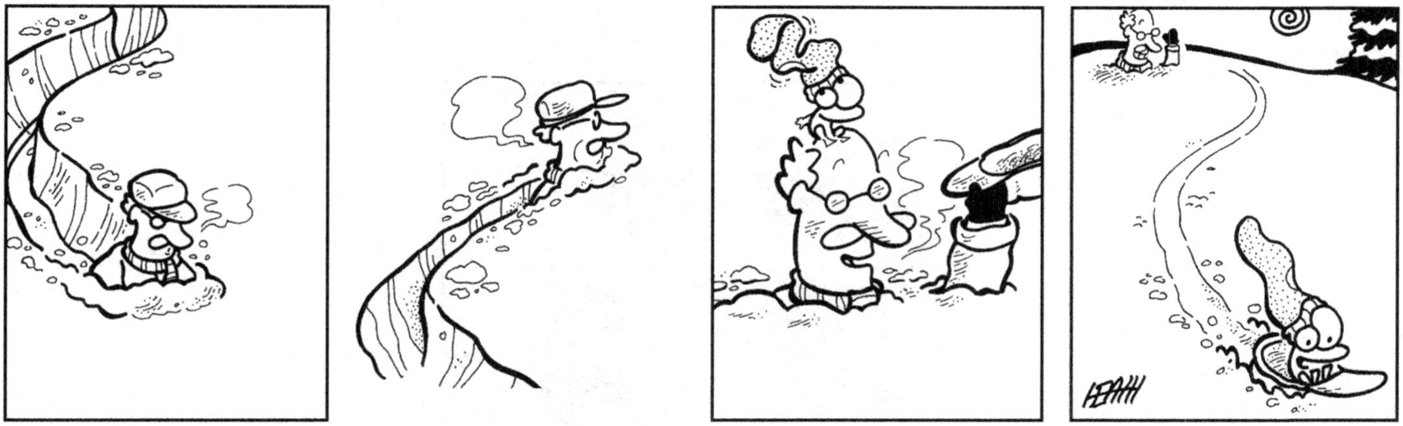

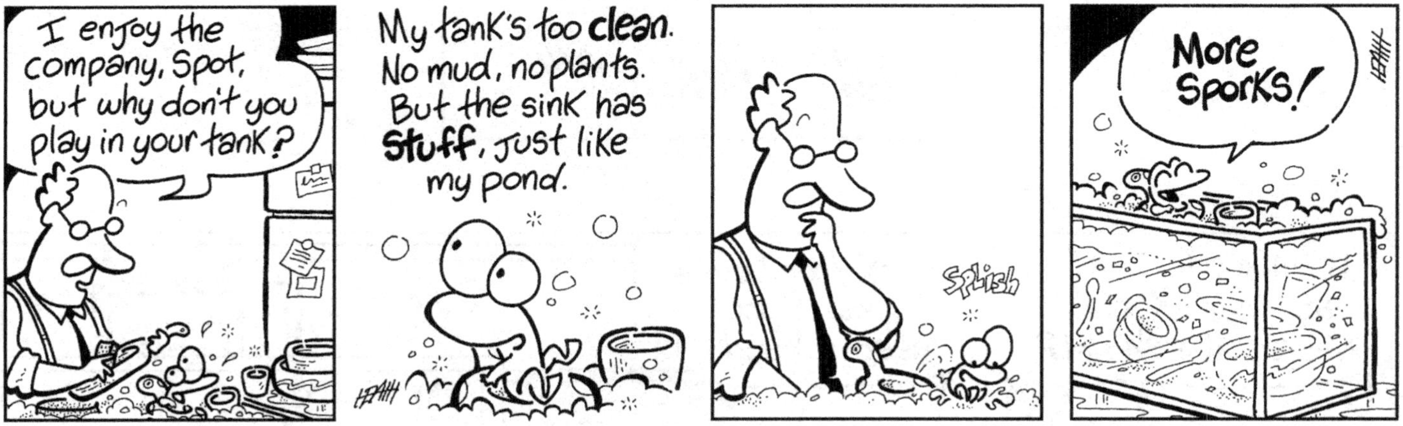
I enjoy the company, Spot, but why don't you play in your tank?
My tank's too **clean**. No mud, no plants. But the sink has **Stuff**, just like my pond.
Splish
More Sporks!

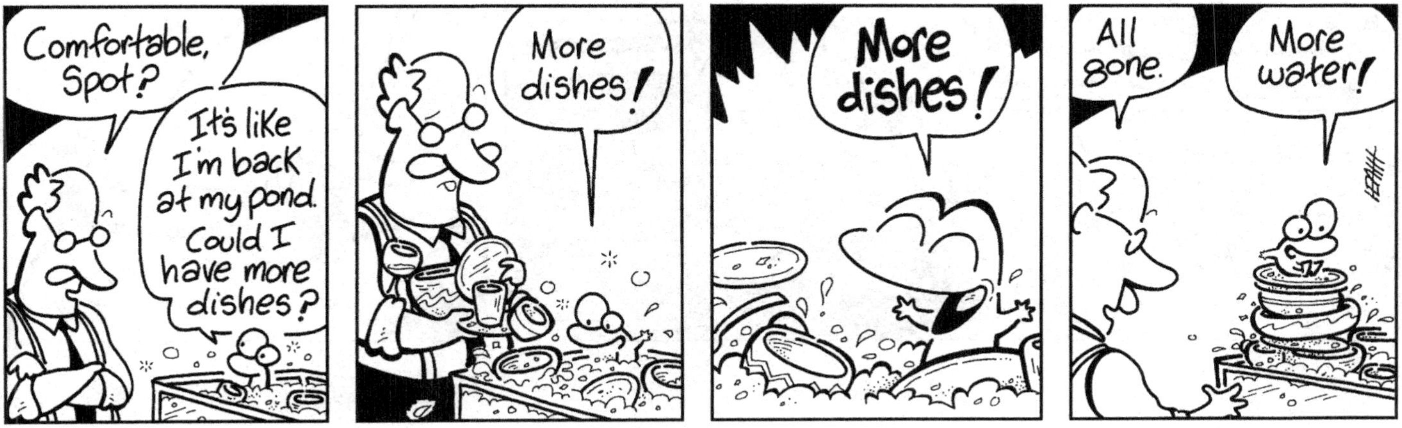
Comfortable, Spot?
It's like I'm back at my pond. Could I have more dishes?
More dishes!
More dishes!
All gone.
More water!

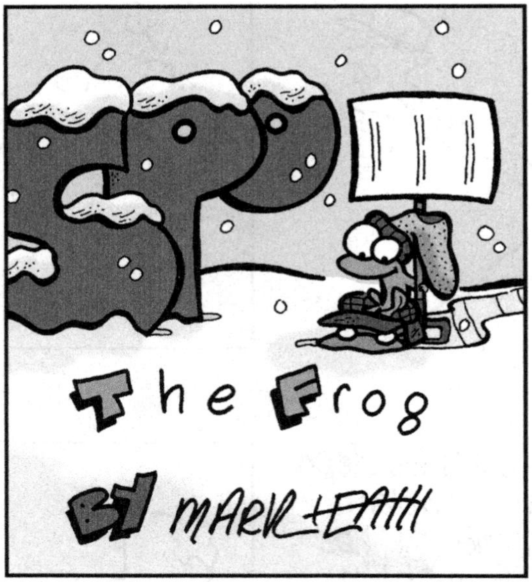

The Frog
By Mark Leahy

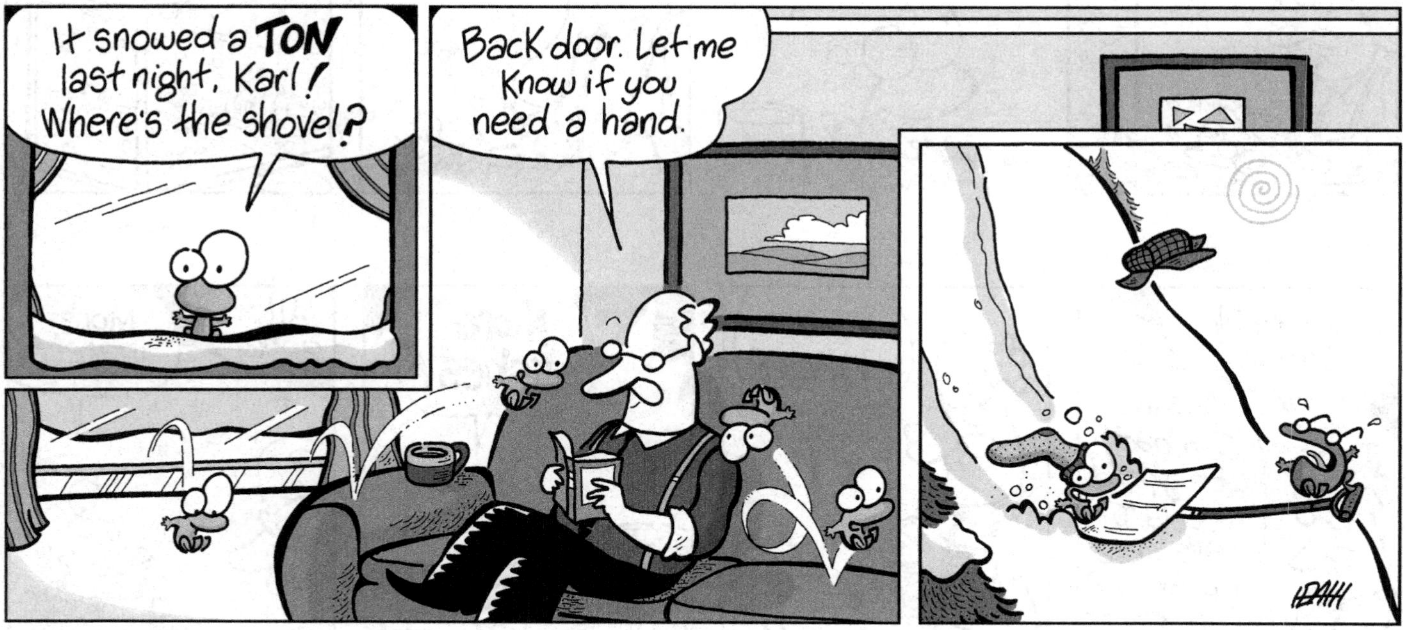

It snowed a TON last night, Karl! Where's the shovel?
Back door. Let me know if you need a hand.

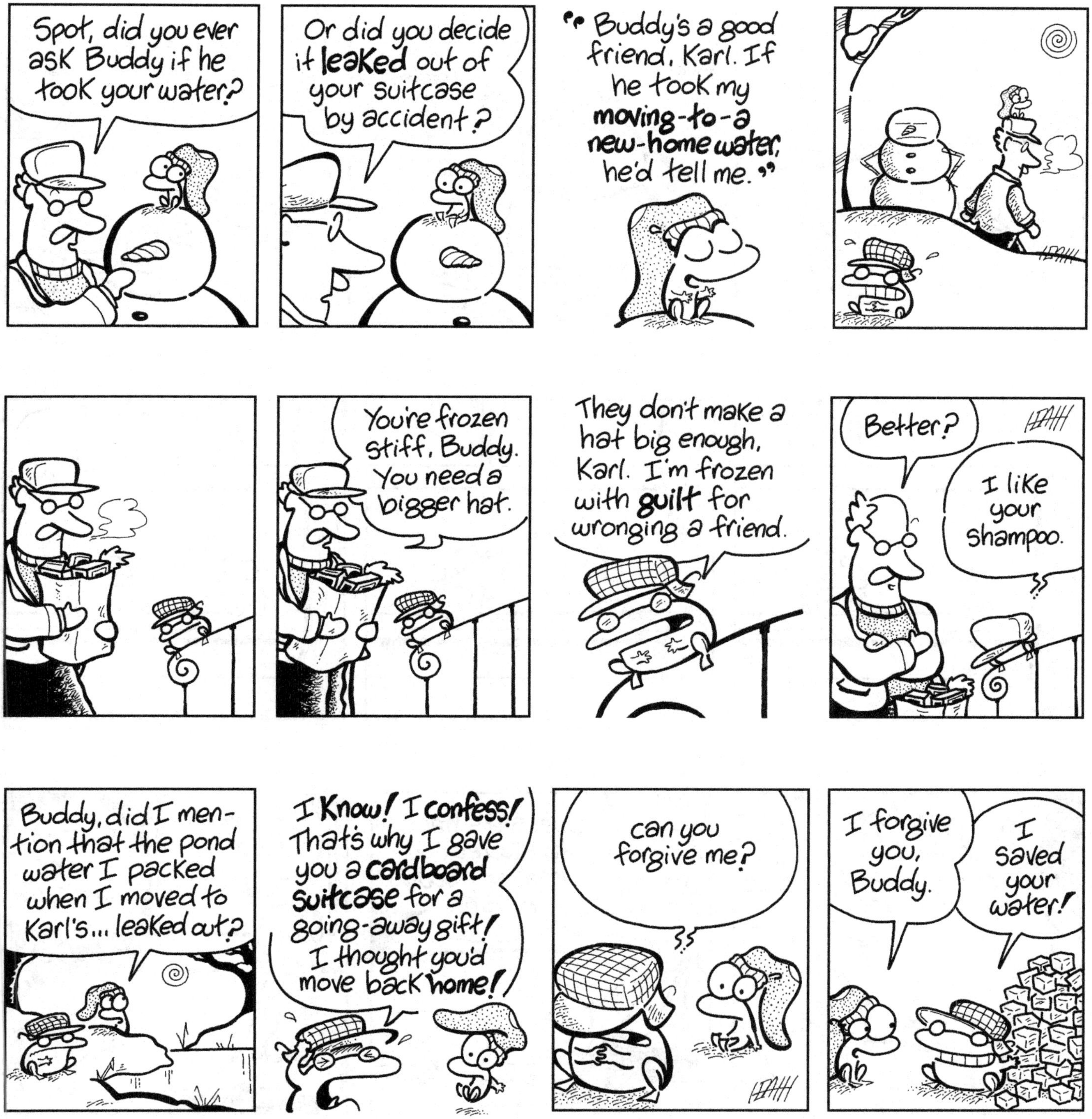
Spot, did you ever ask Buddy if he took your water?
Or did you decide if leaked out of your suitcase by accident?
"Buddy's a good friend, Karl. If he took my moving-to-a new-home water, he'd tell me."
You're frozen stiff, Buddy. You need a bigger hat.
They don't make a hat big enough, Karl. I'm frozen with guilt for wronging a friend.
Better?
I like your shampoo.
Buddy, did I mention that the pond water I packed when I moved to Karl's... leaked out?
I Know! I confess! That's why I gave you a cardboard suitcase for a going-away gift! I thought you'd move back home!
can you forgive me?
I forgive you, Buddy.
I saved your water!

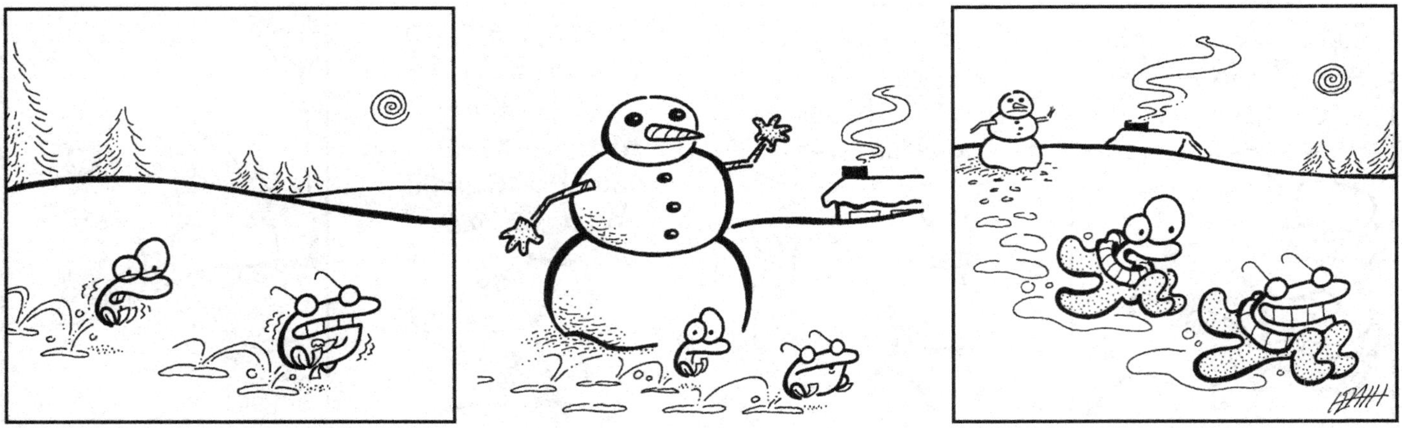

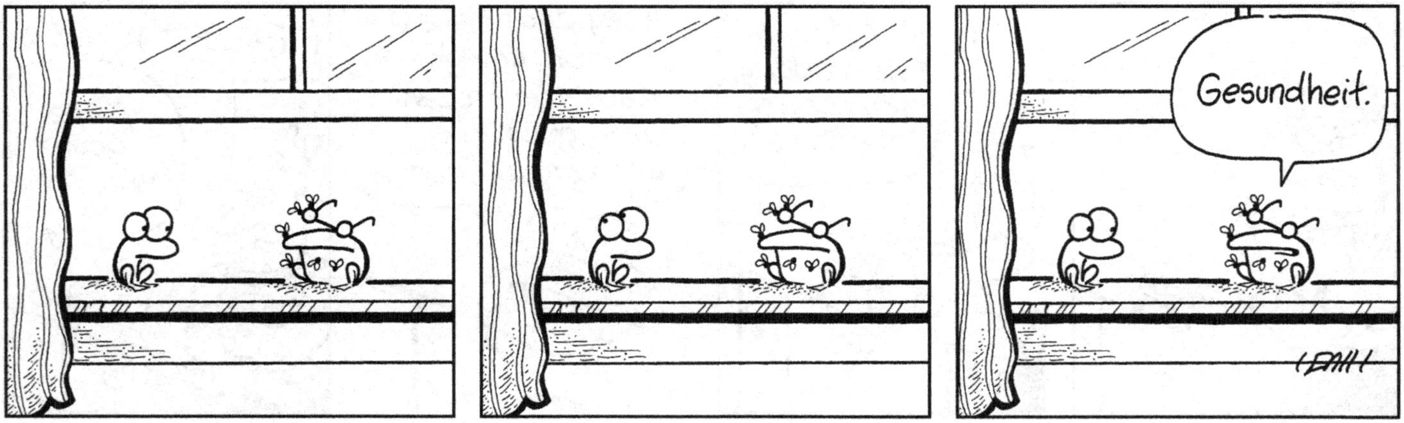
Gesundheit.

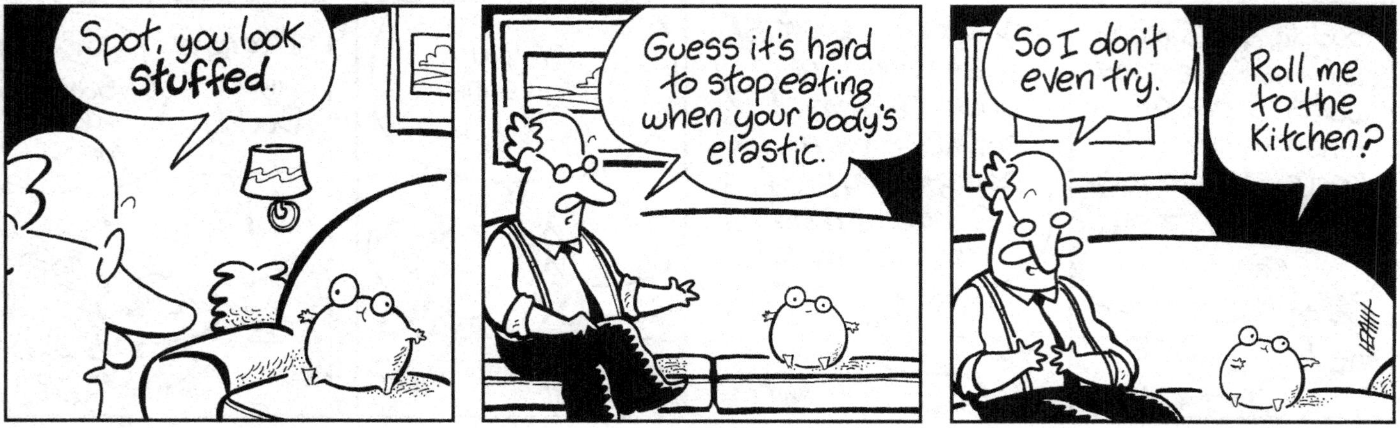
Spot, you look **stuffed**.
Guess it's hard to stop eating when your body's elastic.
So I don't even try.
Roll me to the Kitchen?

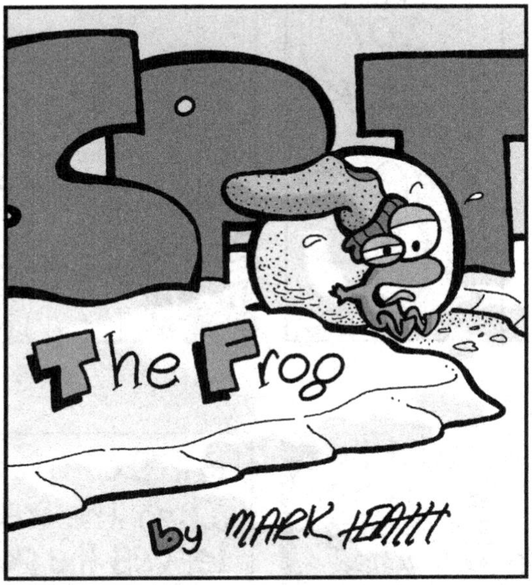
SPOT
The Frog
by MARK HEATH

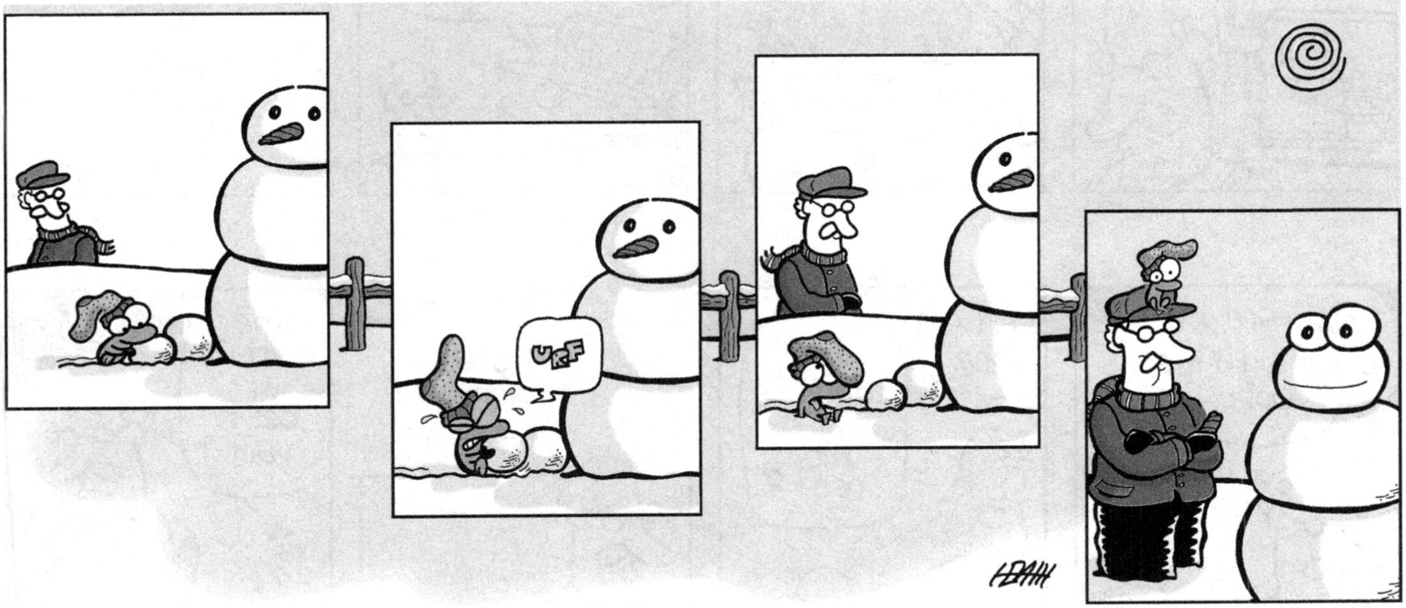
URF
HEATH

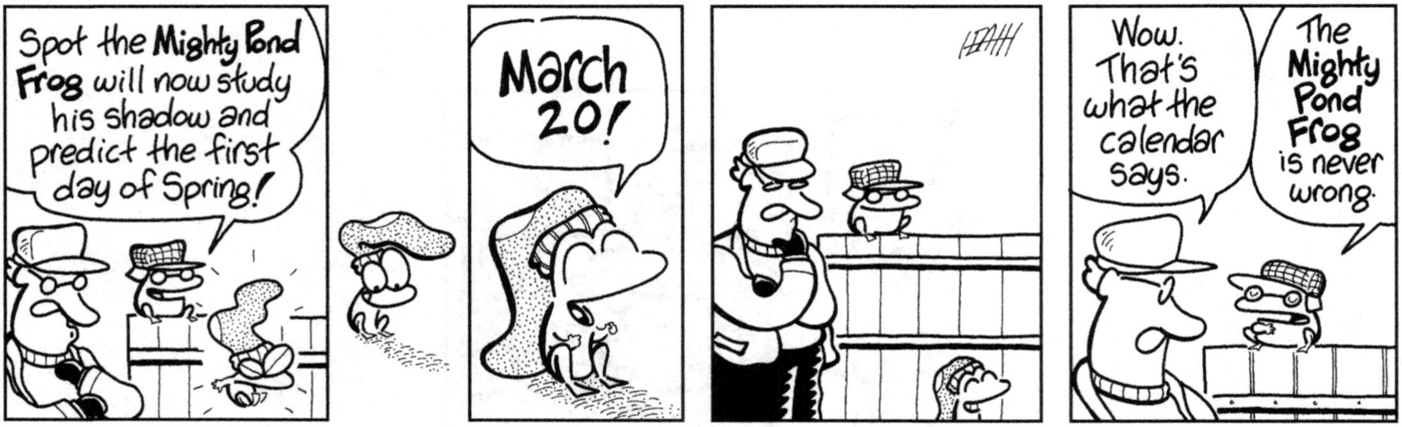
Spot the Mighty Pond Frog will now study his shadow and predict the first day of Spring!
March 20!
Wow. That's what the calendar says.
The Mighty Pond Frog is never wrong.

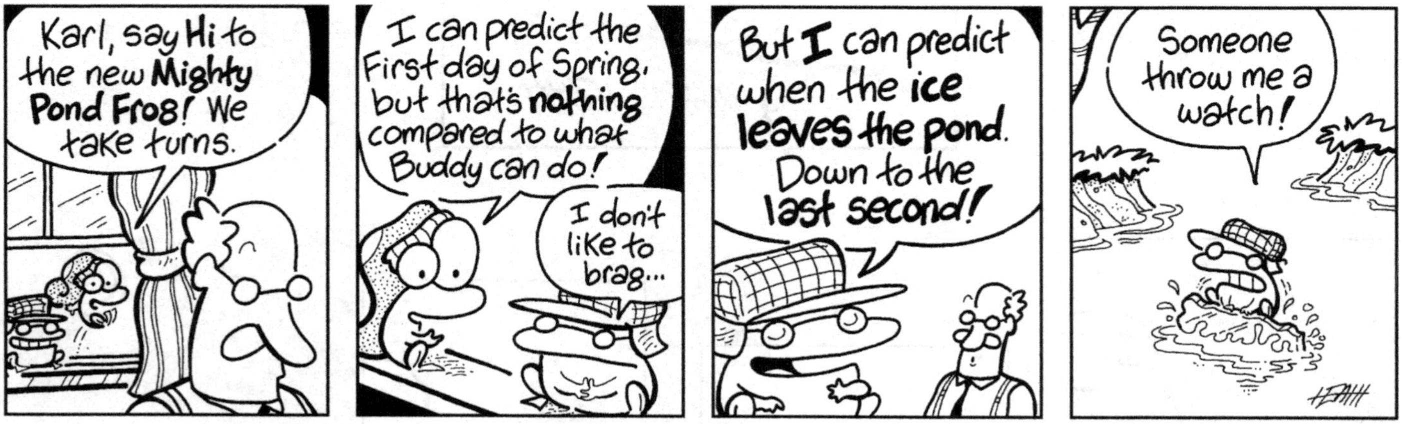
Karl, say Hi to the new Mighty Pond Frog! We take turns.
I can predict the First day of Spring, but that's nothing compared to what Buddy can do!
I don't like to brag...
But I can predict when the ice leaves the pond. Down to the last second!
Someone throw me a watch!

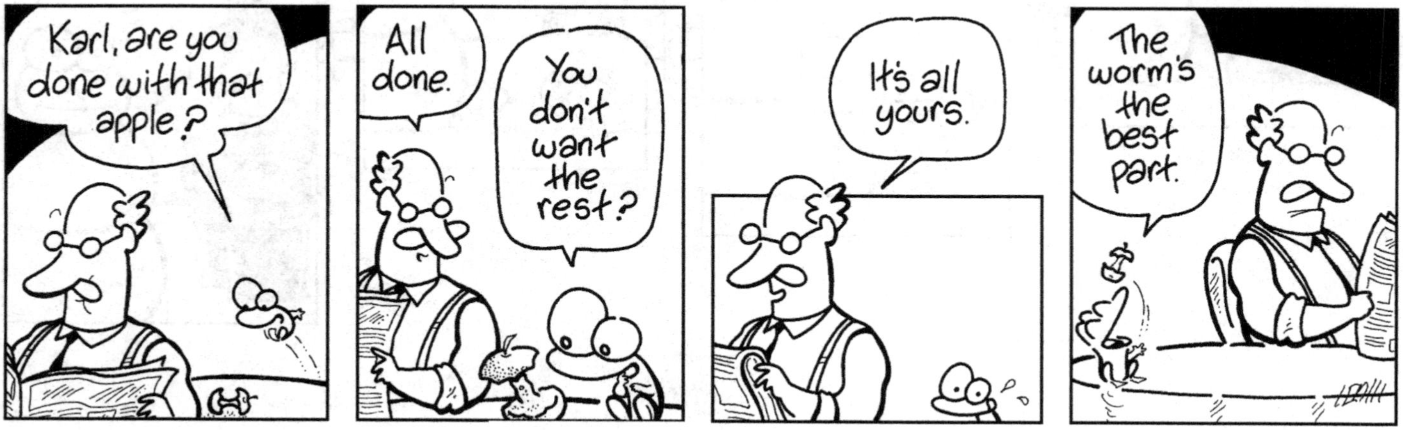
Karl, are you done with that apple?
All done.
You don't want the rest?
It's all yours.
The worm's the best part.

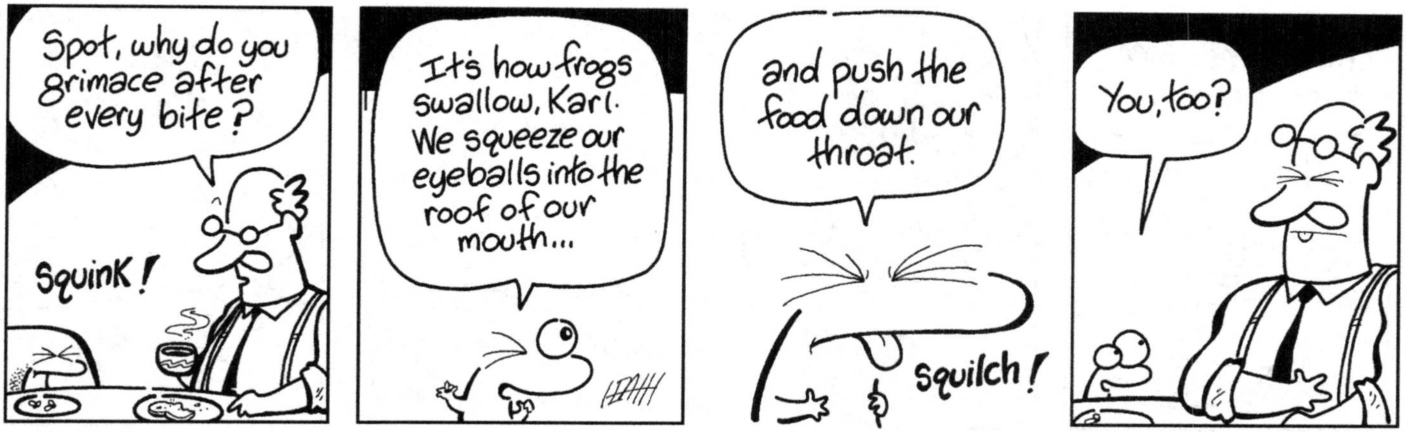
Spot, why do you grimace after every bite?
Squink!
It's how frogs swallow, Karl. We squeeze our eyeballs into the roof of our mouth...
and push the food down our throat.
Squilch!
You, too?

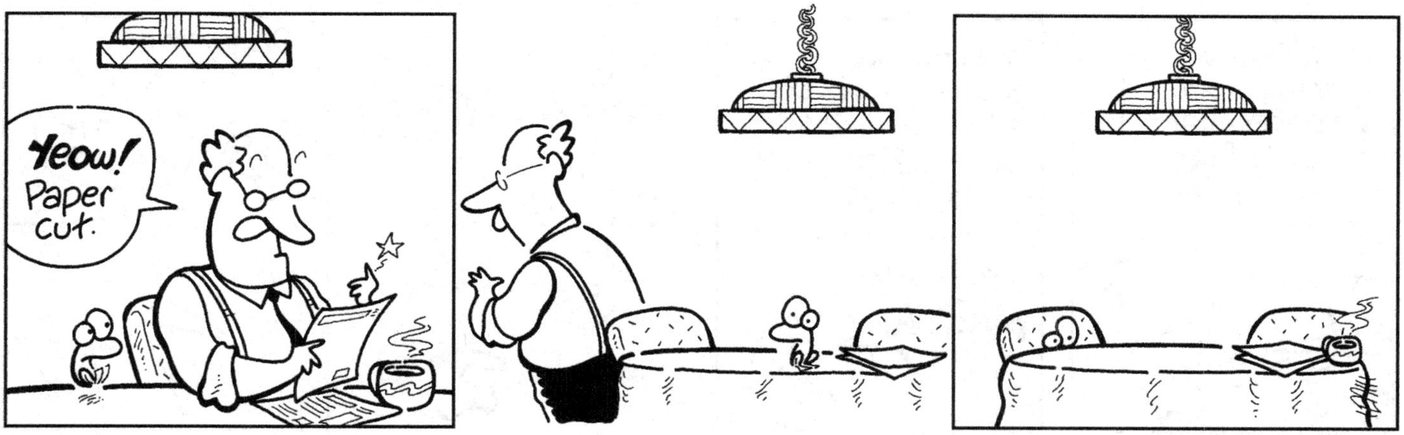
Yeow! Paper cut.

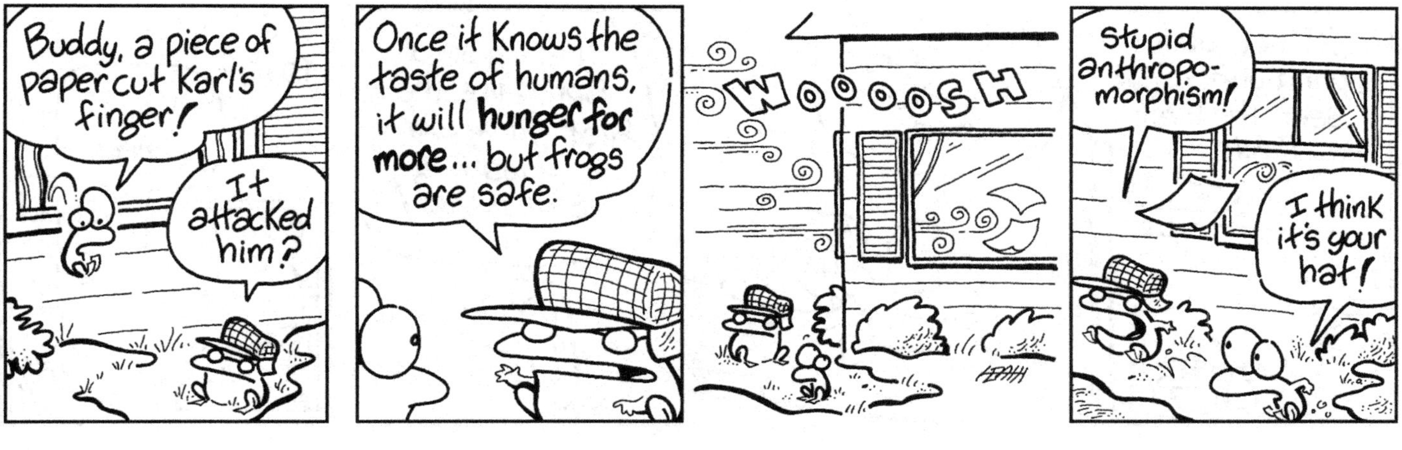
Buddy, a piece of paper cut Karl's finger!
It attacked him?
Once it knows the taste of humans, it will **hunger for more**... but frogs are safe.
WOOOOSH
Stupid anthropo-morphism!
I think it's your hat!

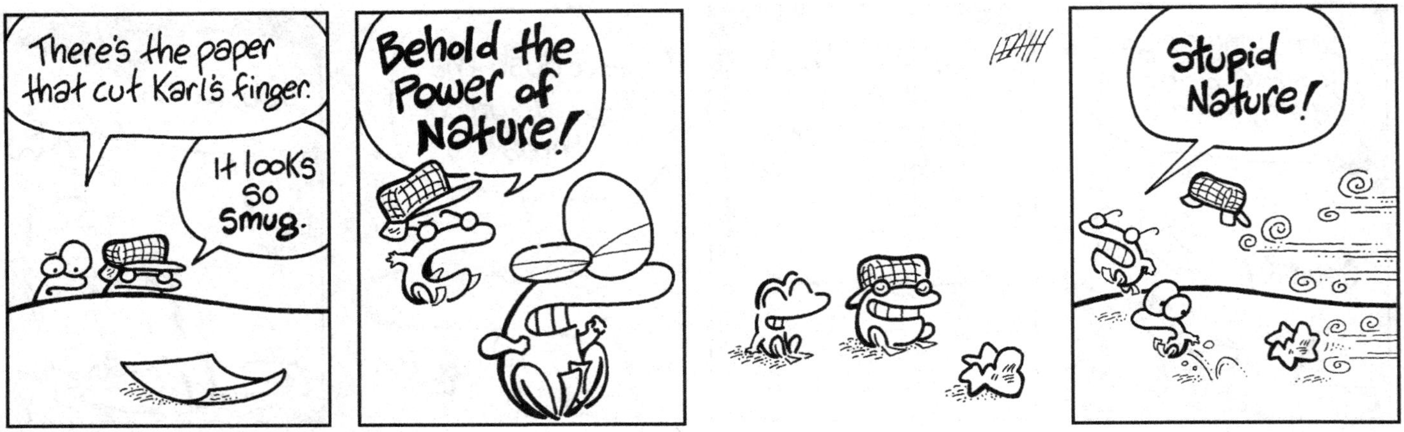
There's the paper that cut Karl's finger.
It looks so smug.
Behold the Power of Nature!
Stupid Nature!

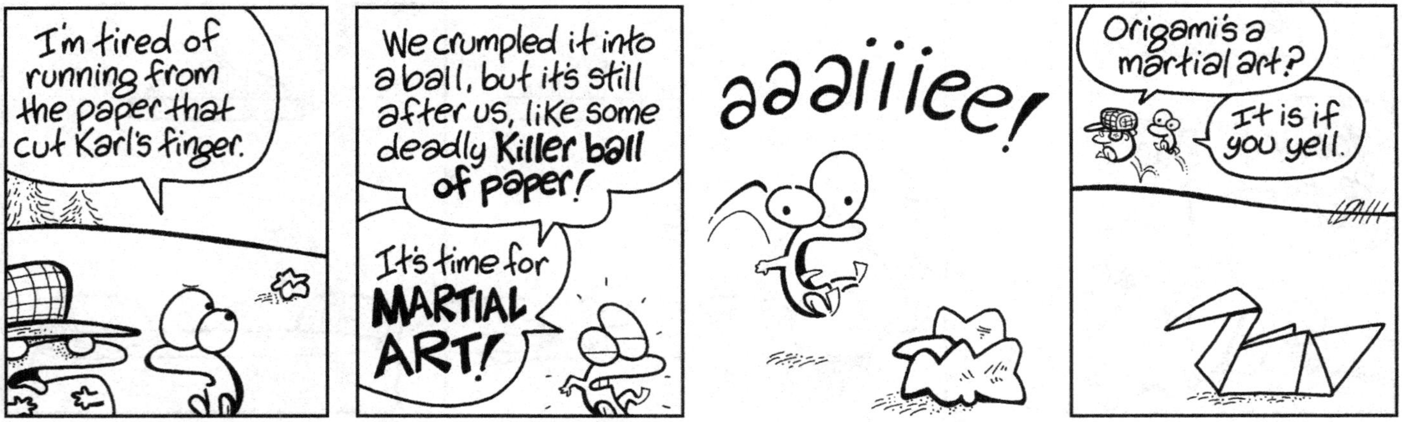
I'm tired of running from the paper that cut Karl's finger.
We crumpled it into a ball, but it's still after us, like some deadly Killer ball of paper!
It's time for MARTIAL ART!
aaaiiiee!
Origami's a martial art?
It is if you yell.

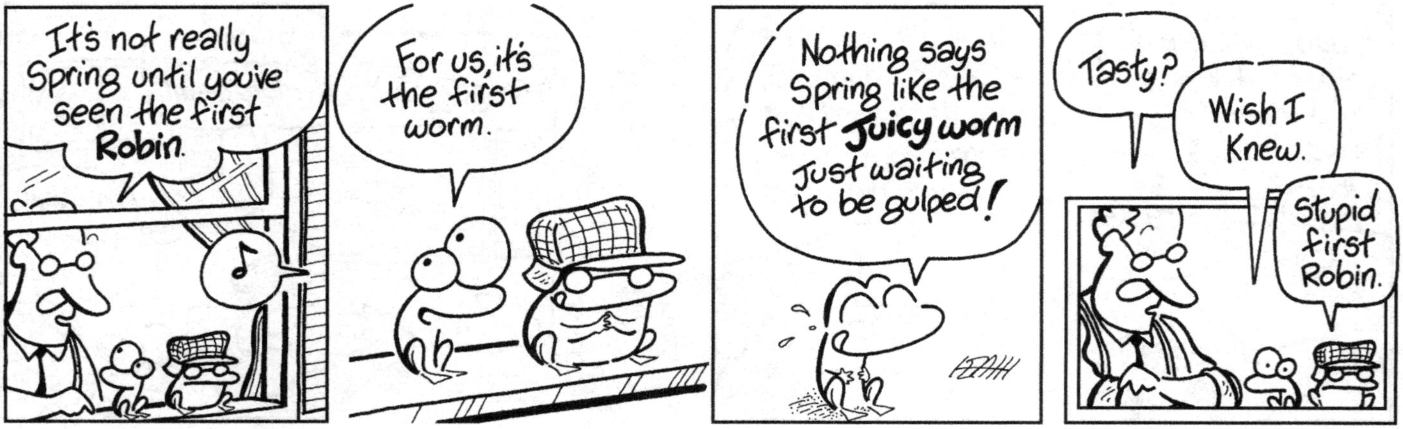
It's not really Spring until you've seen the first Robin.
For us, it's the first worm.
Nothing says Spring like the first Juicy worm Just waiting to be gulped!
Tasty?
Wish I Knew.
Stupid first Robin.

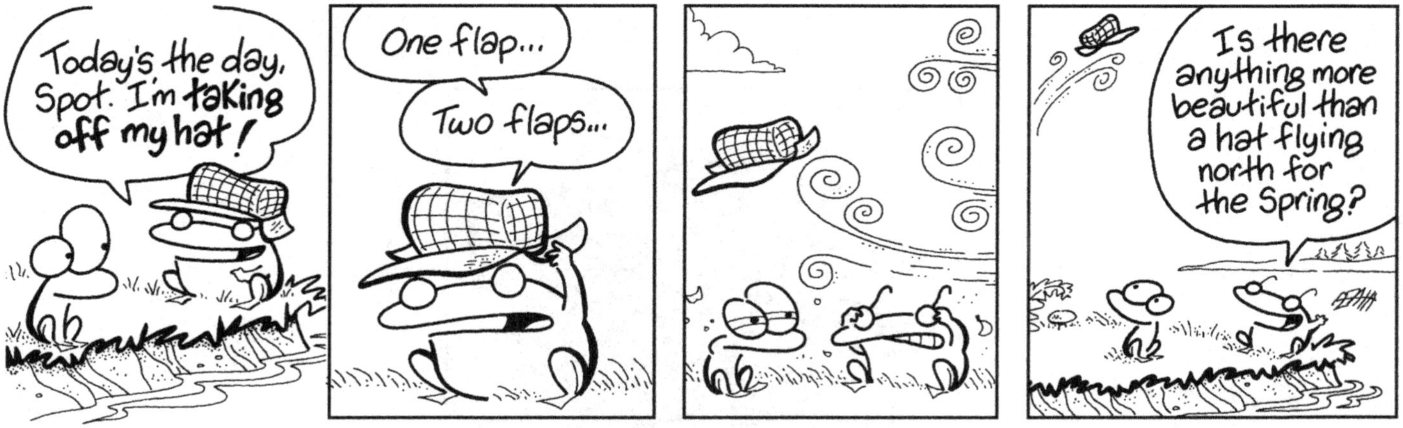
Today's the day, Spot. I'm **taking off my hat!**
One flap...
Two flaps...
Is there anything more beautiful than a hat flying north for the Spring?

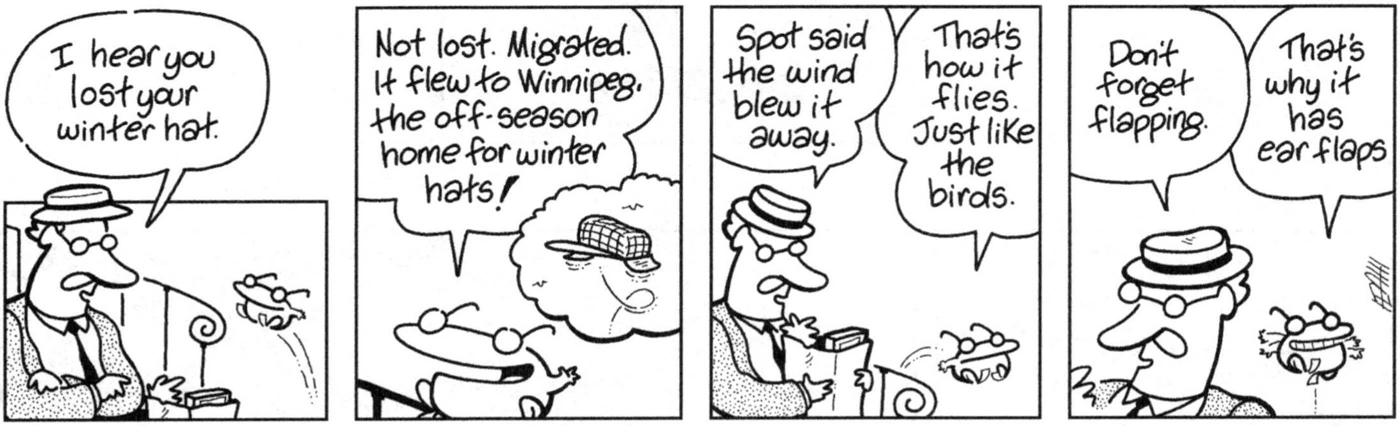
I hear you lost your winter hat.
Not lost. Migrated. It flew to Winnipeg, the off-season home for winter hats!
Spot said the wind blew it away.
That's how it flies. Just like the birds.
Don't forget flapping.
That's why it has ear flaps

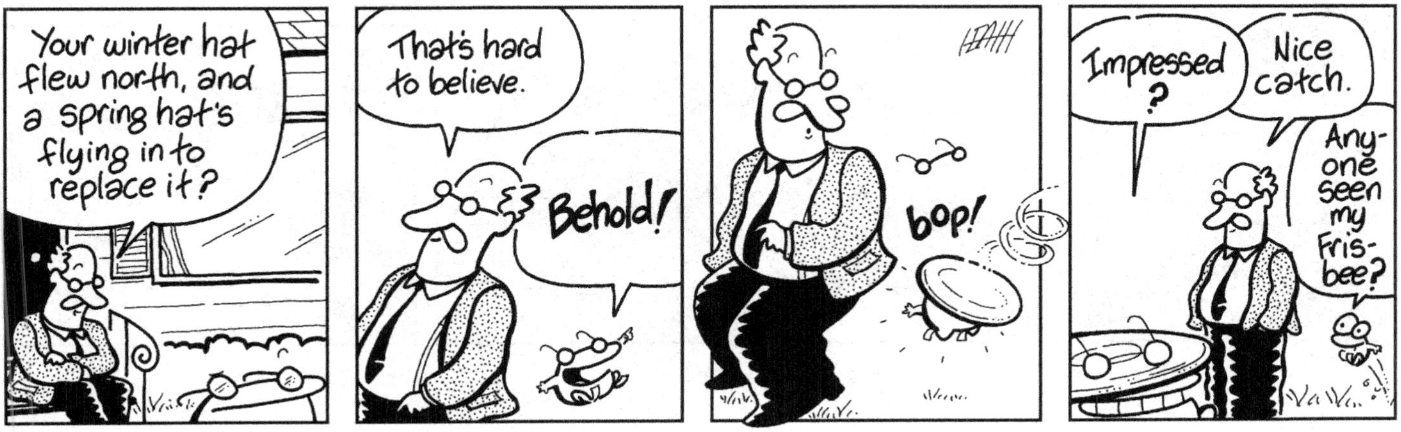
Your winter hat flew north, and a spring hat's flying in to replace it?
That's hard to believe.
Behold!
bop!
Impressed?
Nice catch.
Any-one seen my Fris-bee?

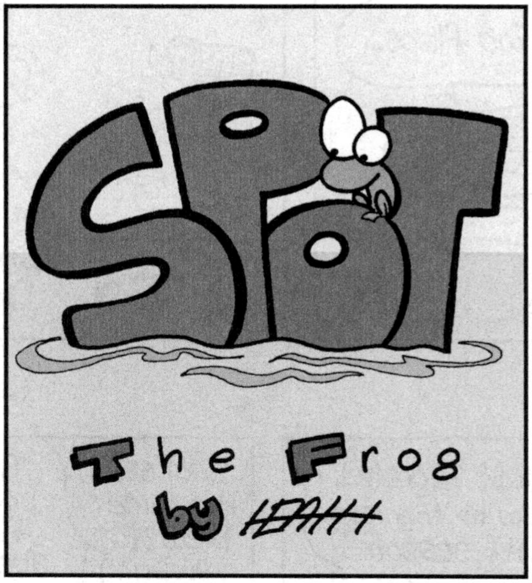
SPOT
The Frog
by

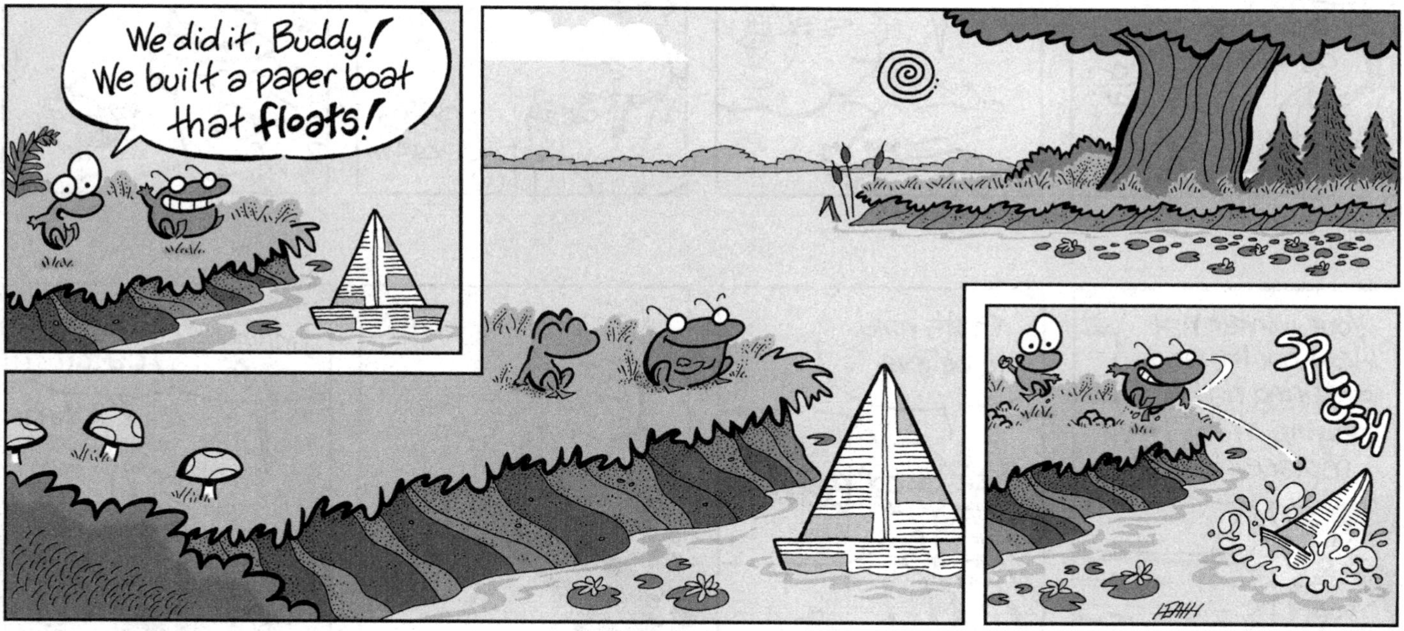
We did it, Buddy! We built a paper boat that floats!
SPLOOSH

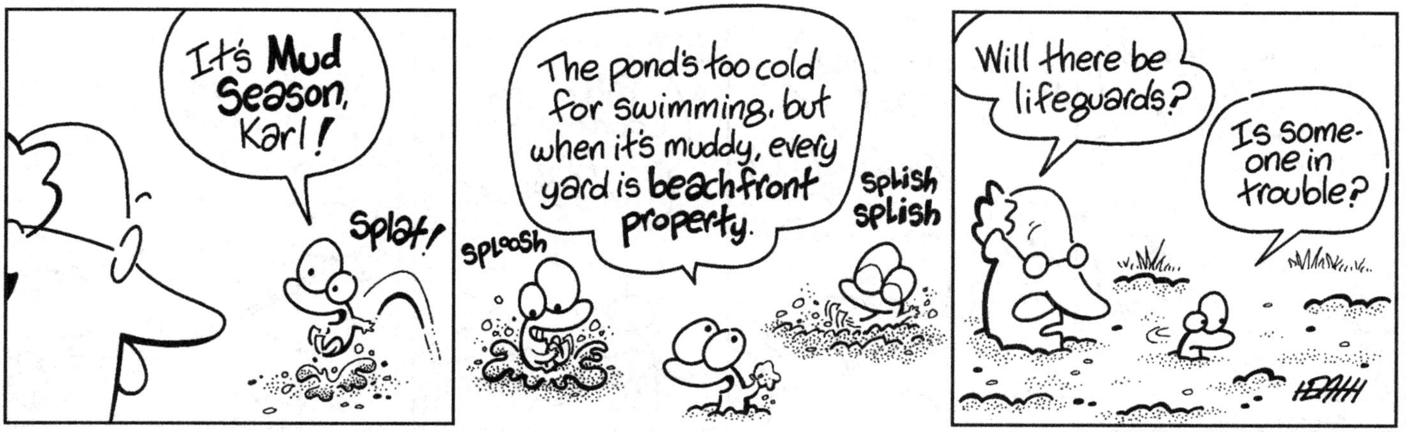
It's **Mud Season**, Karl!
Splat!
sploosh
The pond's too cold for swimming, but when it's muddy, every yard is **beachfront property**.
splish splish
Will there be lifeguards?
Is some-one in trouble?

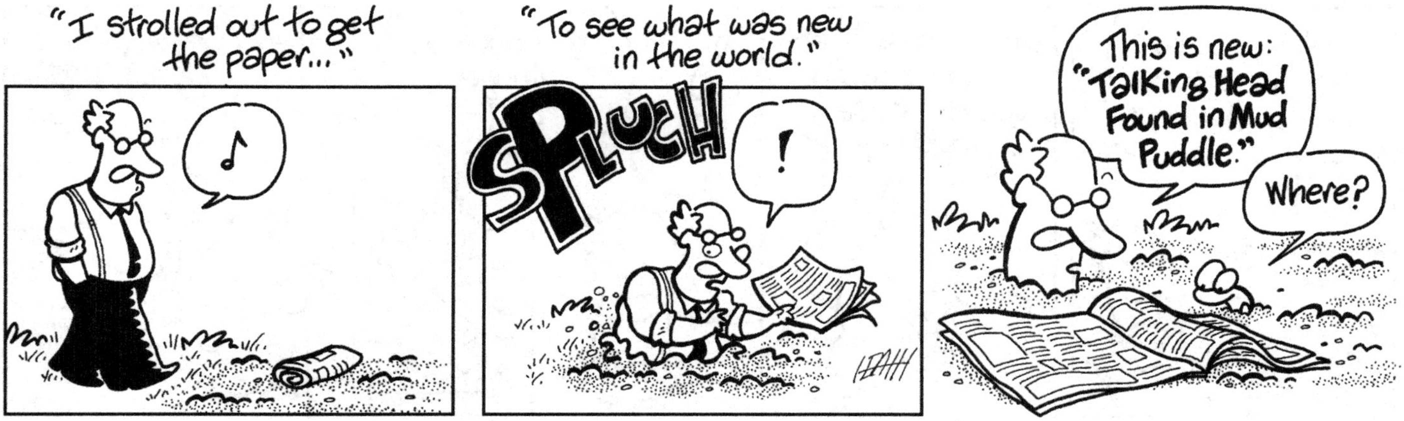
"I strolled out to get the paper..."
♪
"To see what was new in the world."
SPLUCH
!
This is new: **"Talking Head Found in Mud Puddle."**
Where?

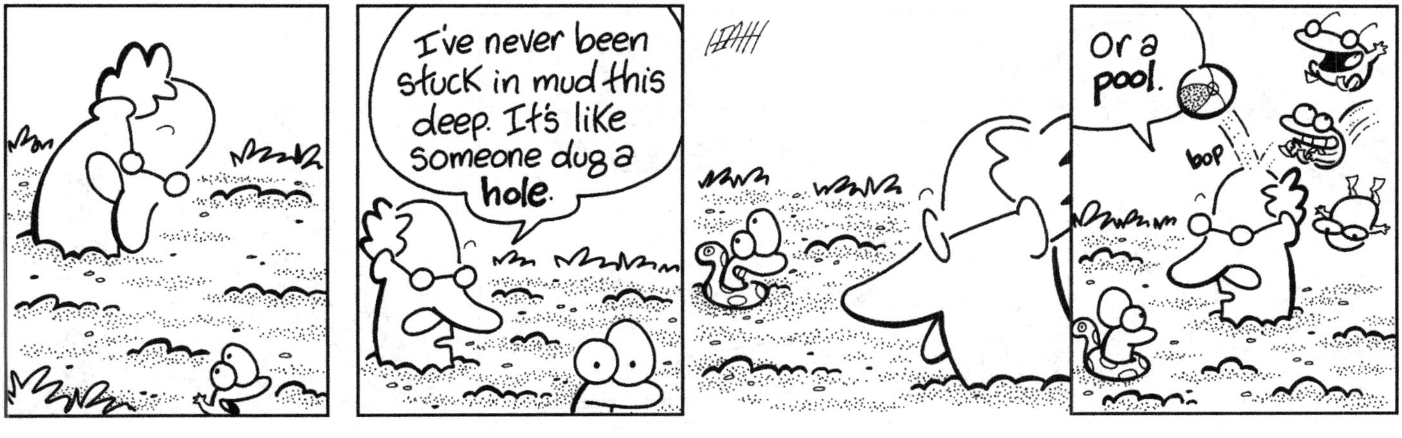
I've never been stuck in mud this deep. It's like someone dug a **hole**.
Or a **pool**.
bop

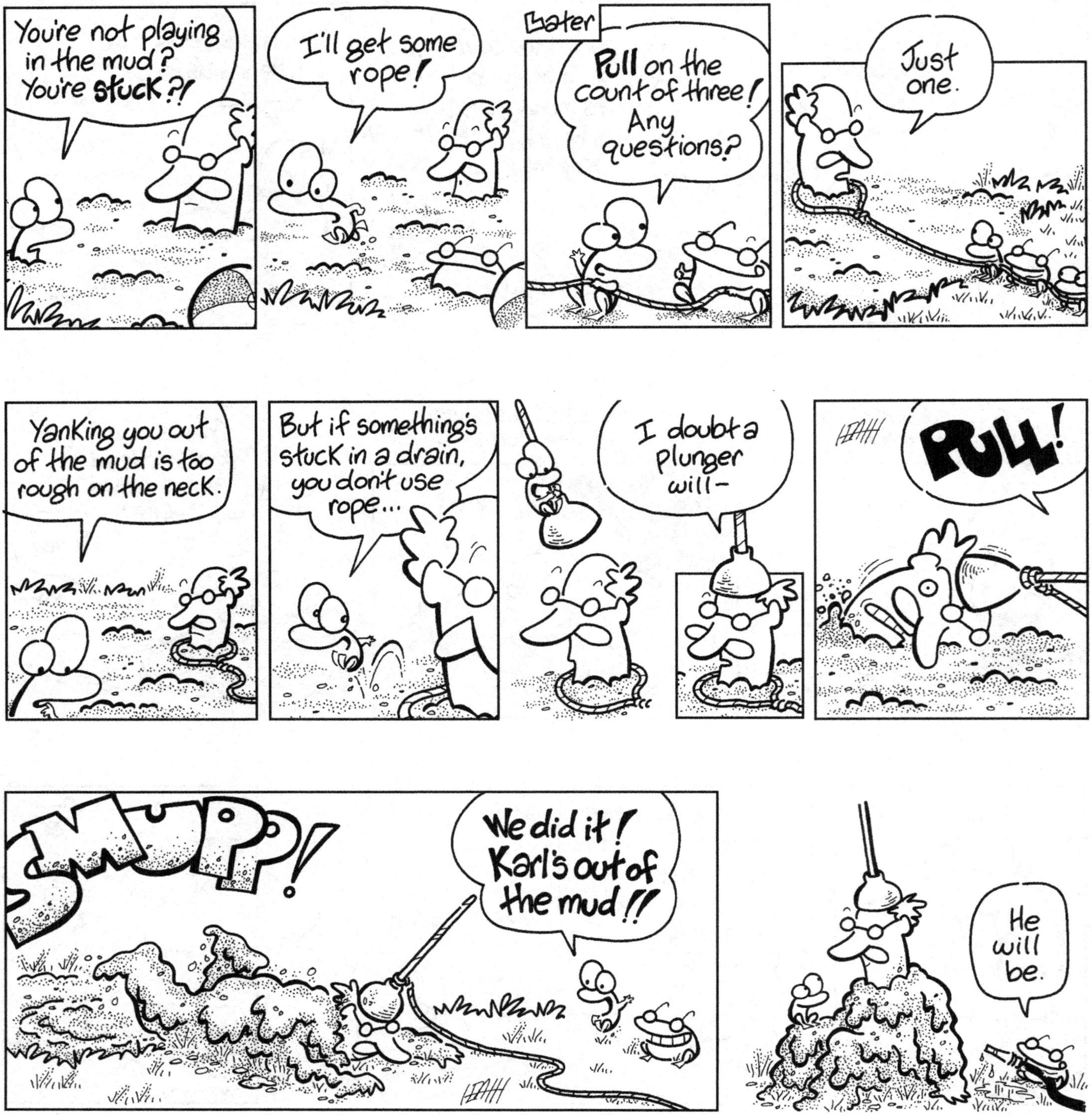
You're not playing in the mud? You're stuck?!
I'll get some rope!
Later
Pull on the count of three! Any questions?
Just one.
Yanking you out of the mud is too rough on the neck.
But if something's stuck in a drain, you don't use rope...
I doubt a plunger will-
PULL!
SMUPP!
We did it! Karl's out of the mud!!
He will be.

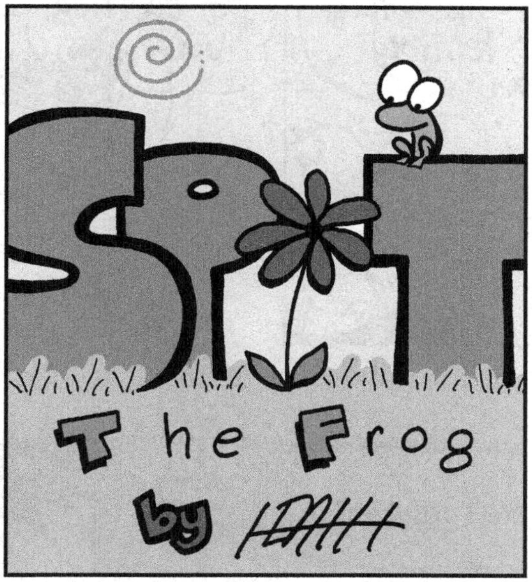
Spot
The Frog
by

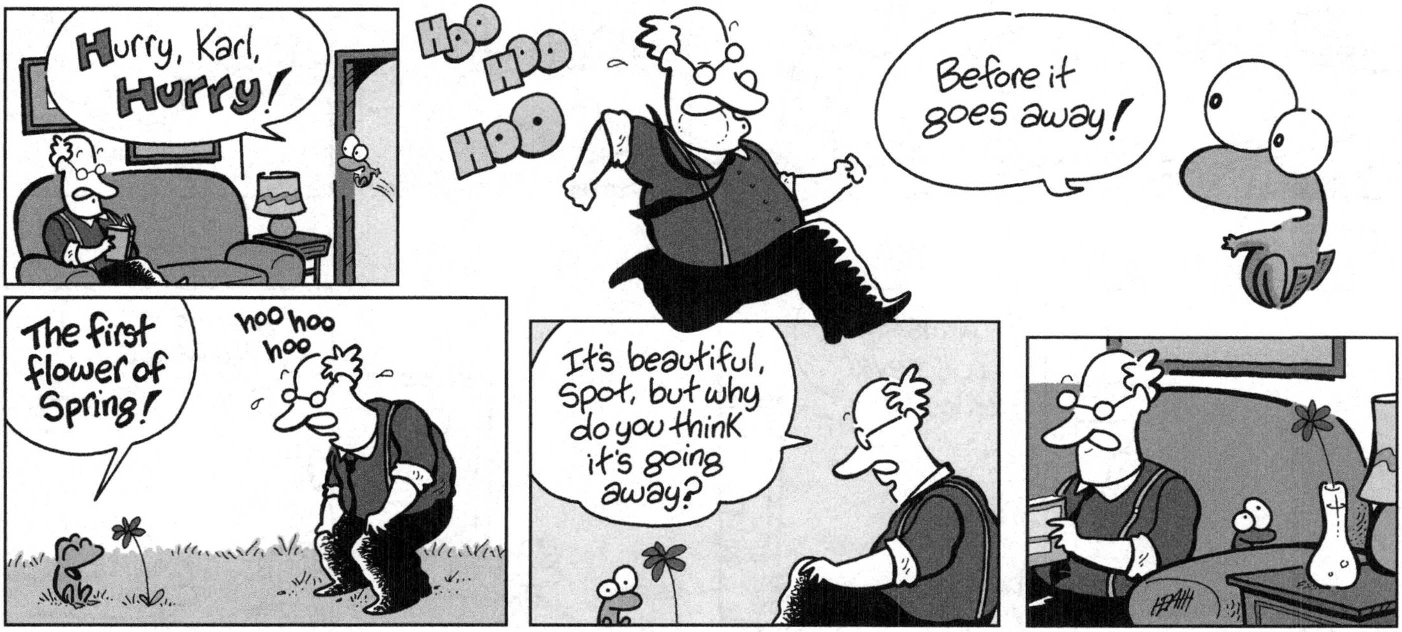
Hurry, Karl, Hurry!
HOO HOO HOO
Before it goes away!
The first flower of Spring!
hoo hoo hoo
It's beautiful, Spot, but why do you think it's going away?

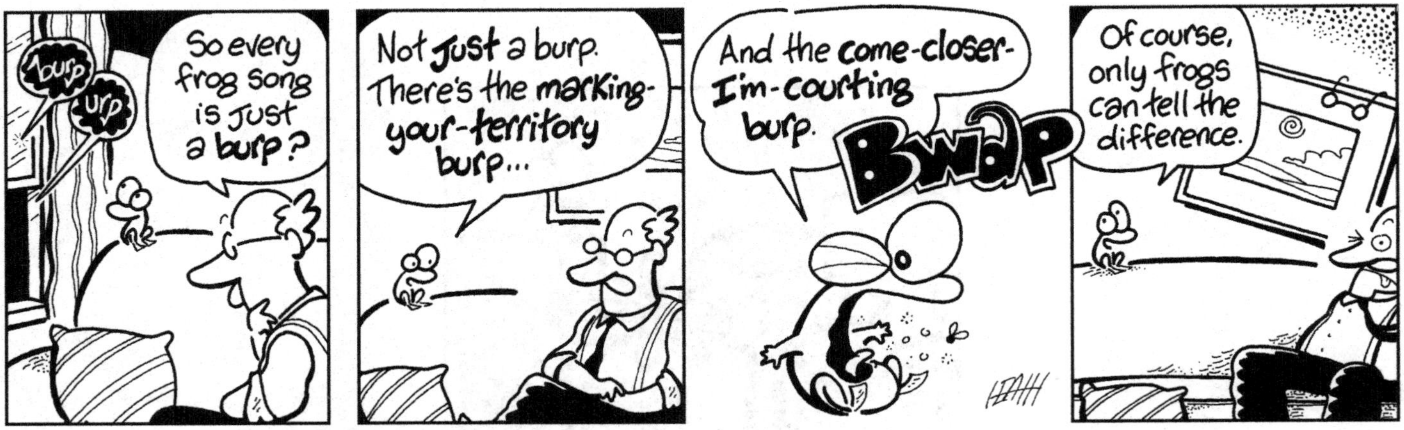
burp
urp
So every frog song is just a burp?
Not just a burp. There's the marking-your-territory burp...
And the come-closer-I'm-courting burp.
BWAP
Of course, only frogs can tell the difference.

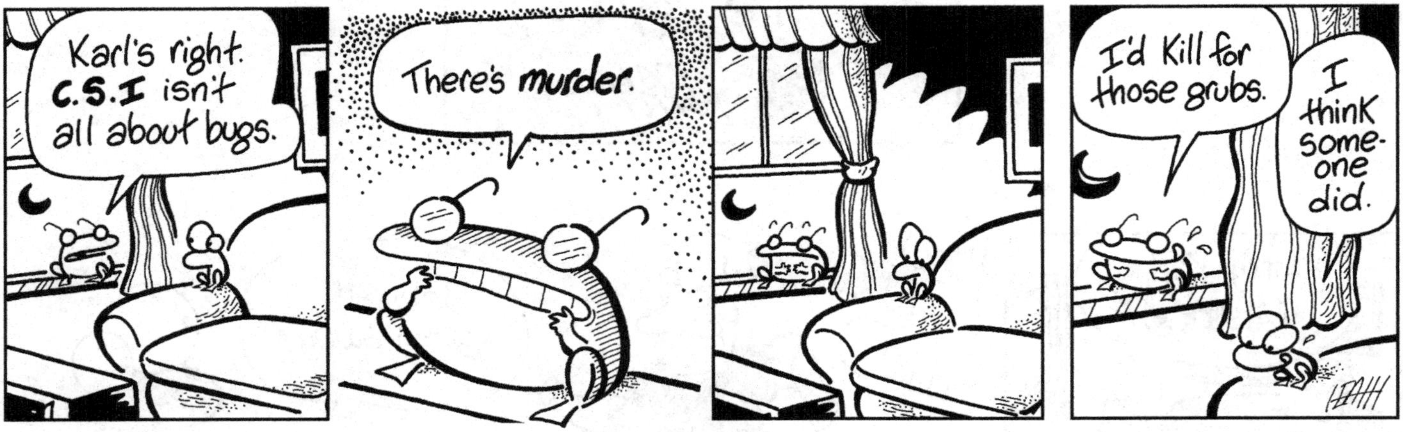
Karl's right. C.S.I isn't all about bugs.
There's murder.
I'd kill for those grubs.
I think someone did.

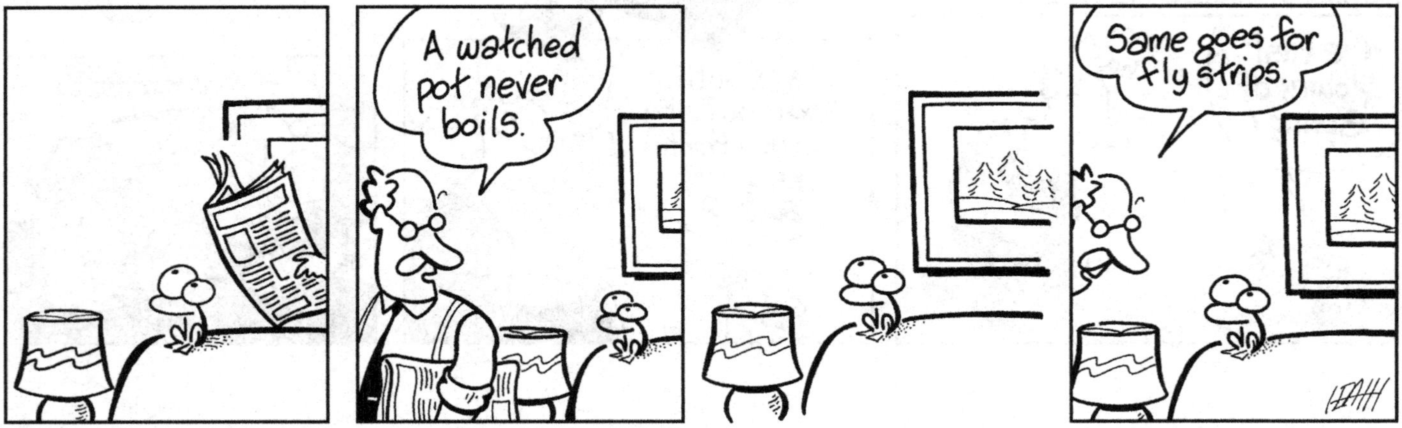
A watched pot never boils.
Same goes for fly strips.

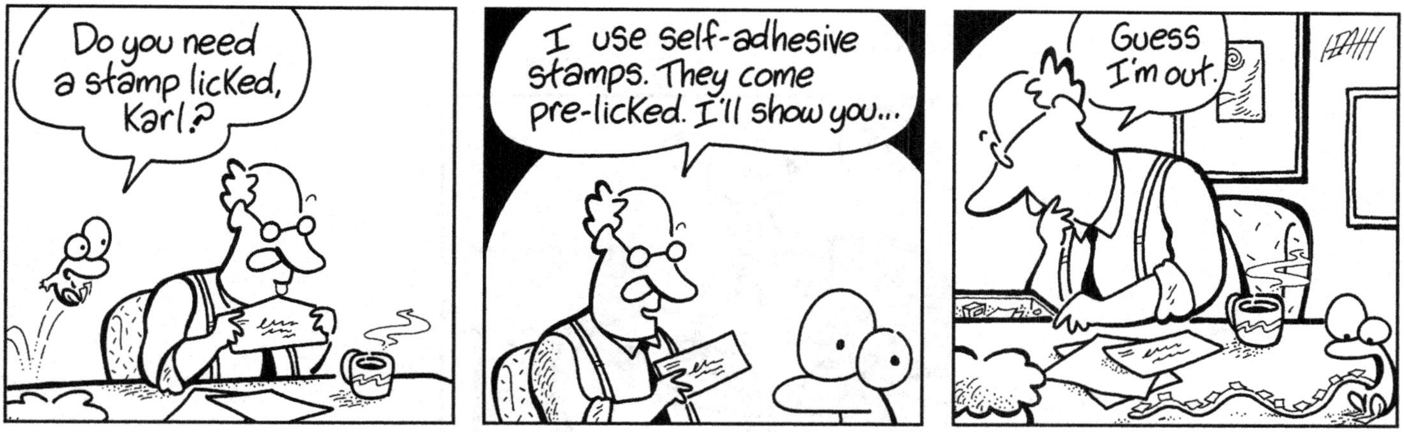
Do you need a stamp licked, Karl?
I use self-adhesive stamps. They come pre-licked. I'll show you...
Guess I'm out.

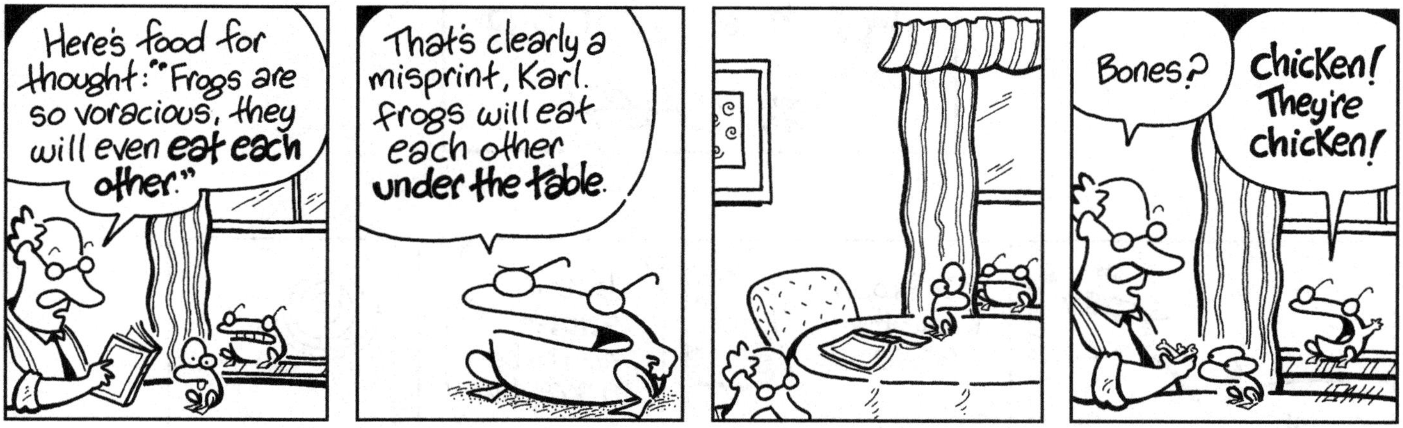
Here's food for thought: "Frogs are so voracious, they will even **eat each other**."
That's clearly a misprint, Karl. Frogs will eat each other **under the table**.
Bones?
Chicken! They're chicken!

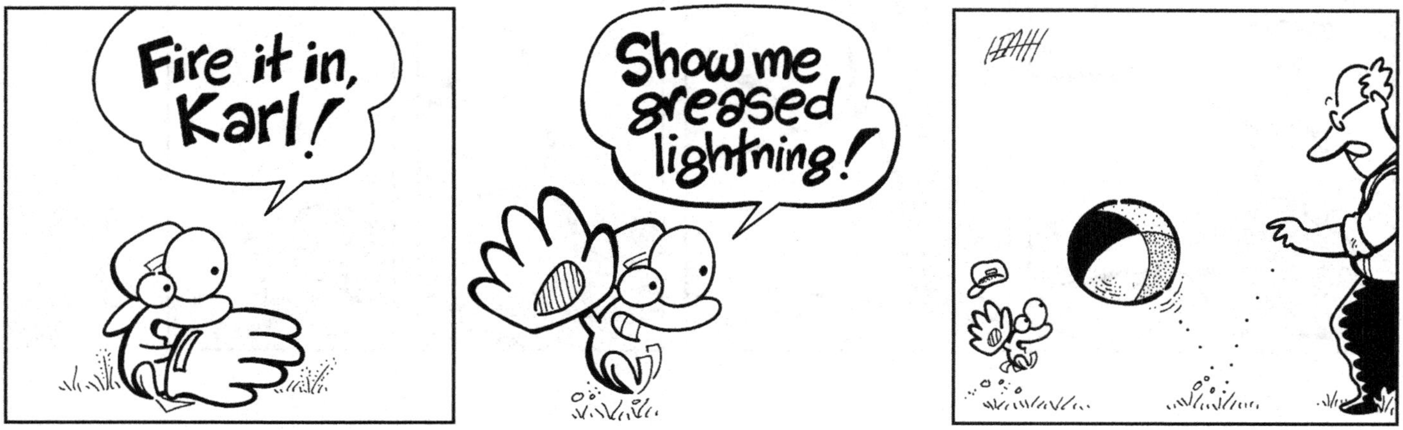
Fire it in, Karl!
Show me greased lightning!

Spot The Frog

by HEATH

I wish I had a giant umbrella to keep you out of the sun.

But Frogs know the score.

Life is **short,** and it's best to accept it.

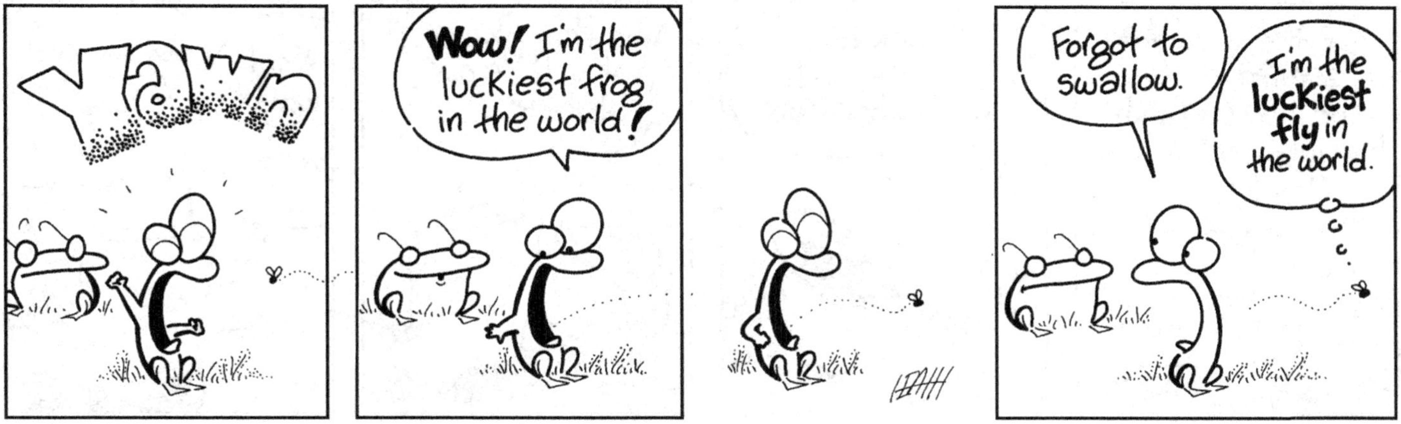
Yawn
Wow! I'm the luckiest frog in the world!
Forgot to swallow.
I'm the luckiest fly in the world.

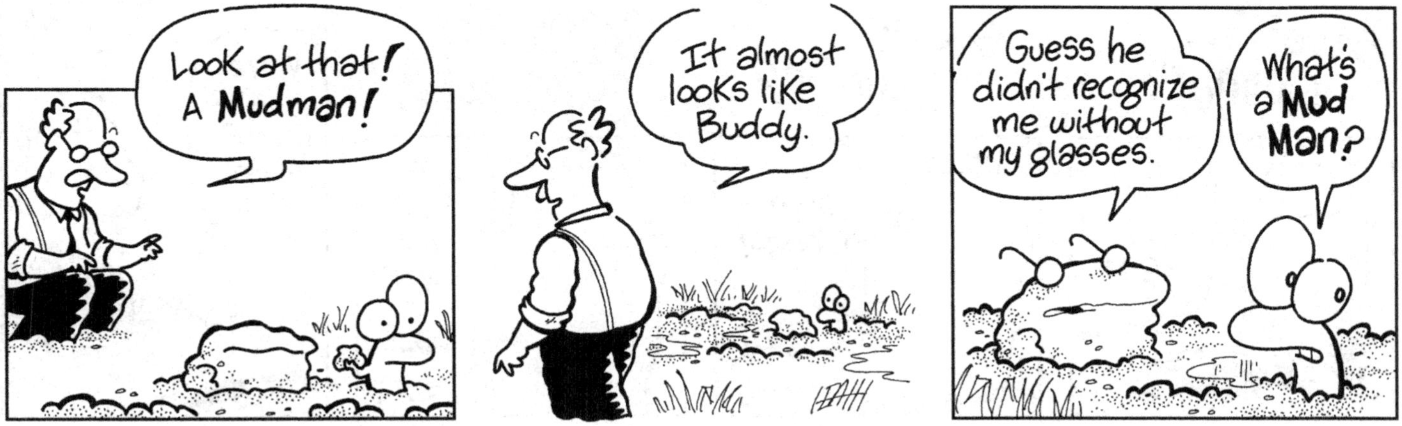
Look at that! A Mudman!
It almost looks like Buddy.
Guess he didn't recognize me without my glasses.
What's a Mud Man?

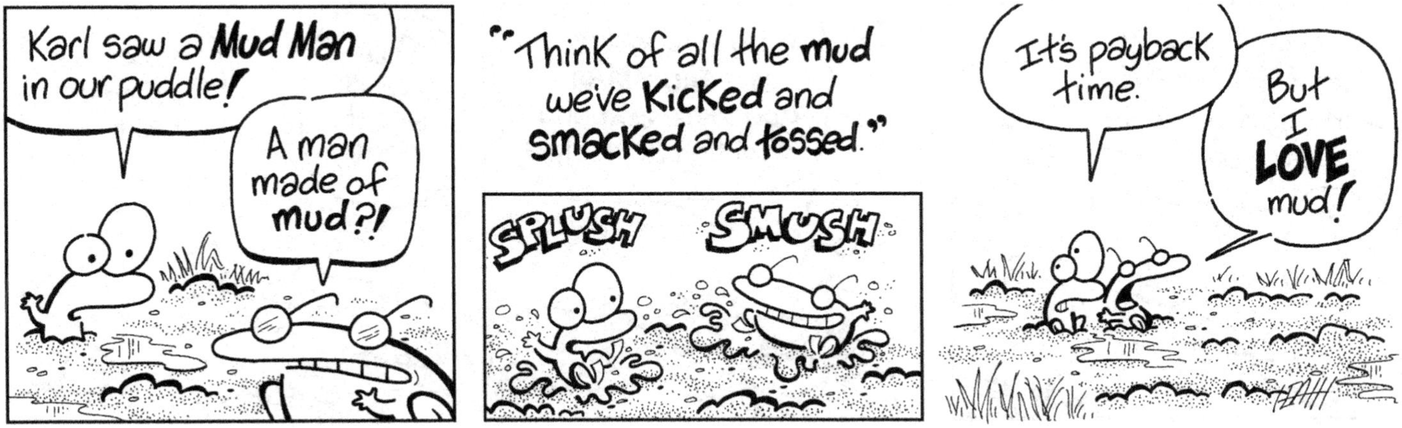
Karl saw a Mud Man in our puddle!
A man made of mud?!
"Think of all the mud we've kicked and smacked and tossed."
SPLUSH
SMUSH
It's payback time.
But I LOVE mud!

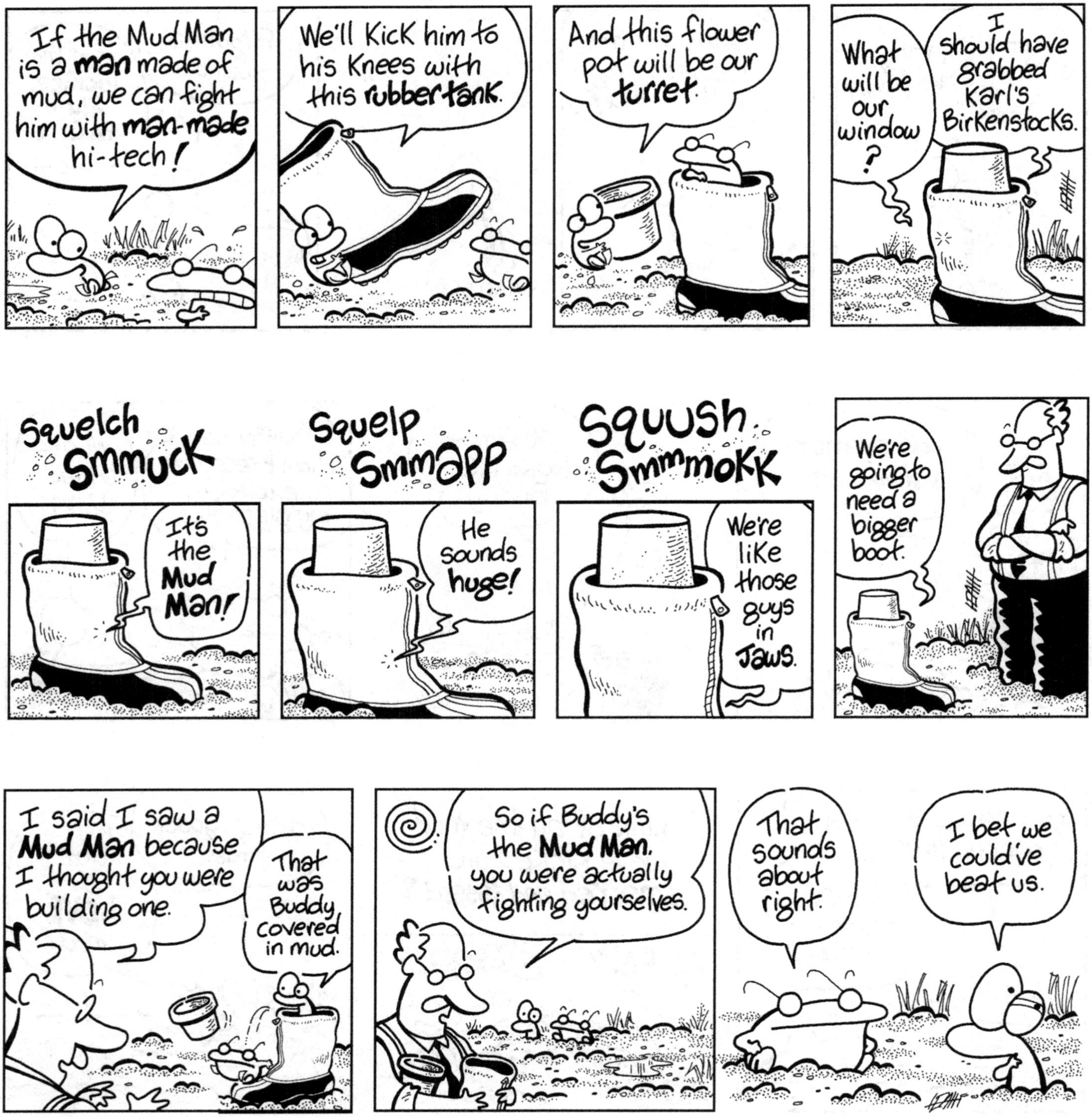
If the Mud Man is a man made of mud, we can fight him with man-made hi-tech!
We'll Kick him to his Knees with this rubber tank.
And this flower pot will be our turret.
What will be our window?
I should have grabbed Karl's Birkenstocks.
Squelch
Smmuck
It's the Mud Man!
Squelp
Smmapp
He sounds huge!
Squush.
Smmmokk
We're like those guys in Jaws.
We're going to need a bigger boot.
I said I saw a Mud Man because I thought you were building one.
That was Buddy covered in mud.
So if Buddy's the Mud Man, you were actually fighting yourselves.
That sounds about right.
I bet we could've beat us.

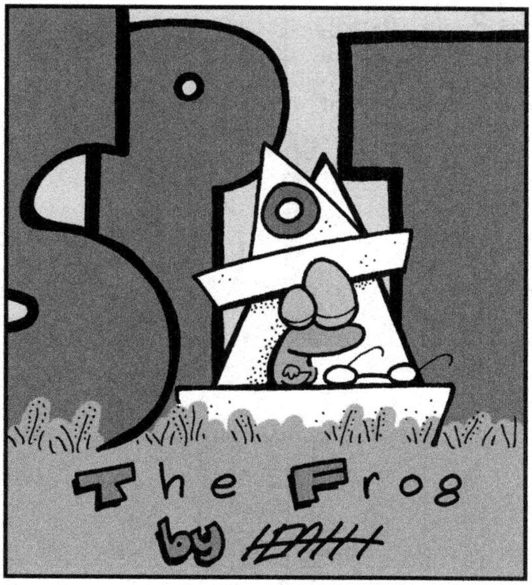
The Frog
by

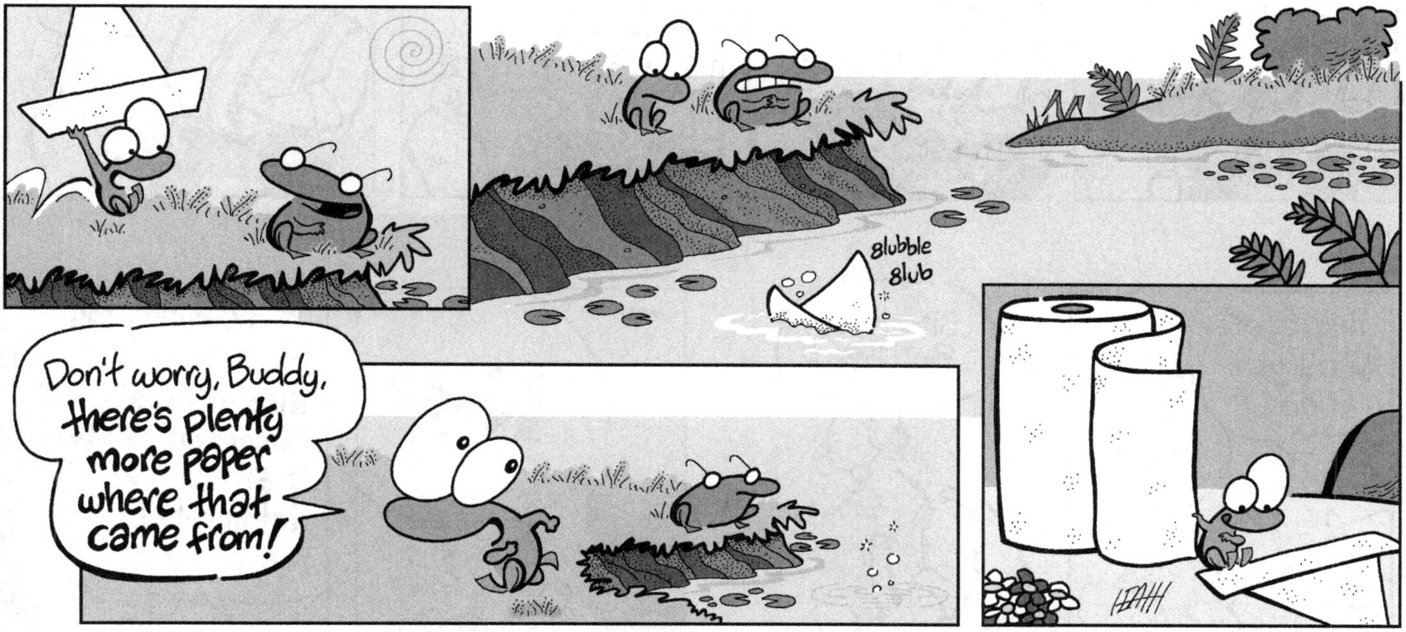
Blubble
Blub
Don't worry, Buddy, there's plenty more paper where that came from!

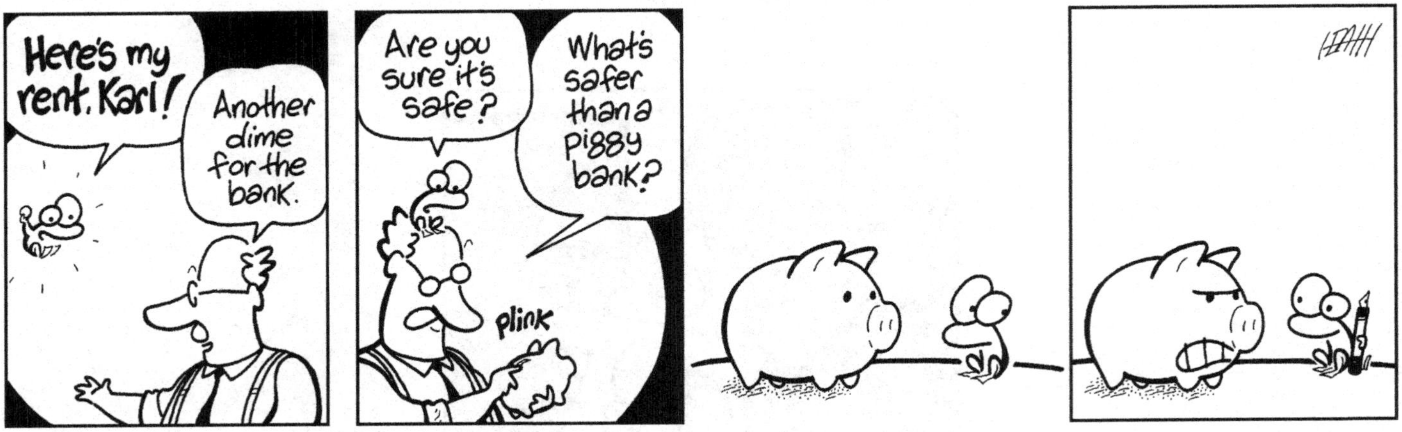
Here's my rent, Karl!
Another dime for the bank.
Are you sure it's safe?
What's safer than a piggy bank?
plink

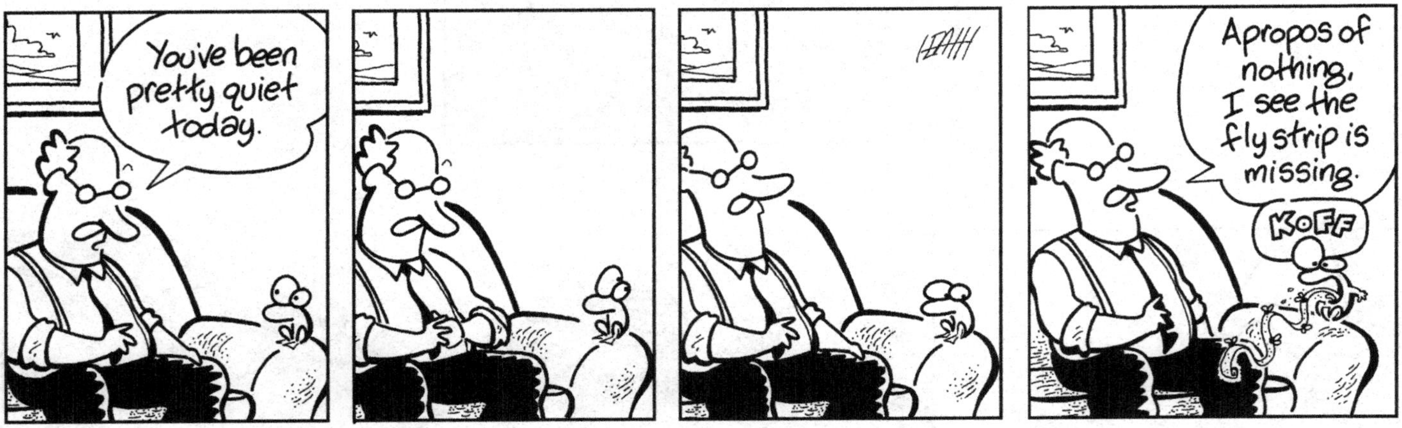
You've been pretty quiet today.
Apropos of nothing, I see the fly strip is missing.
KOFF

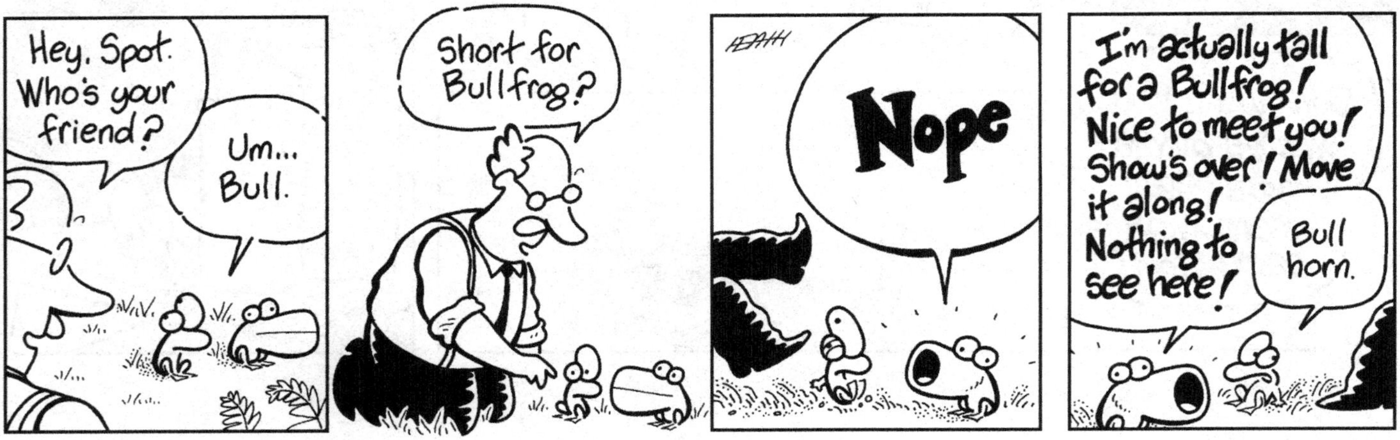
Hey, Spot. Who's your friend?
Um... Bull.
Short for Bullfrog?
Nope
I'm actually tall for a Bullfrog! Nice to meet you! Show's over! Move it along! Nothing to see here!
Bull horn.

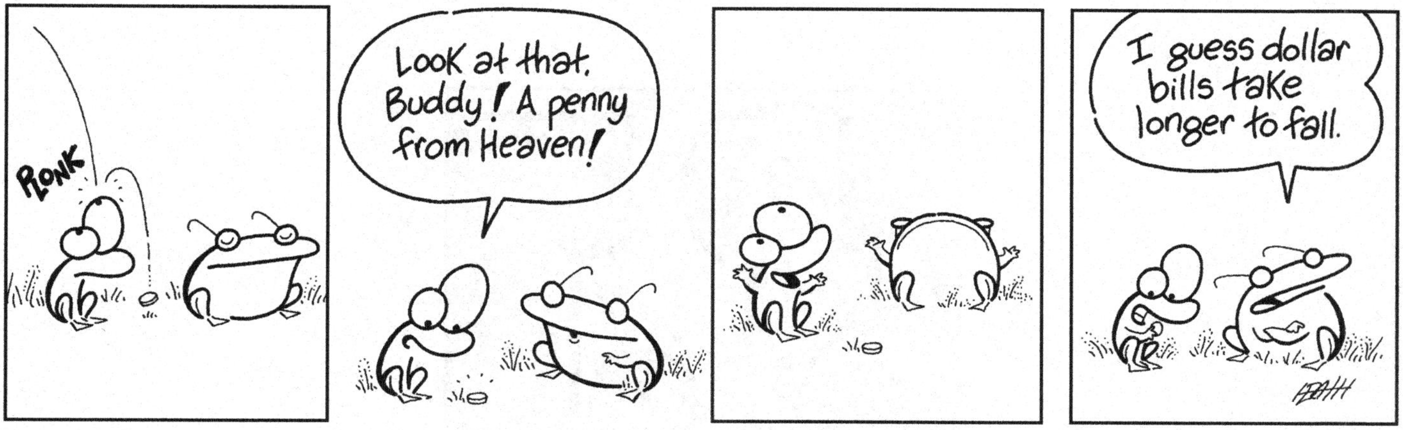
RONK
Look at that, Buddy! A penny from Heaven!
I guess dollar bills take longer to fall.

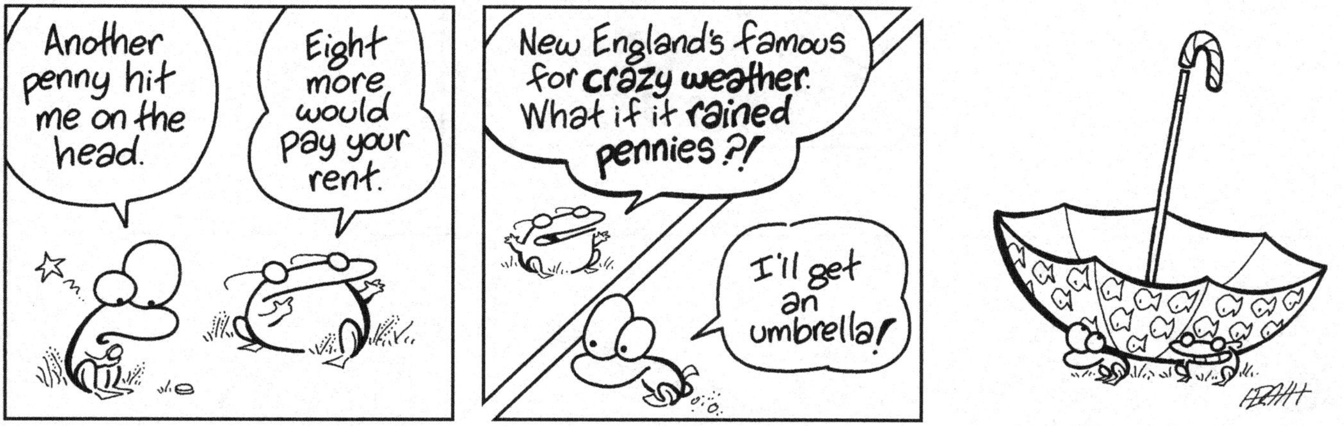
Another penny hit me on the head.
Eight more would pay your rent.
New England's famous for **crazy weather**. What if it **rained pennies**?!
I'll get an umbrella!

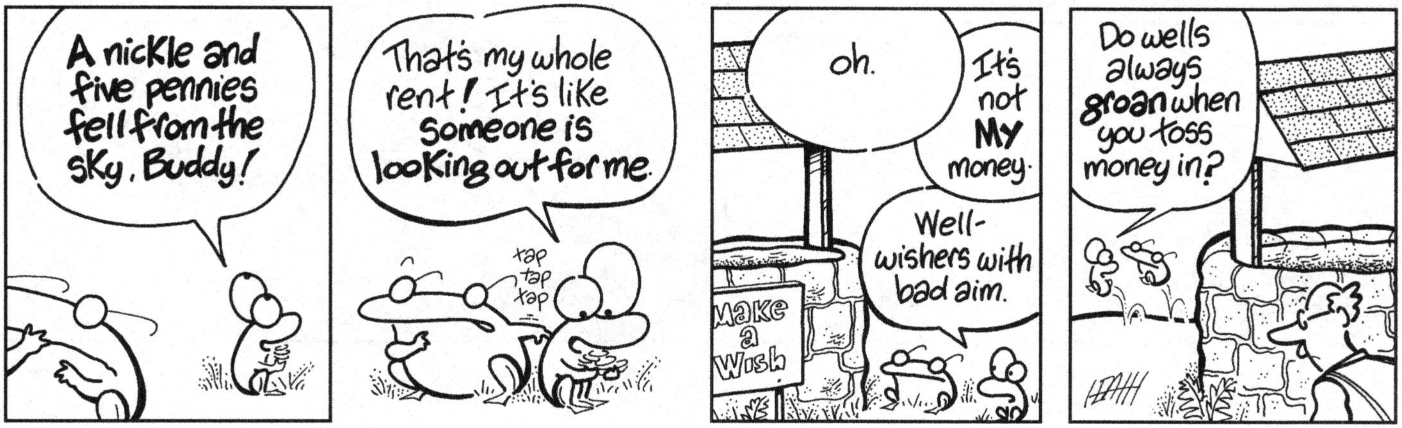
A nickle and five pennies fell from the sky, Buddy!
That's my whole rent! It's like **someone is looking out for me**.
tap tap tap
oh.
It's not **MY** money.
Well-wishers with bad aim.
Make a Wish
Do wells always **groan** when you toss money in?

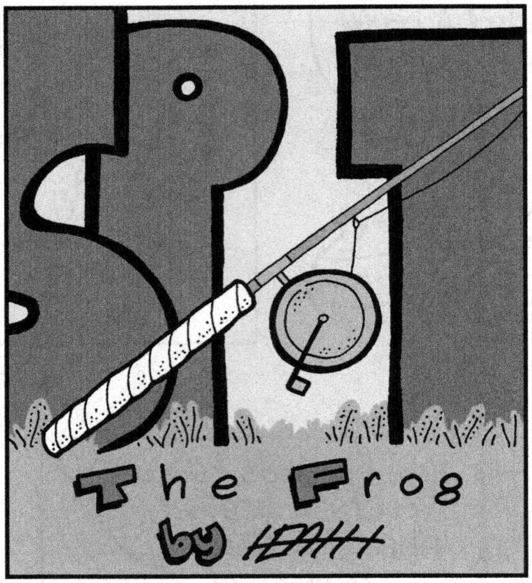
The Frog
by

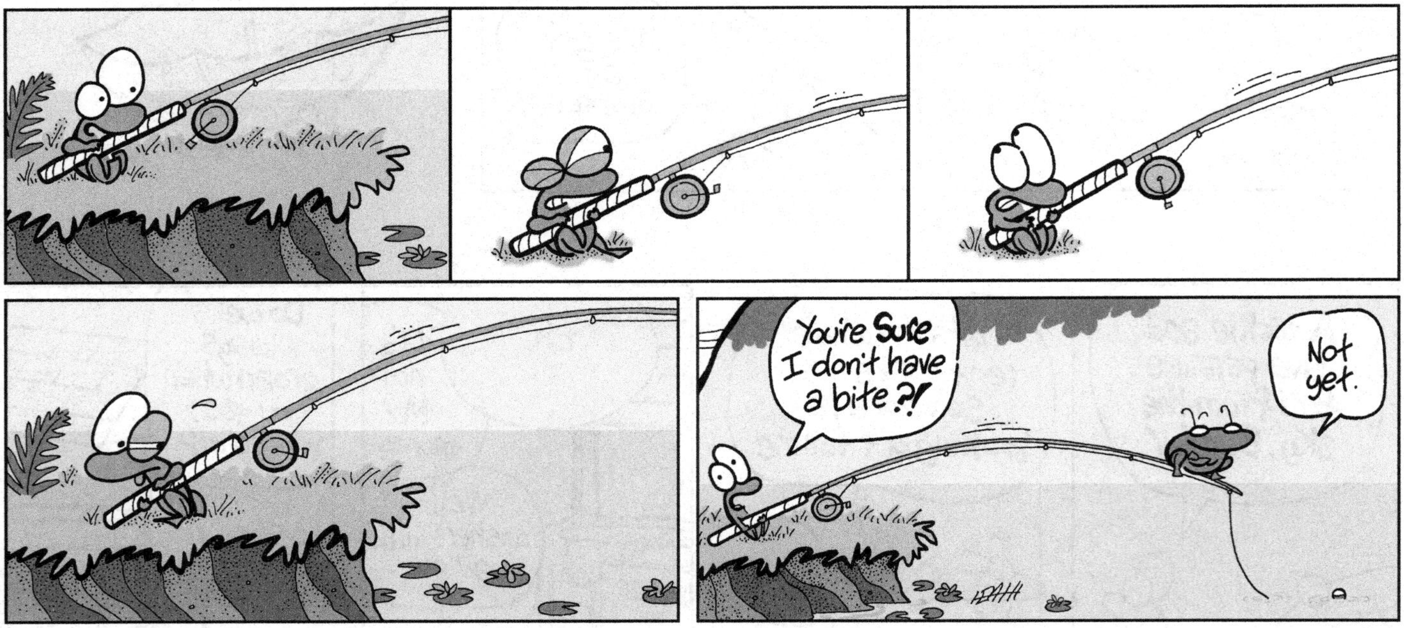
You're Sure I don't have a bite ?!
Not yet.

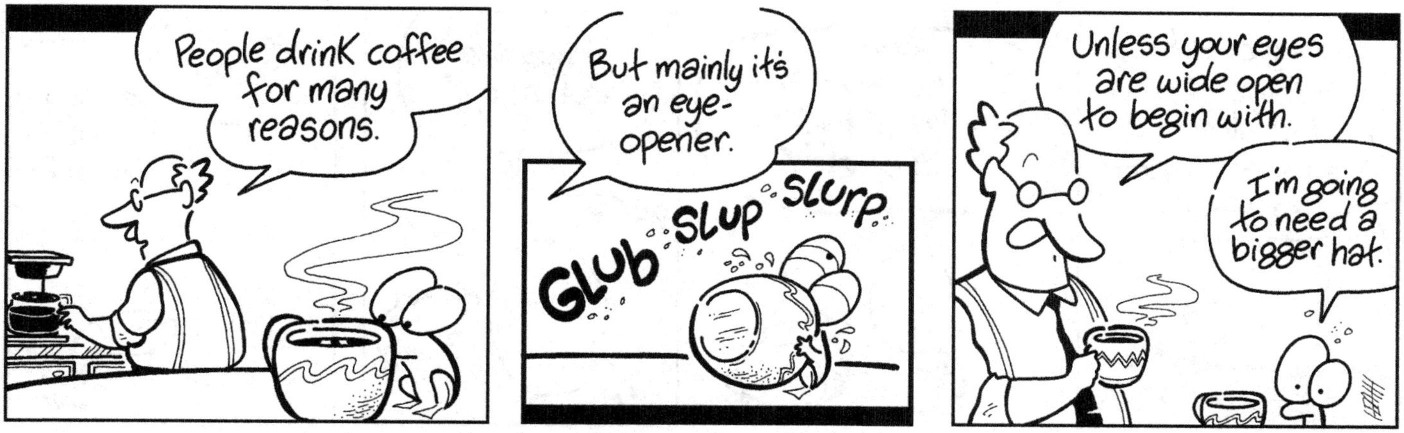
People drink coffee for many reasons.
But mainly it's an eye-opener.
GLUB
SLUP
SLURP
Unless your eyes are wide open to begin with.
I'm going to need a bigger hat.

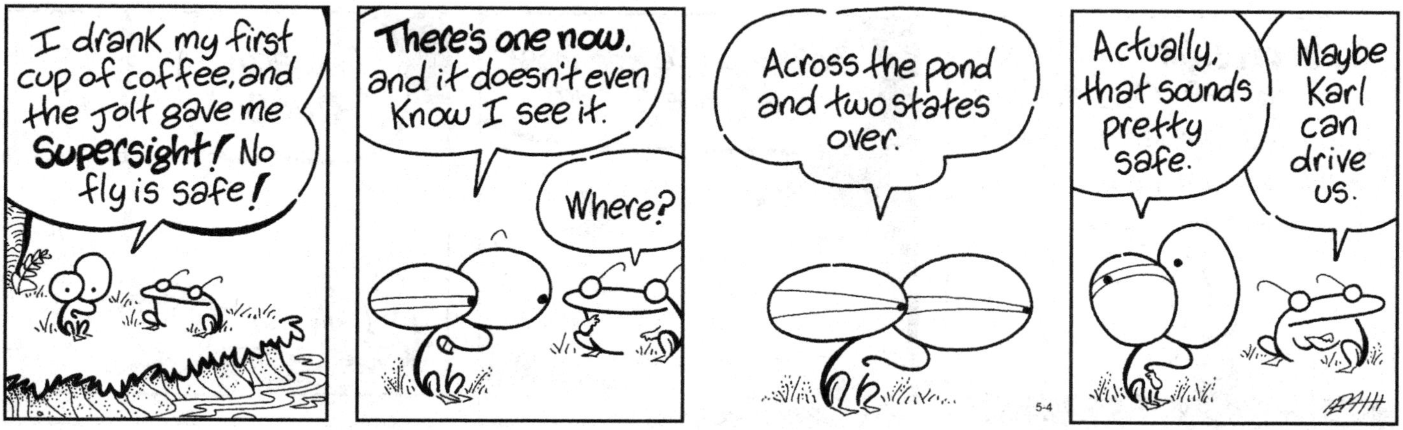
I drank my first cup of coffee, and the jolt gave me Supersight! No fly is safe!
There's one now, and it doesn't even know I see it.
Where?
Across the pond and two states over.
5-4
Actually, that sounds pretty safe.
Maybe Karl can drive us.

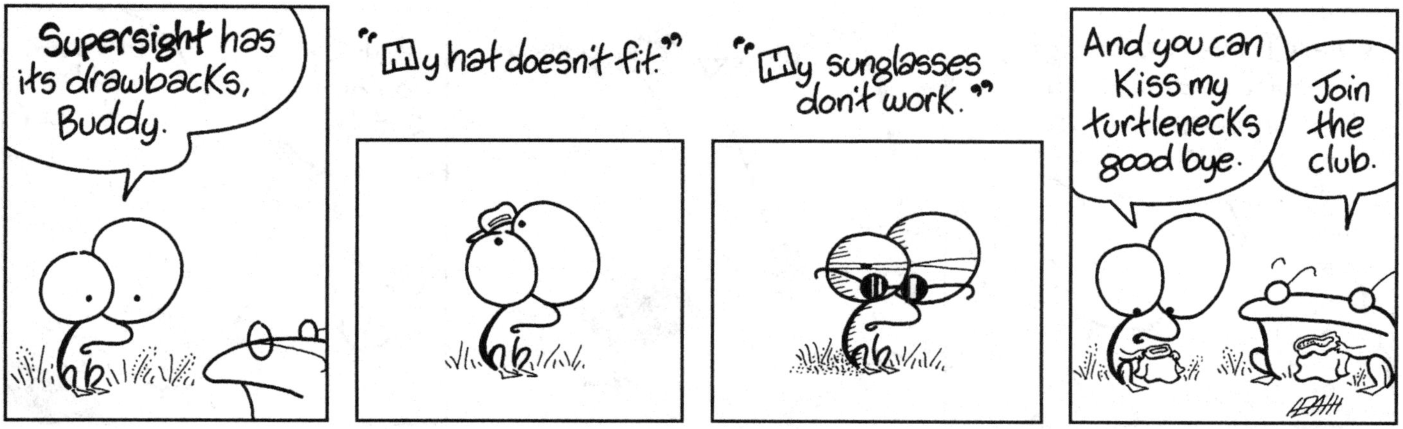
Supersight has its drawbacks, Buddy.
"My hat doesn't fit."
"My sunglasses don't work."
And you can kiss my turtlenecks good bye.
Join the club.

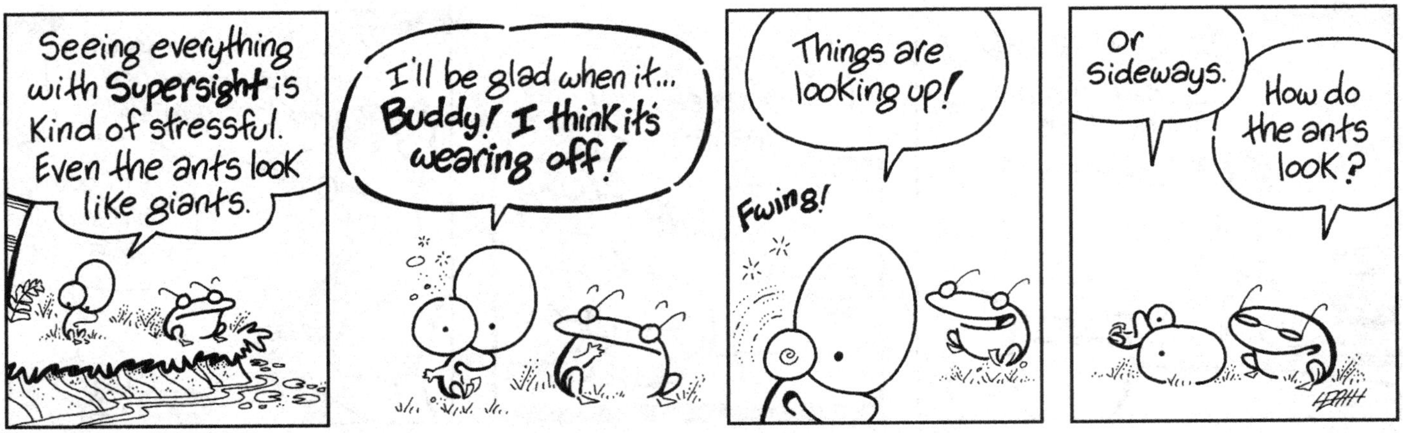
Seeing everything with Supersight is kind of stressful. Even the ants look like giants.
I'll be glad when it... Buddy! I think it's wearing off!
Things are looking up!
Fwing!
Or Sideways.
How do the ants look?

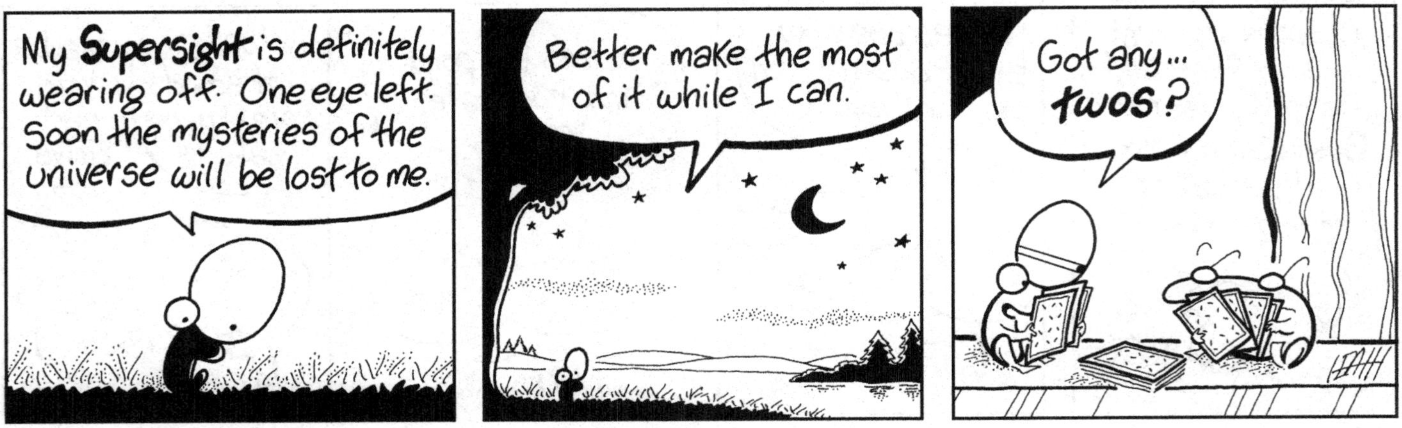
My Supersight is definitely wearing off. One eye left. Soon the mysteries of the universe will be lost to me.
Better make the most of it while I can.
Got any... twos?

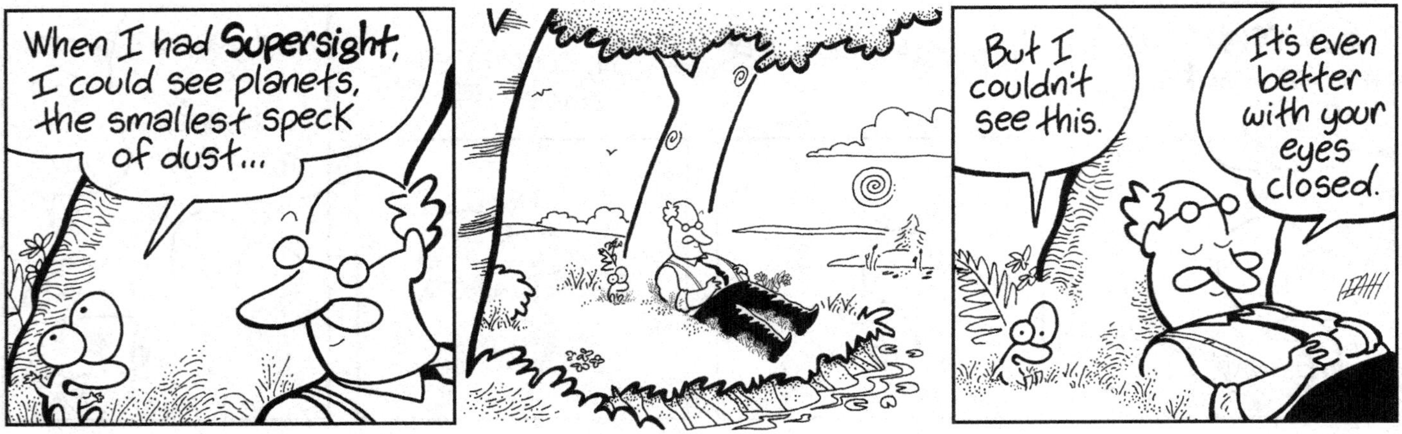
When I had Supersight, I could see planets, the smallest speck of dust...
But I couldn't see this.
It's even better with your eyes closed.

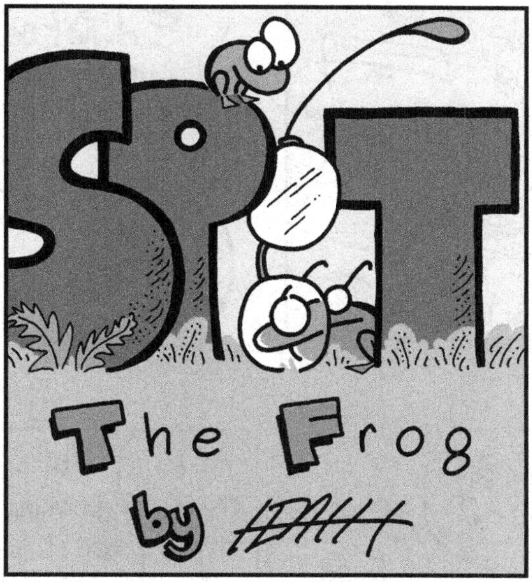
SPOT
The Frog
by

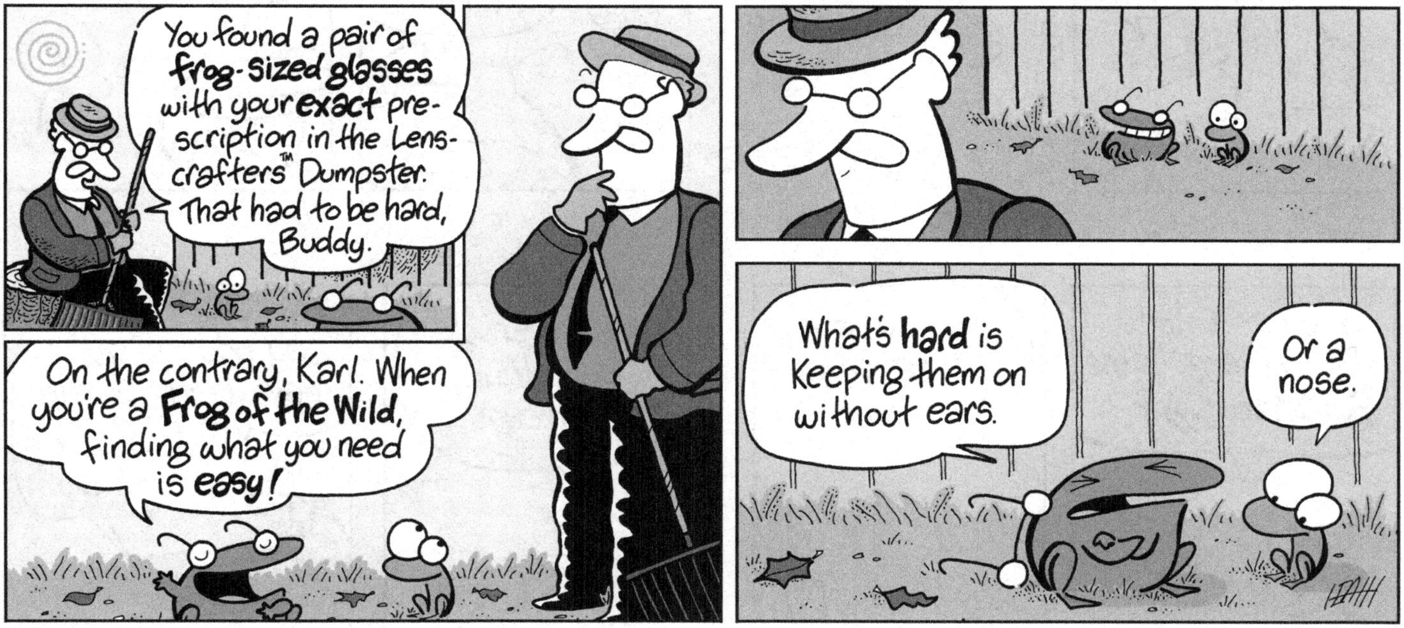
You found a pair of **frog-sized glasses** with your **exact** prescription in the Lenscrafters™ Dumpster. That had to be hard, Buddy.
On the contrary, Karl. When you're a **Frog of the Wild**, finding what you need is **easy**!
What's **hard** is keeping them on without ears.
Or a nose.

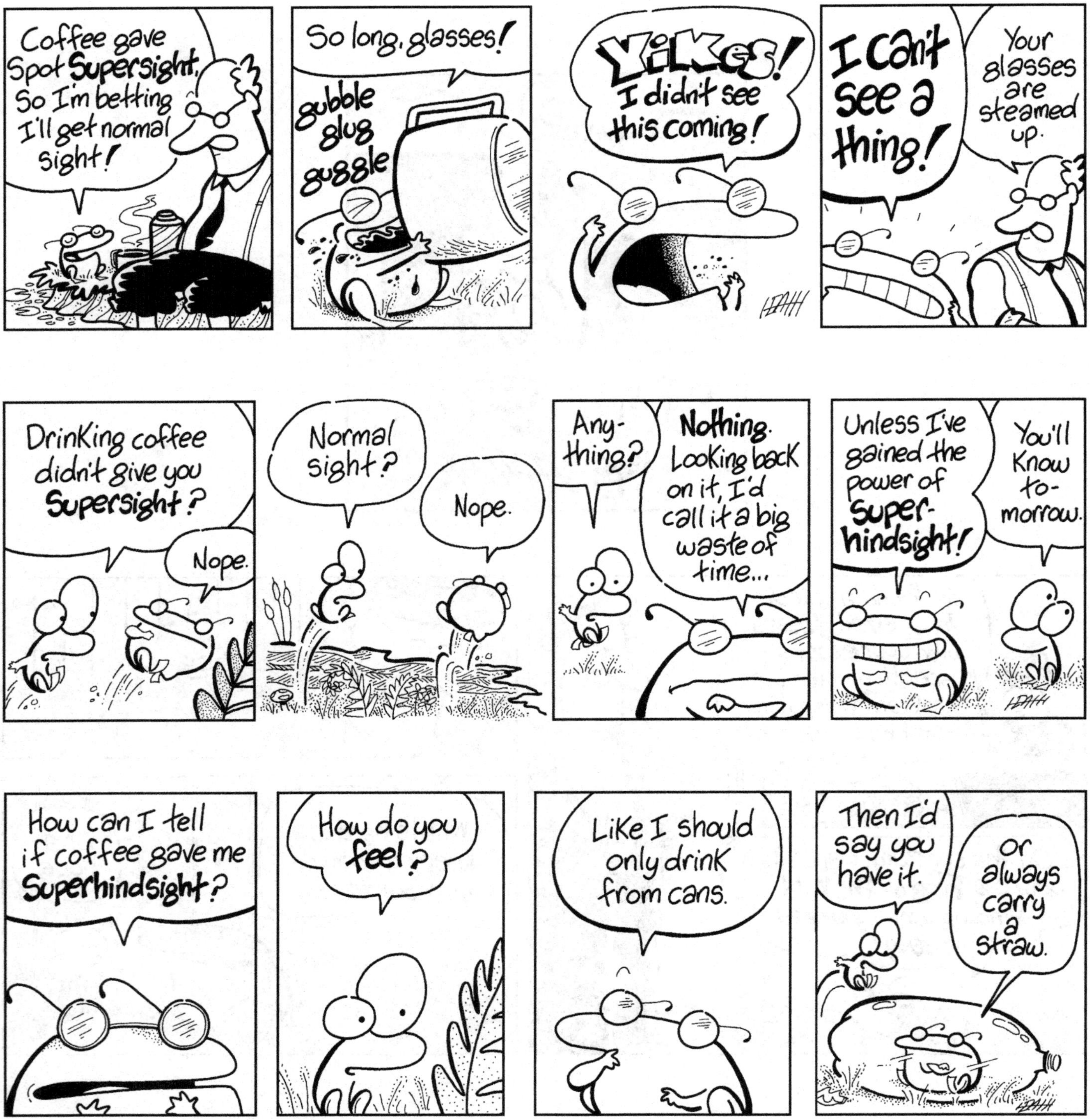
Coffee gave Spot Supersight, So I'm betting I'll get normal sight!
So long, glasses!
gubble glug guggle
YiKes! I didn't see this coming!
I can't see a thing!
Your glasses are steamed up.
Drinking coffee didn't give you Supersight?
Nope.
Normal sight?
Nope.
Any-thing?
Nothing. Looking back on it, I'd call it a big waste of time...
Unless I've gained the power of Super-hindsight!
You'll Know to-morrow.
How can I tell if coffee gave me Superhindsight?
How do you feel?
Like I should only drink from cans.
Then I'd say you have it.
Or always carry a straw.

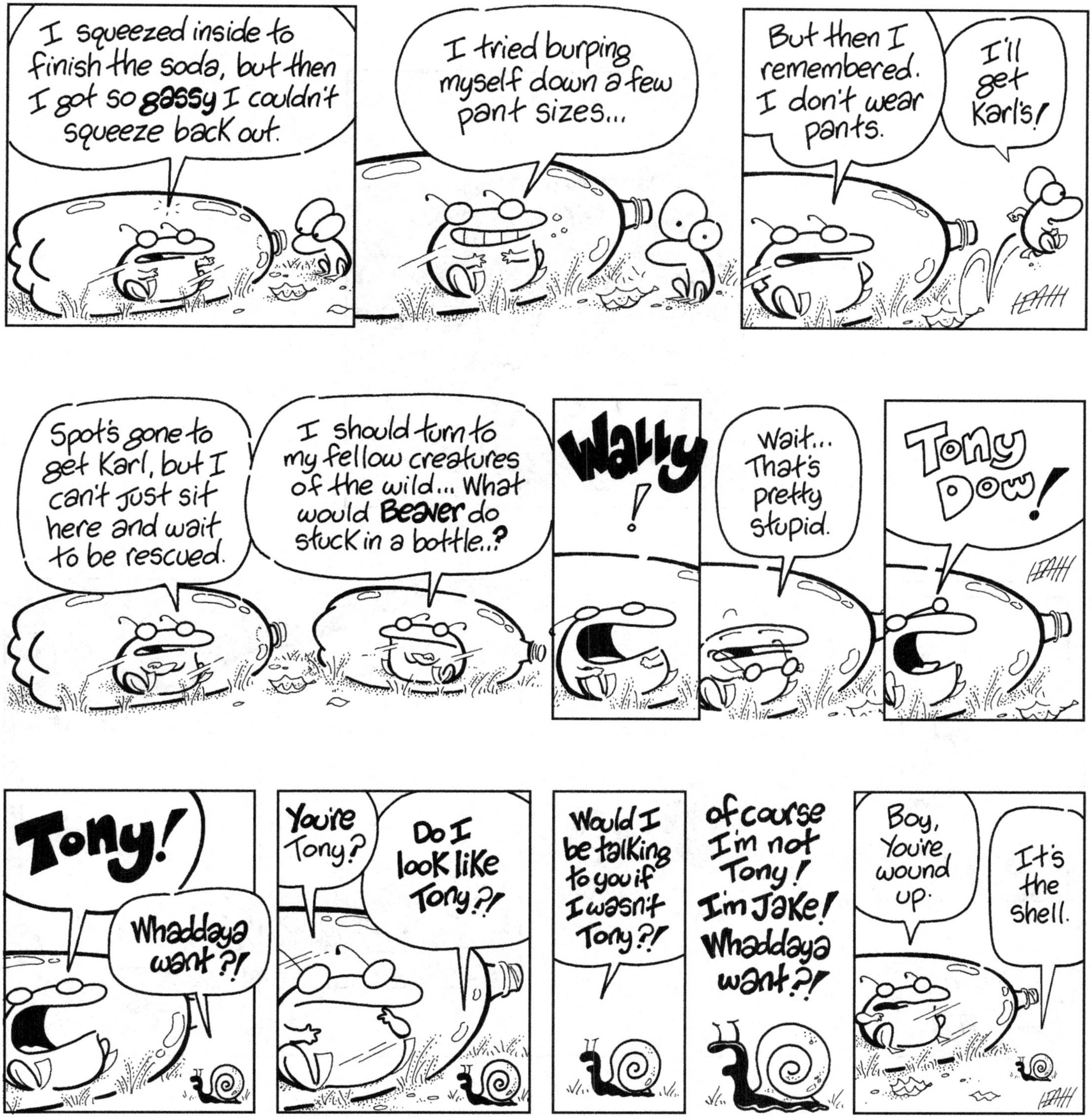
I squeezed inside to finish the soda, but then I got so gassy I couldn't squeeze back out.
I tried burping myself down a few pant sizes...
But then I remembered. I don't wear pants.
I'll get Karl's!
Spot's gone to get Karl, but I can't just sit here and wait to be rescued.
I should turn to my fellow creatures of the wild... What would Beaver do stuck in a bottle..?
Wally!
Wait... That's pretty stupid.
Tony Dow!
Tony!
Whaddaya want?!
You're Tony?
Do I look like Tony?!
Would I be talking to you if I wasn't Tony?!
Of course I'm not Tony! I'm Jake! Whaddaya want?!
Boy, you're wound up.
It's the shell.

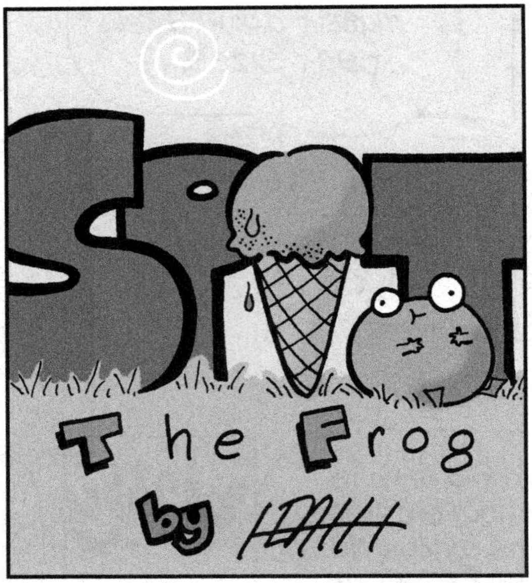
The Frog
by

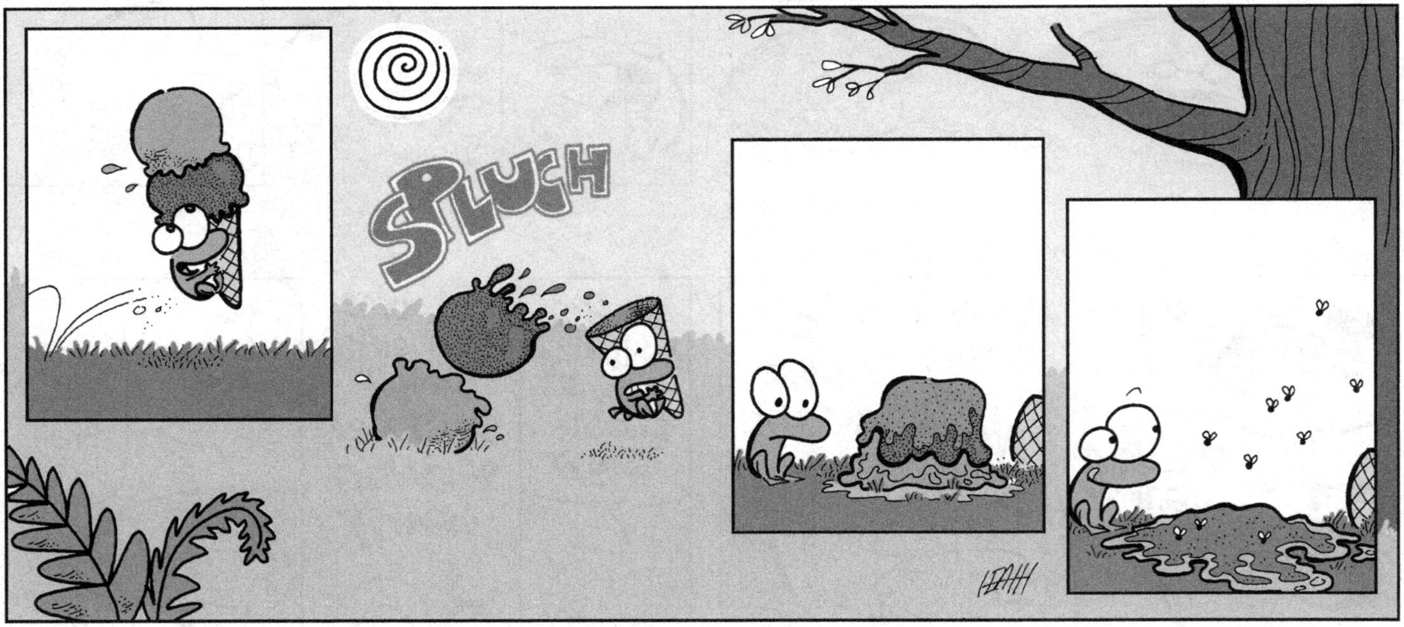
SPLUCH

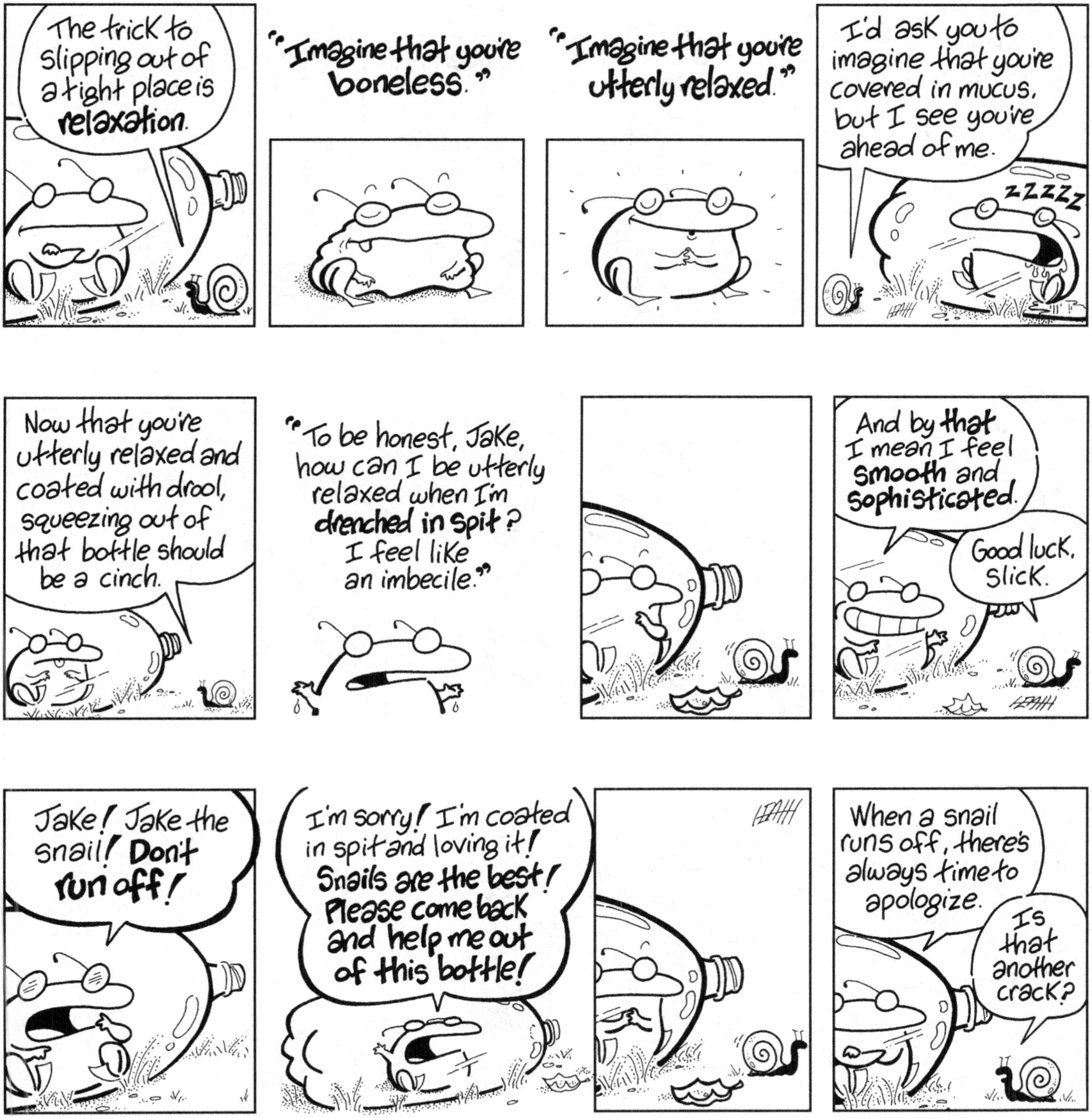

The trick to slipping out of a tight place is **relaxation**.
"Imagine that you're **boneless**."
"Imagine that you're **utterly relaxed**."
I'd ask you to imagine that you're covered in mucus, but I see you're ahead of me.
ZZZZZ
Now that you're utterly relaxed and coated with drool, squeezing out of that bottle should be a cinch.
"To be honest, Jake, how can I be utterly relaxed when I'm **drenched in spit**? I feel like an imbecile."
And by **that** I mean I feel **smooth** and **sophisticated**.
Good luck, Slick.
Jake! Jake the snail! **Don't run off!**
I'm sorry! I'm coated in spit and loving it! **Snails are the best! Please come back and help me out of this bottle!**
When a snail runs off, there's always time to apologize.
Is that another crack?

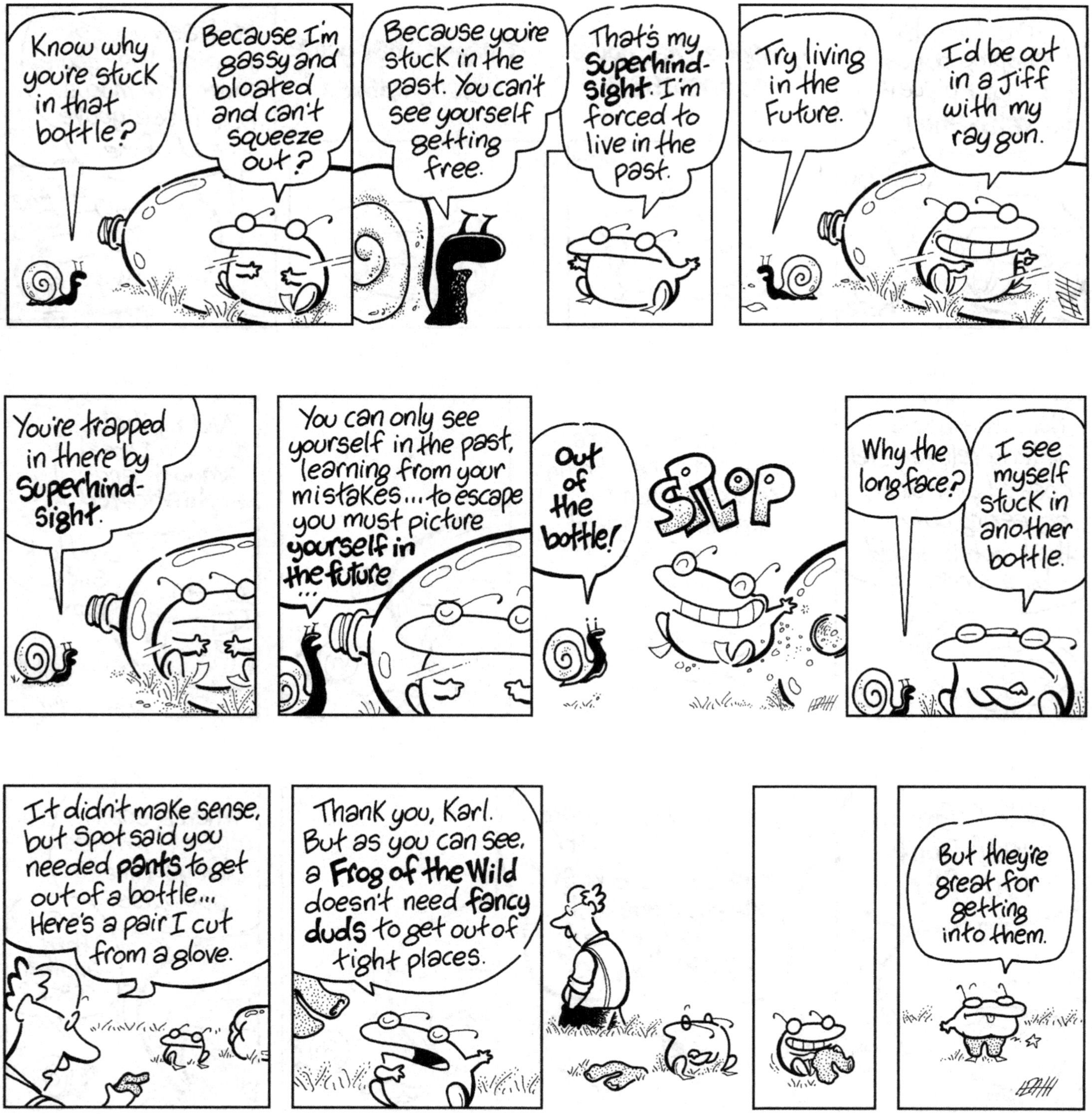
Know why you're stuck in that bottle?
Because I'm gassy and bloated and can't squeeze out?
Because you're stuck in the past. You can't see yourself getting free.
That's my **Superhind-sight**. I'm forced to live in the past.
Try living in the Future.
I'd be out in a jiff with my ray gun.
You're trapped in there by **Superhind-sight**.
You can only see yourself in the past, learning from your mistakes... to escape you must picture **yourself in the future**...
Out of the bottle!
SPLOP
Why the long face?
I see myself stuck in another bottle.
It didn't make sense, but Spot said you needed **pants** to get out of a bottle... Here's a pair I cut from a glove.
Thank you, Karl. But as you can see, a **Frog of the Wild** doesn't need **fancy duds** to get out of tight places.
But they're great for getting into them.

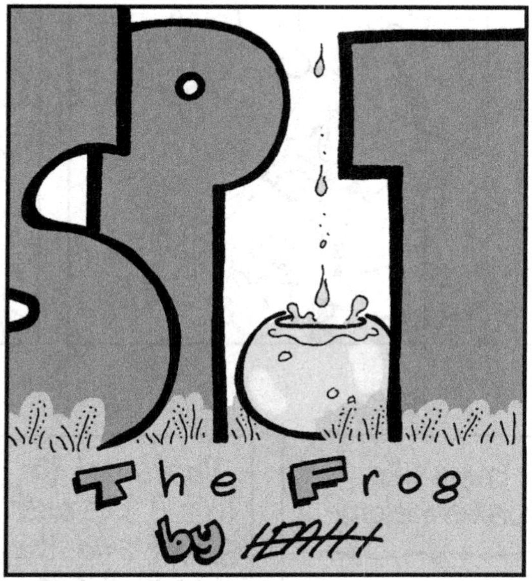

SPIT
The Frog
by HEAHY

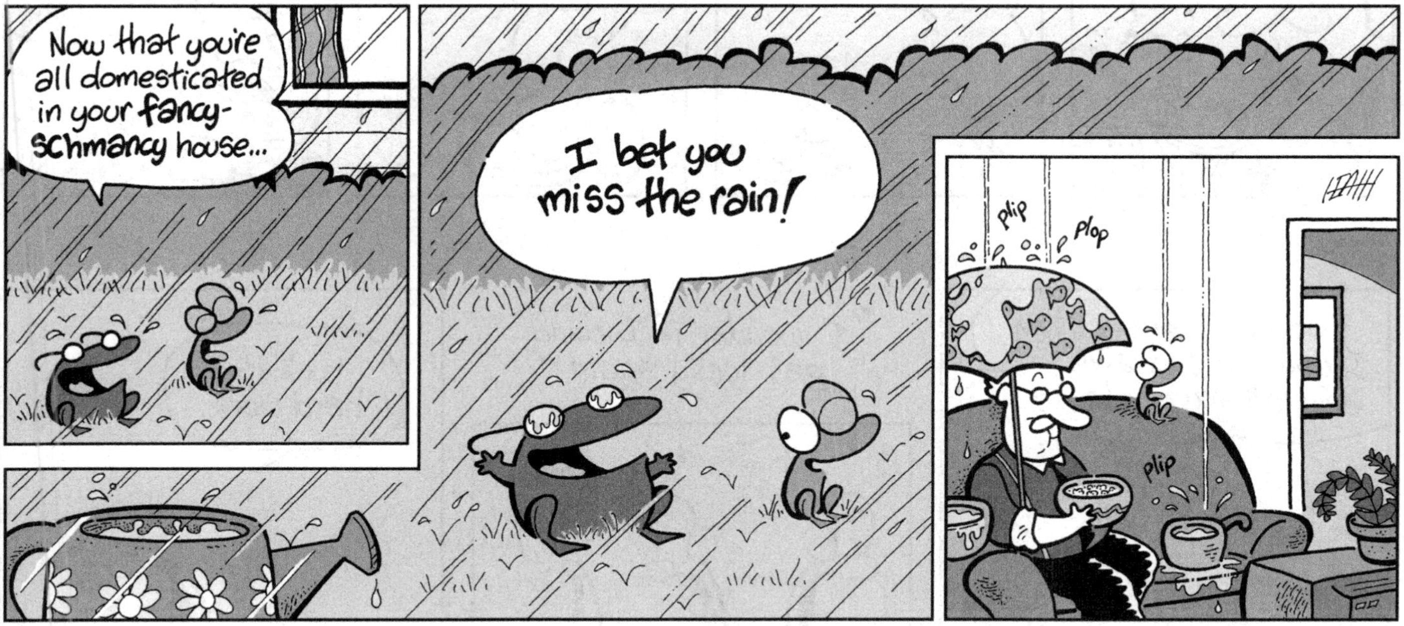

Now that you're all domesticated in your fancy-schmancy house...
I bet you miss the rain!
plip
plop
plip

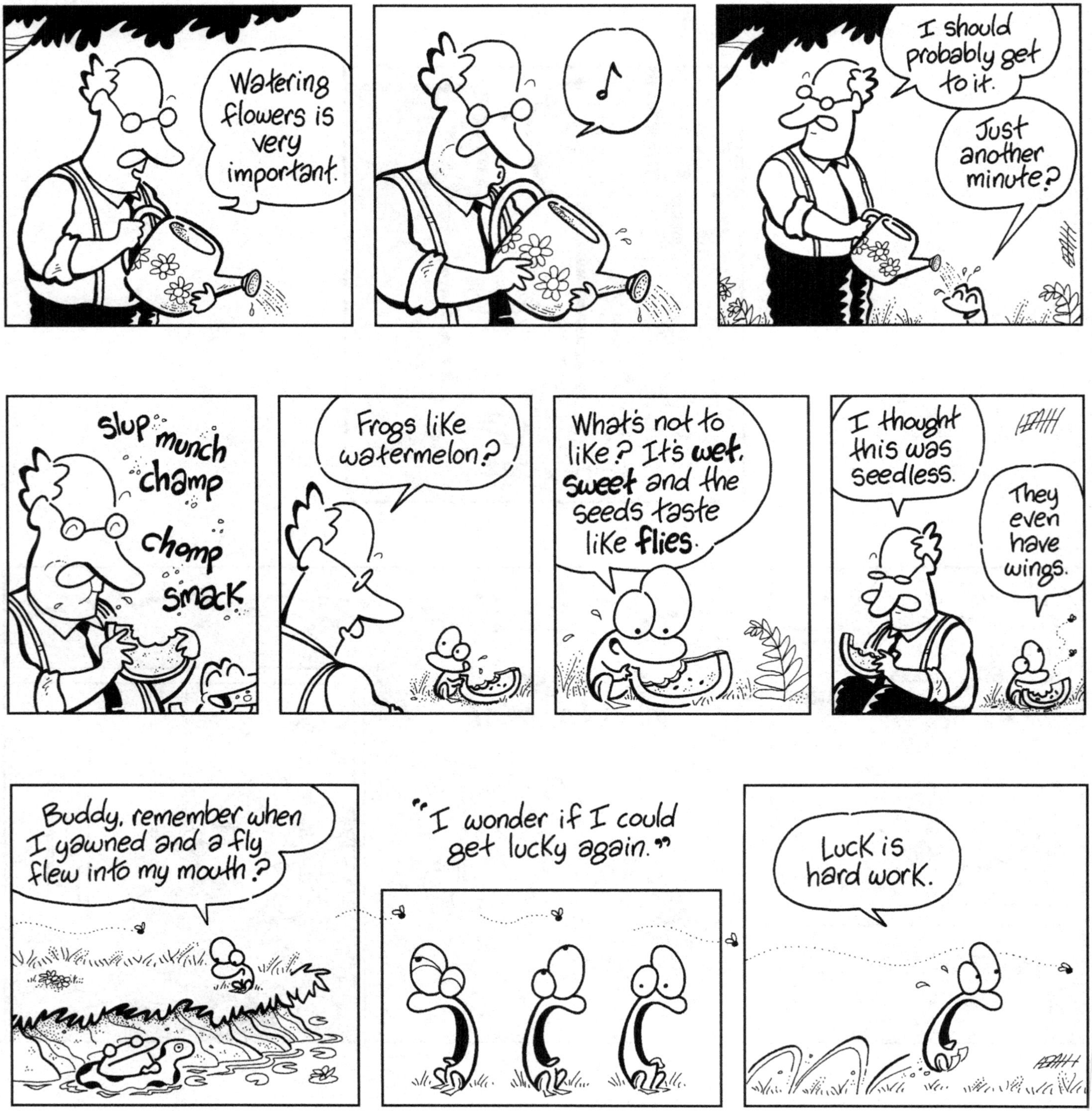

Watering flowers is very important.
♪
I should probably get to it.
Just another minute?
Slup
munch
champ
chomp
smack
Frogs like watermelon?
What's not to like? It's **wet**, **sweet** and the seeds taste like **flies**.
I thought this was seedless.
They even have wings.
Buddy, remember when I yawned and a fly flew into my mouth?
"I wonder if I could get lucky again."
Luck is hard work.

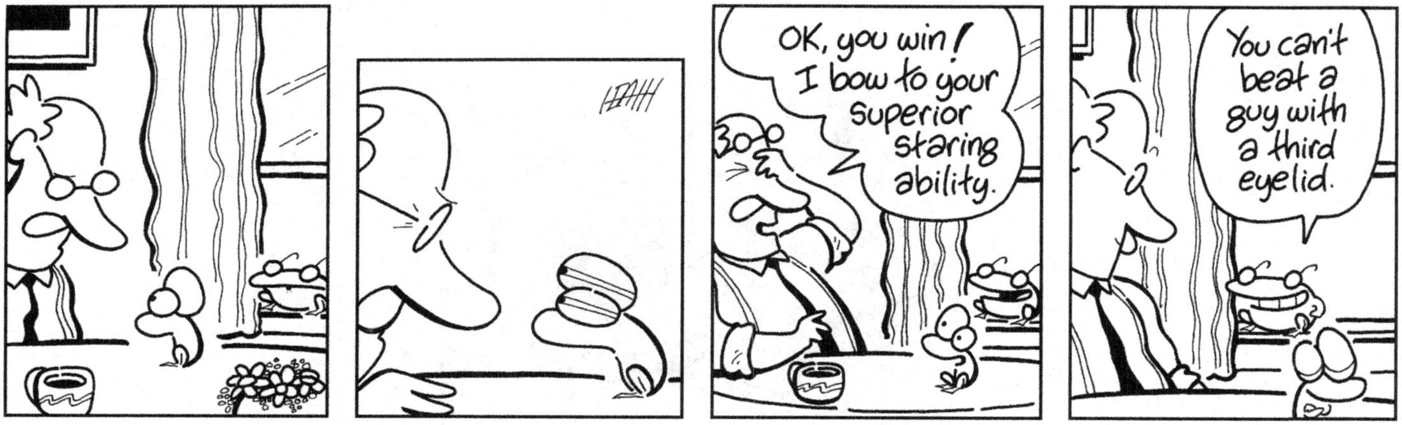
OK, you win! I bow to your superior staring ability.
You can't beat a guy with a third eyelid.

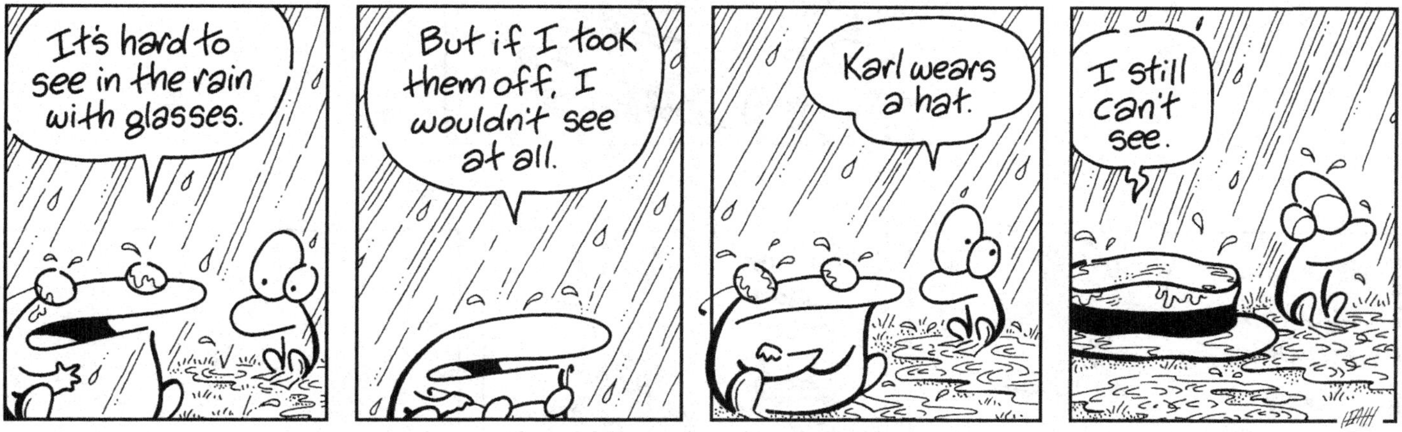
It's hard to see in the rain with glasses.
But if I took them off, I wouldn't see at all.
Karl wears a hat.
I still can't see.

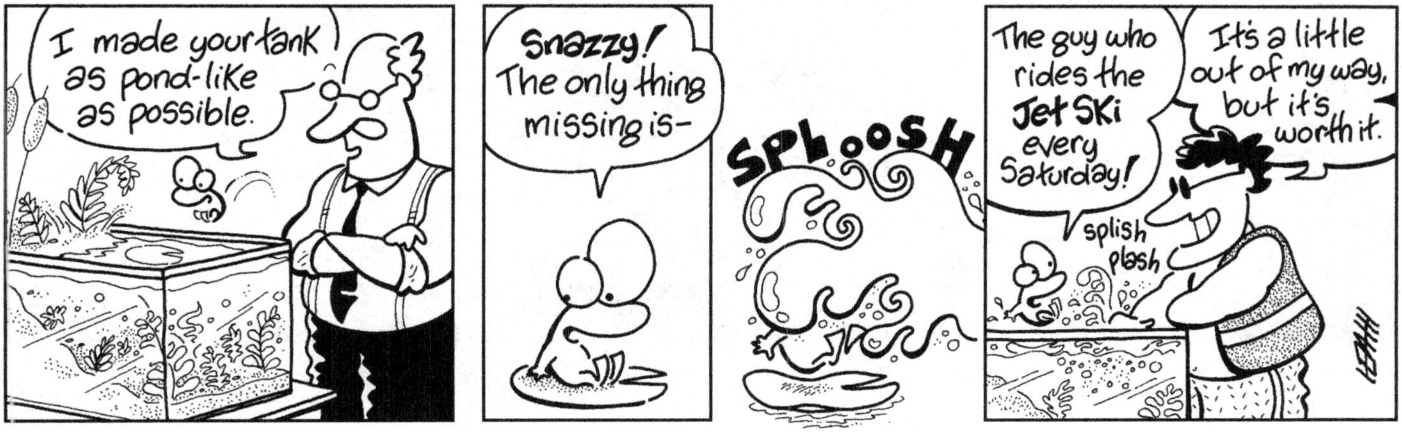
I made your tank as pond-like as possible.
Snazzy! The only thing missing is-
SPLOOSH
The guy who rides the Jet Ski every Saturday!
It's a little out of my way, but it's worth it.
splish plash

The Frog
by

Here you go, boys. You'll have to take turns.
You first, Buddy.
You first.
After you.
After you.
I insist.
OK!
sss

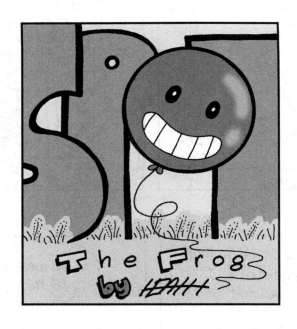

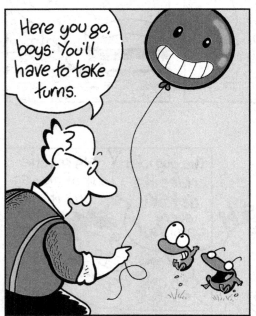

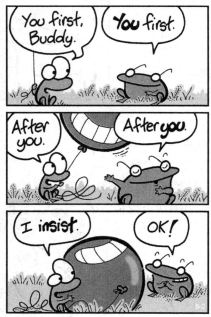

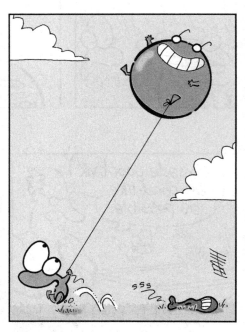

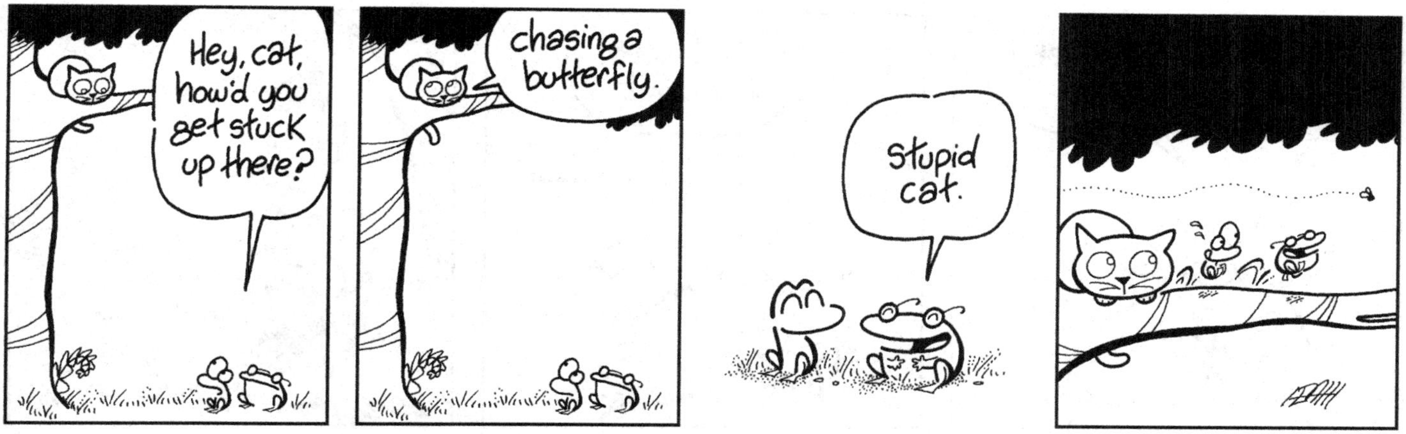
Hey, cat, how'd you get stuck up there?
chasing a butterfly.
Stupid cat.

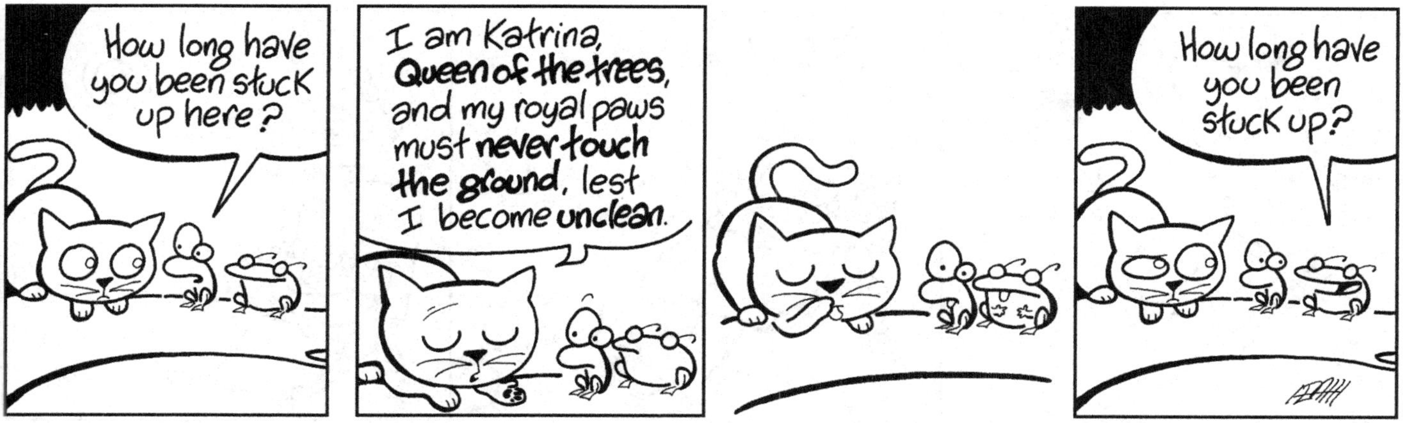
How long have you been stuck up here?
I am Katrina, **Queen of the trees**, and my royal paws must **never touch the ground**, lest I become **unclean**.
How long have you been stuck up?

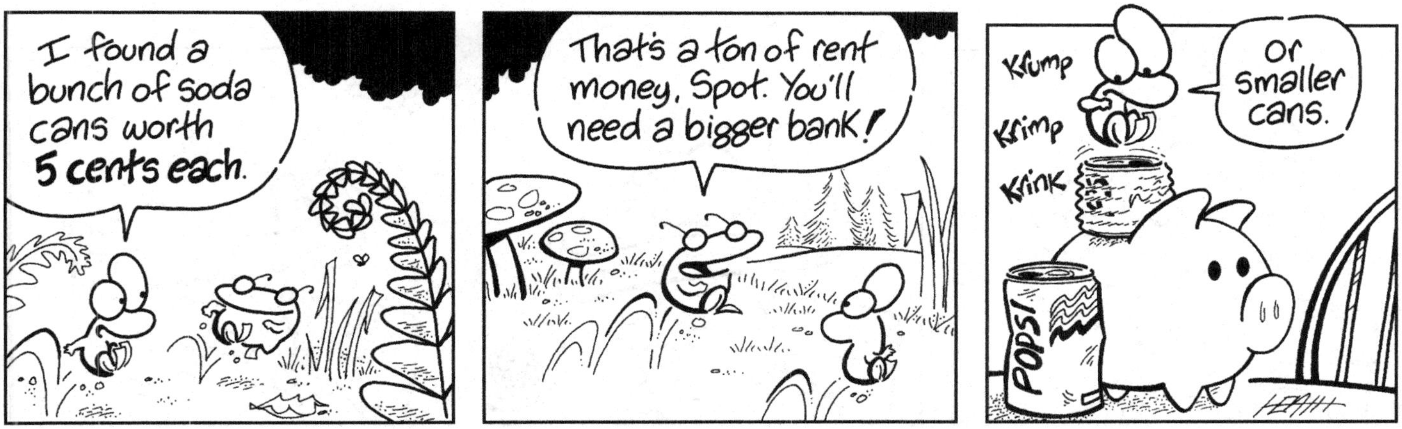
I found a bunch of soda cans worth **5 cents each**.
That's a ton of rent money, Spot. You'll need a bigger bank!
Krump
Krimp
Krink
Or smaller cans.
POPSI

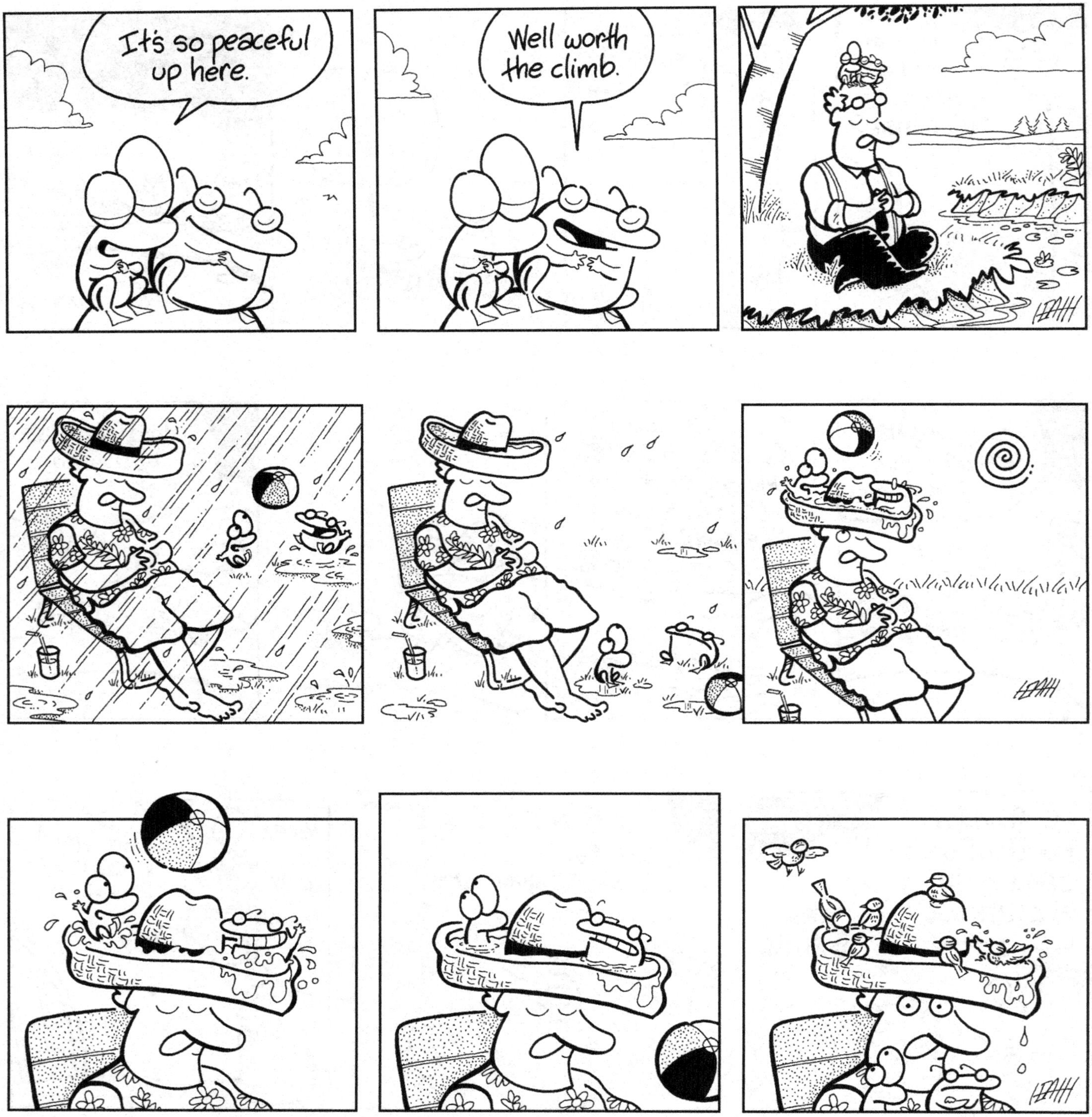

It's so peaceful up here.
Well worth the climb.

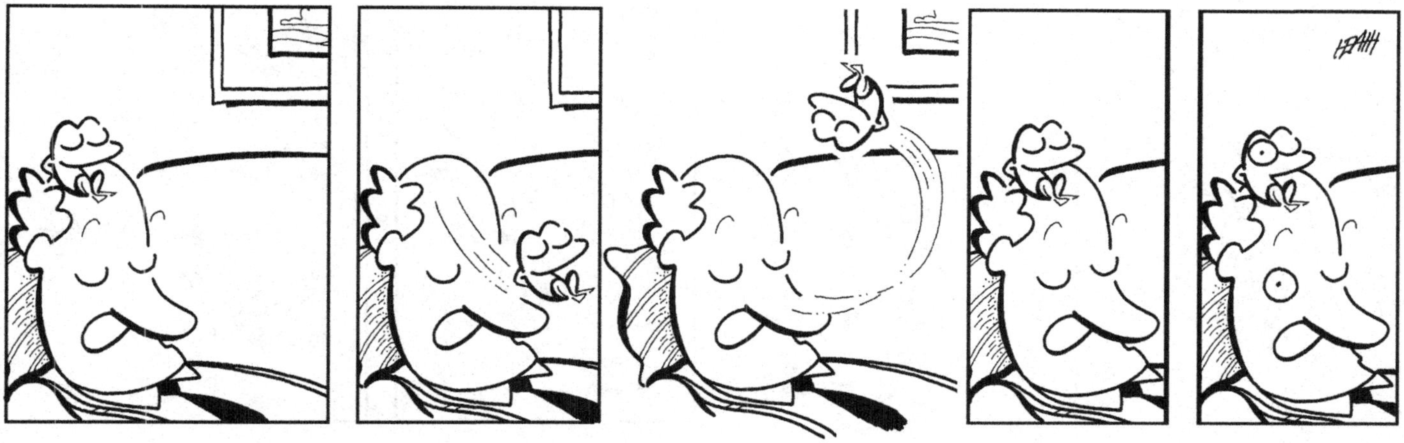

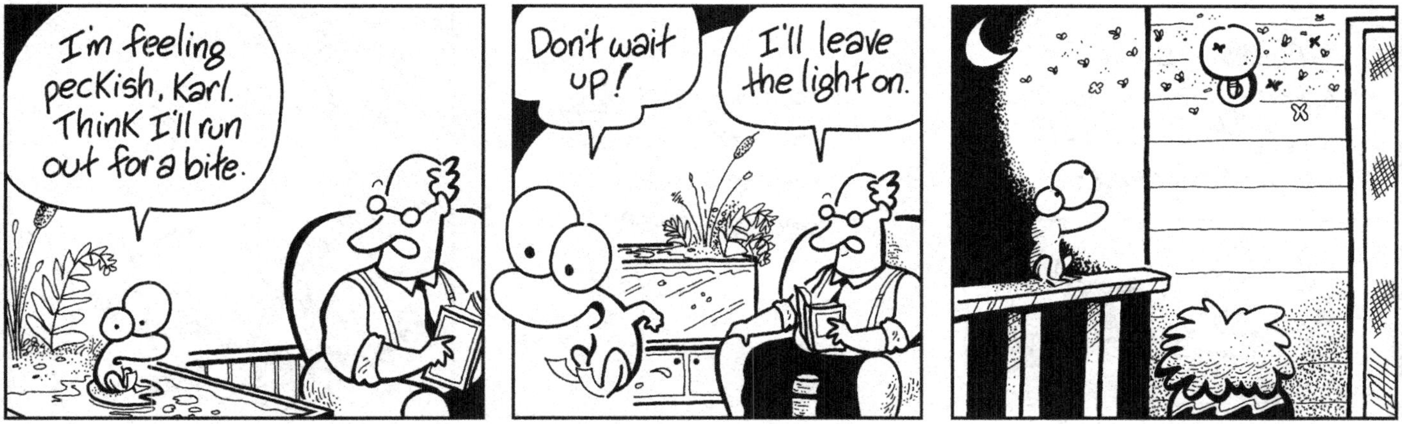
I'm feeling peckish, Karl. Think I'll run out for a bite.
Don't wait up!
I'll leave the light on.

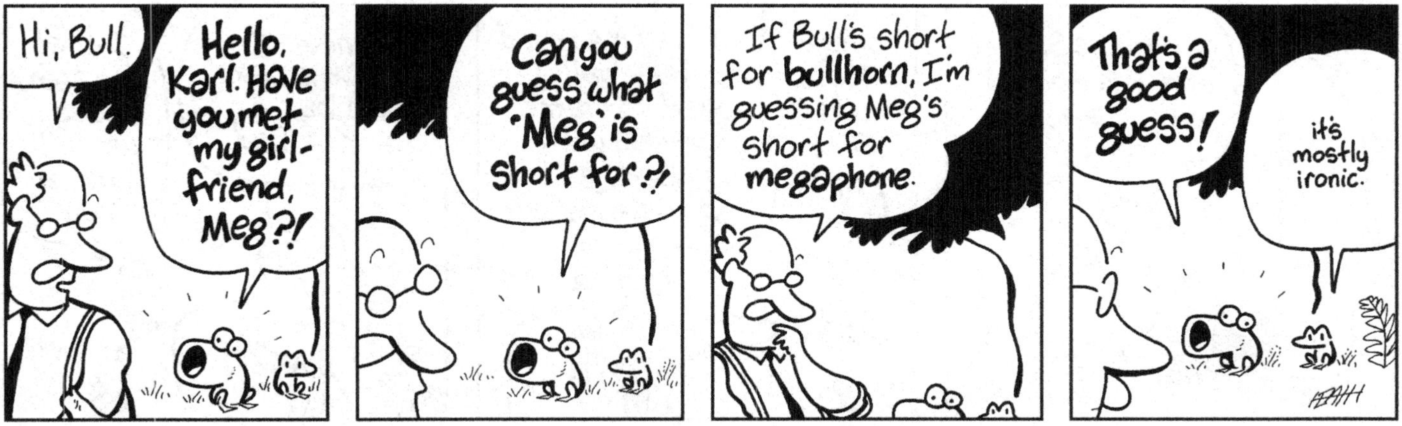
Hi, Bull.
Hello, Karl. Have you met my girl-friend, Meg?!
Can you guess what "Meg" is short for?!
If Bull's short for bullhorn, I'm guessing Meg's short for megaphone.
That's a good guess!
it's mostly ironic.

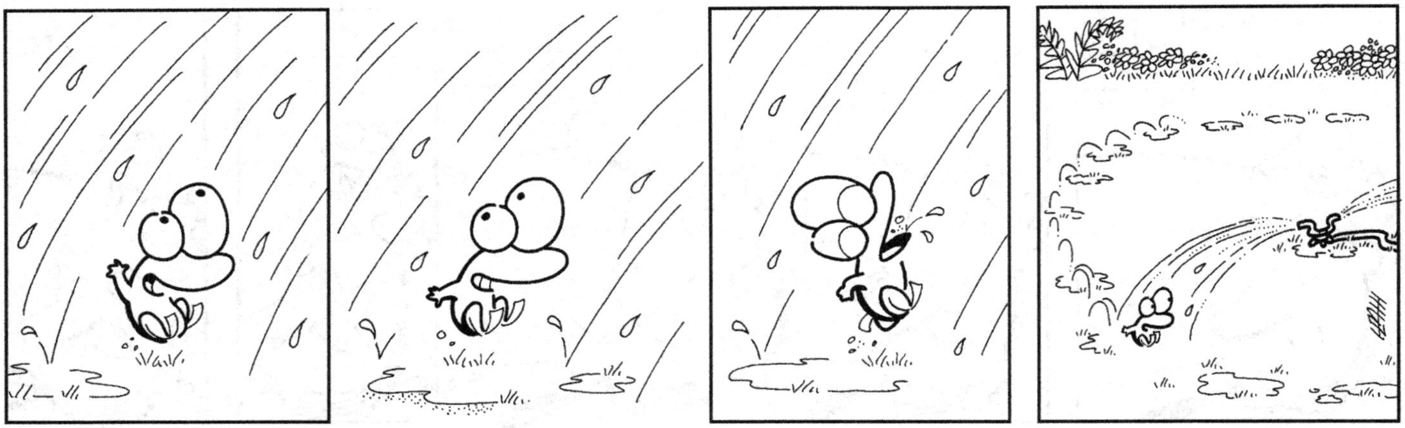

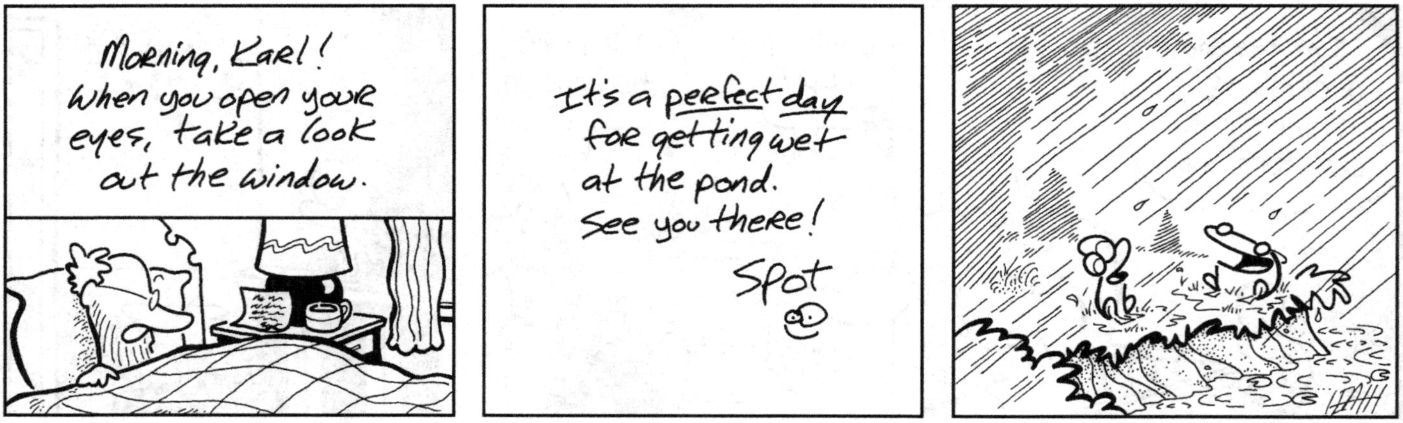
Morning, Karl! When you open your eyes, take a look out the window.
It's a perfect day for getting wet at the pond. See you there!
Spot

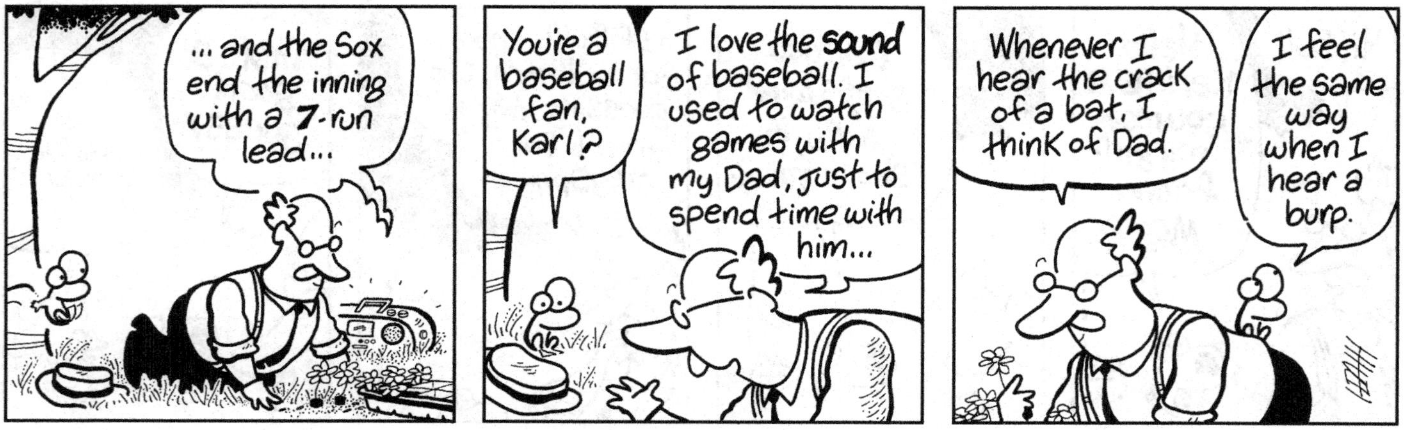
... and the Sox end the inning with a 7-run lead...
You're a baseball fan, Karl?
I love the sound of baseball. I used to watch games with my Dad, just to spend time with him...
Whenever I hear the crack of a bat, I think of Dad.
I feel the same way when I hear a burp.

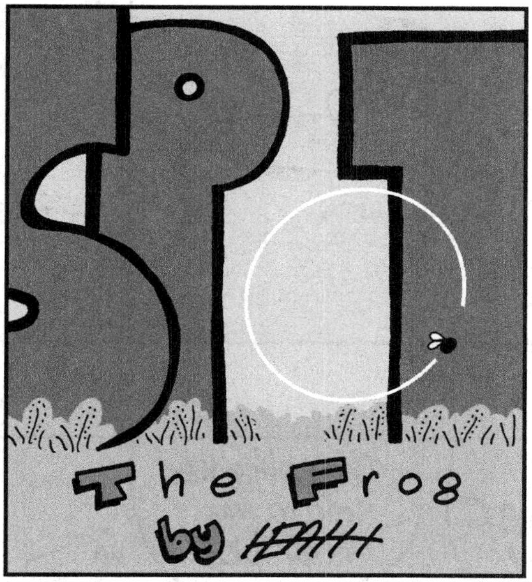
The Frog
by

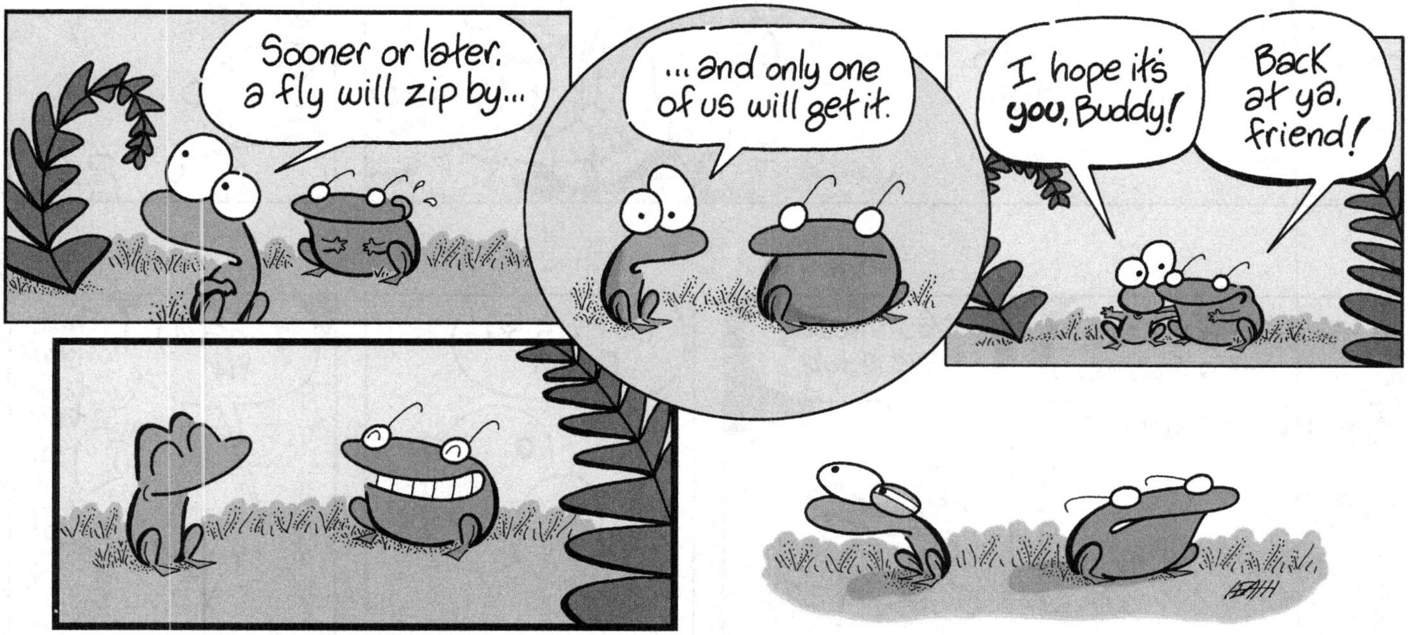
Sooner or later, a fly will zip by...
...and only one of us will get it.
I hope it's **you**, Buddy!
Back at ya, friend!

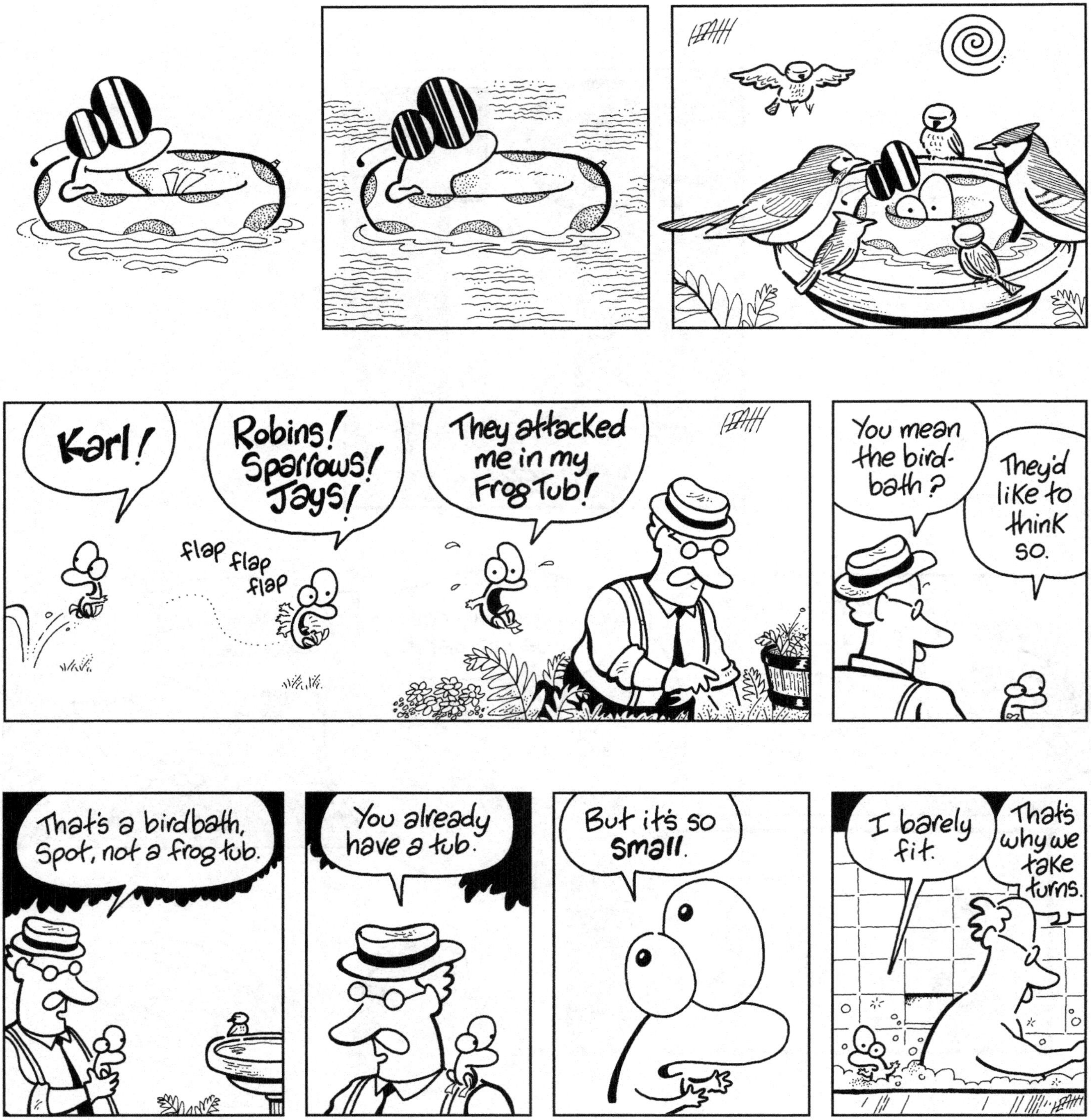
Karl!
Robins! Sparrows! Jays!
flap flap flap
They attacked me in my Frog Tub!
You mean the bird-bath?
They'd like to think so.
That's a birdbath, Spot, not a frog tub.
You already have a tub.
But it's so small.
I barely fit.
That's why we take turns.

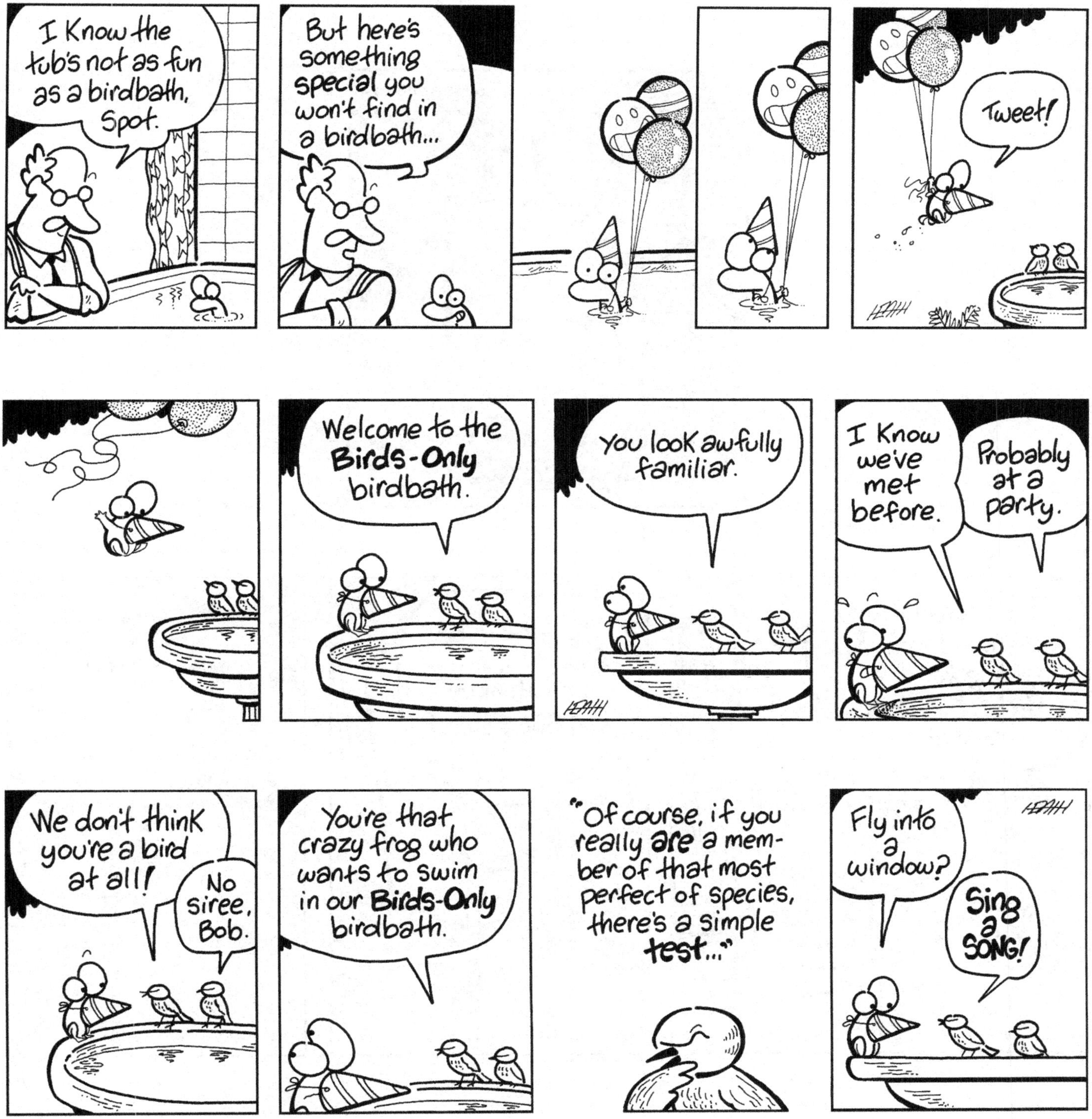
I Know the tub's not as fun as a birdbath, Spot.
But here's something special you won't find in a birdbath...
Tweet!
Welcome to the **Birds-Only** birdbath.
You look awfully familiar.
I Know we've met before.
Probably at a party.
We don't think you're a bird at all!
No siree, Bob.
You're that crazy frog who wants to swim in our **Birds-Only** birdbath.
"Of course, if you really **are** a member of that most perfect of species, there's a simple **test**..."
Fly into a window?
Sing a SONG!

The Frog
by

I've been watching this fly all morning, waiting for the Perfect Moment to strike.
Wouldn't it be funny if the fly was thinking the same thing?

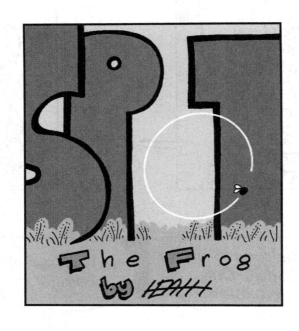

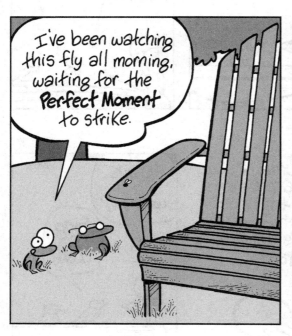

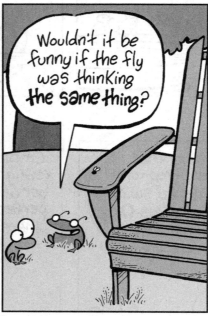

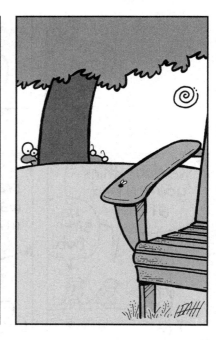

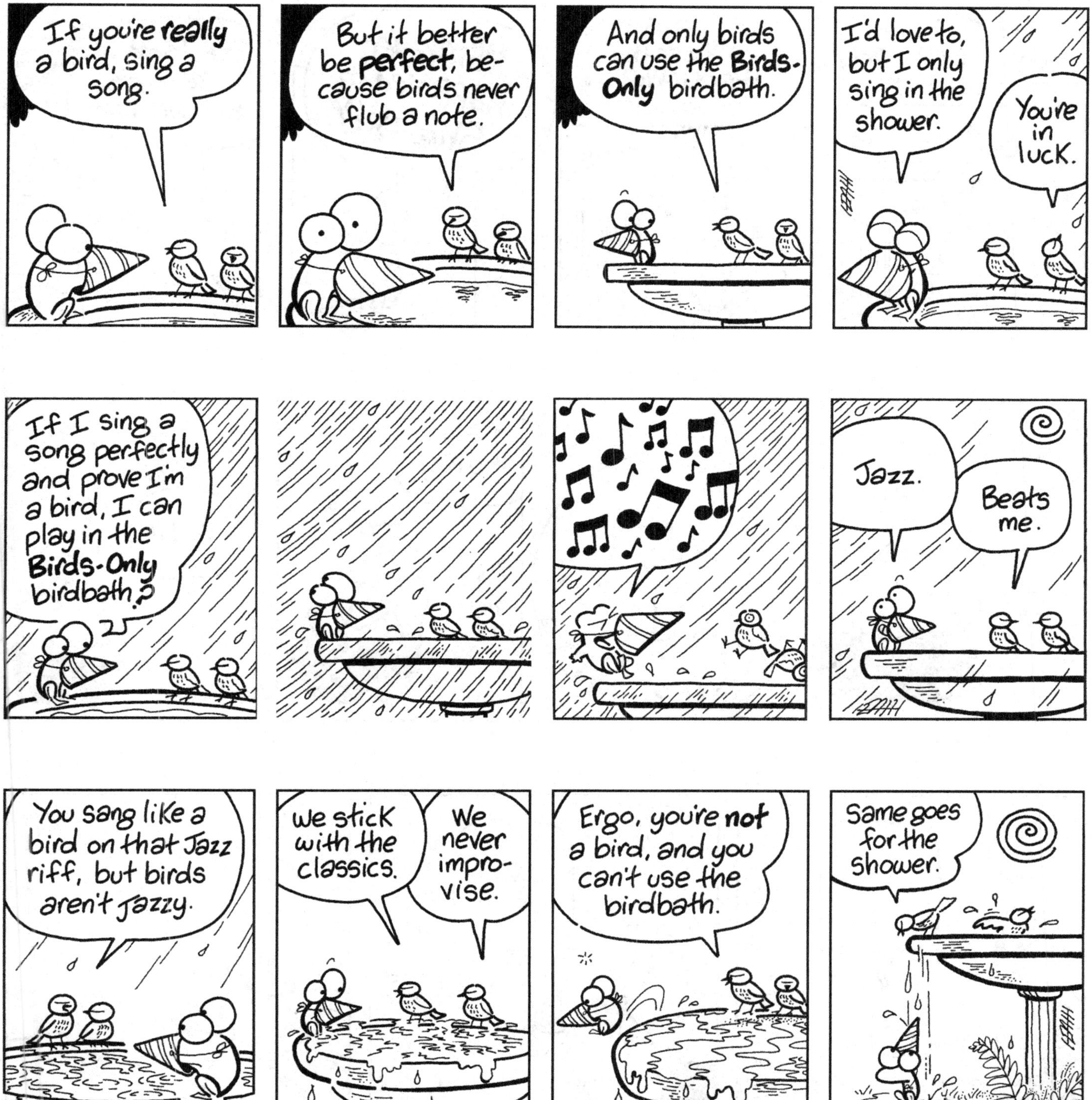
If you're really a bird, sing a song.
But it better be perfect, because birds never flub a note.
And only birds can use the Birds-Only birdbath.
I'd love to, but I only sing in the shower.
You're in luck.
If I sing a song perfectly and prove I'm a bird, I can play in the Birds-Only birdbath?
Jazz.
Beats me.
You sang like a bird on that Jazz riff, but birds aren't Jazzy.
We stick with the classics.
We never improvise.
Ergo, you're not a bird, and you can't use the birdbath.
Same goes for the shower.

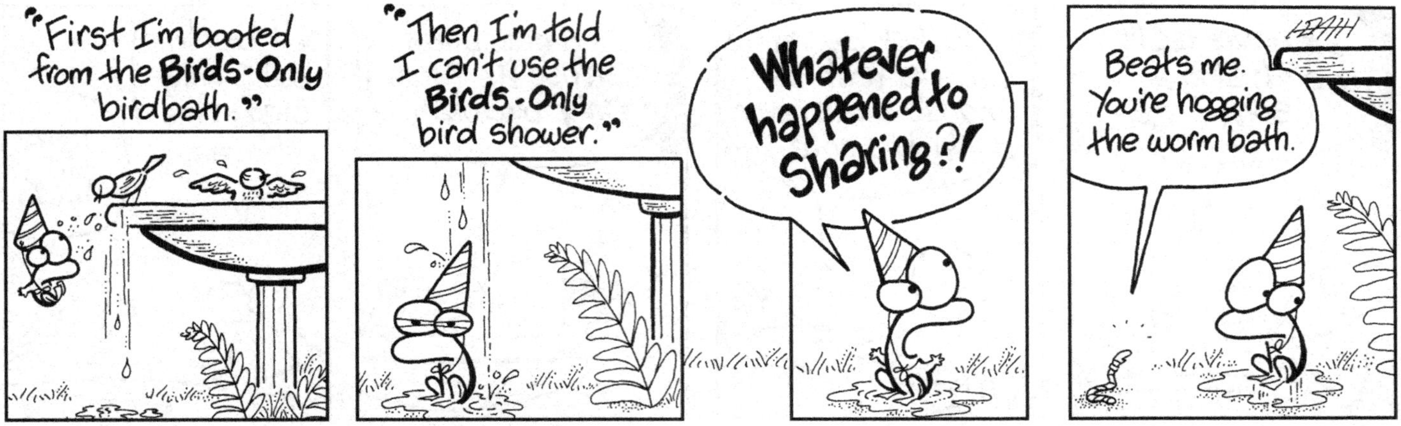
"First I'm booted from the **Birds-Only** birdbath."
"Then I'm told I can't use the **Birds-Only** bird shower."
Whatever happened to Sharing?!
Beats me. You're hogging the worm bath.

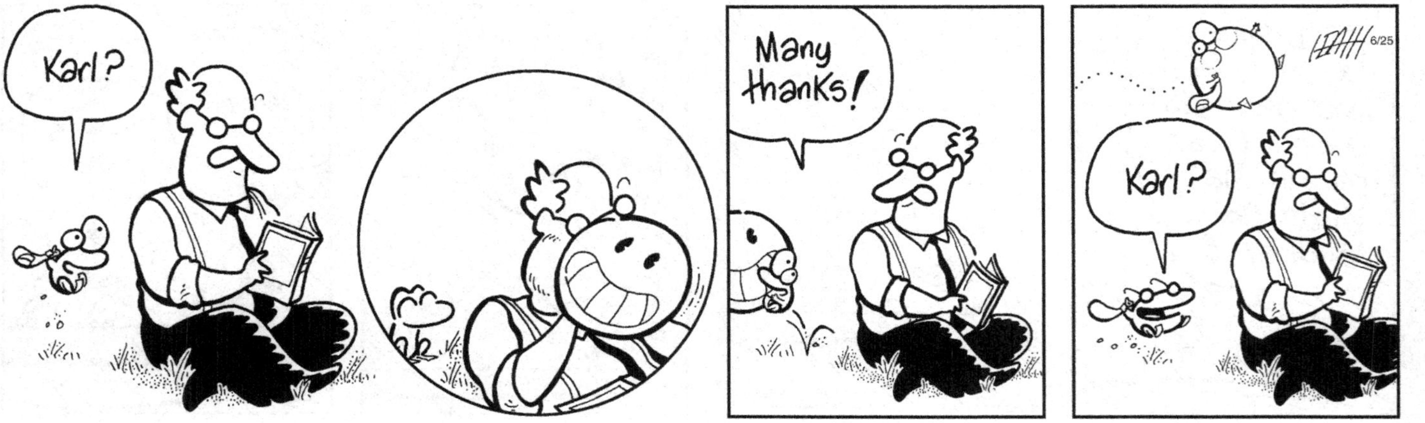
Karl?
Many thanks!
Karl?

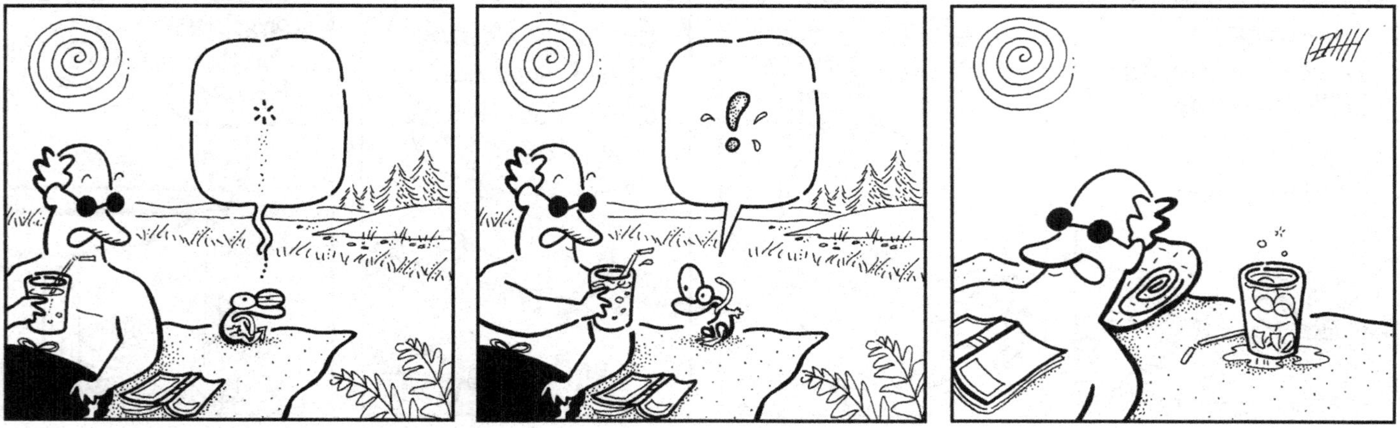
!

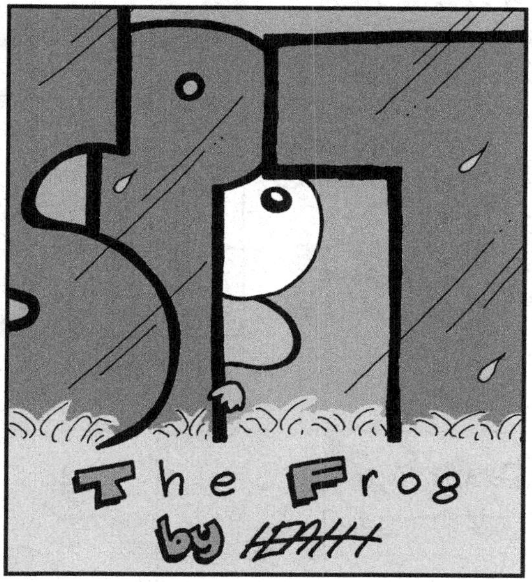
The Frog
by

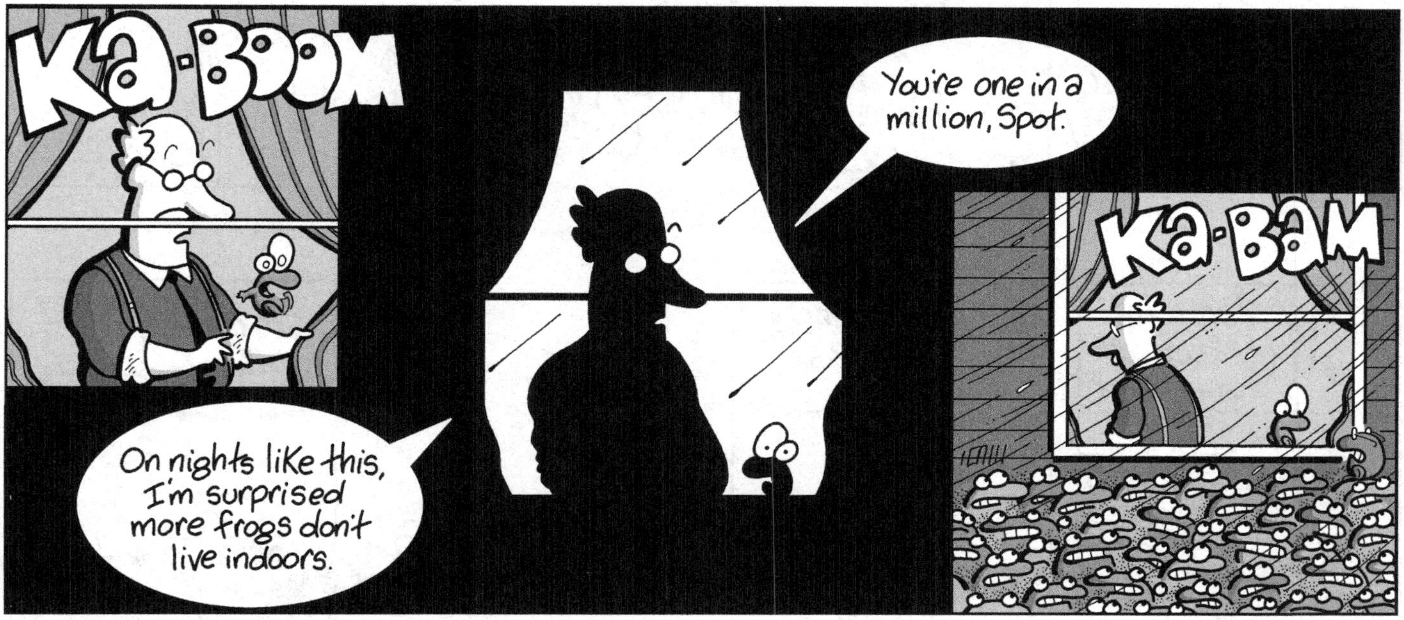
KA-BOOM
On nights like this, I'm surprised more frogs don't live indoors.
You're one in a million, Spot.
KA-BAM

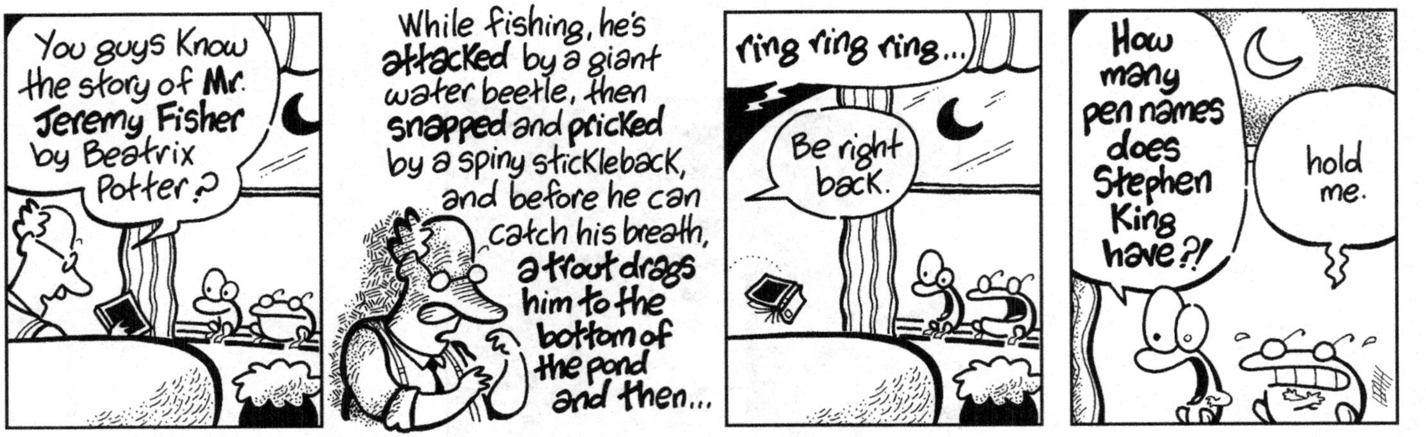
You guys Know the story of Mr. Jeremy Fisher by Beatrix Potter?
While fishing, he's attacked by a giant water beetle, then snapped and pricked by a spiny stickleback, and before he can catch his breath, a trout drags him to the bottom of the pond and then...
ring ring ring...
Be right back.
How many pen names does Stephen King have?!
hold me.

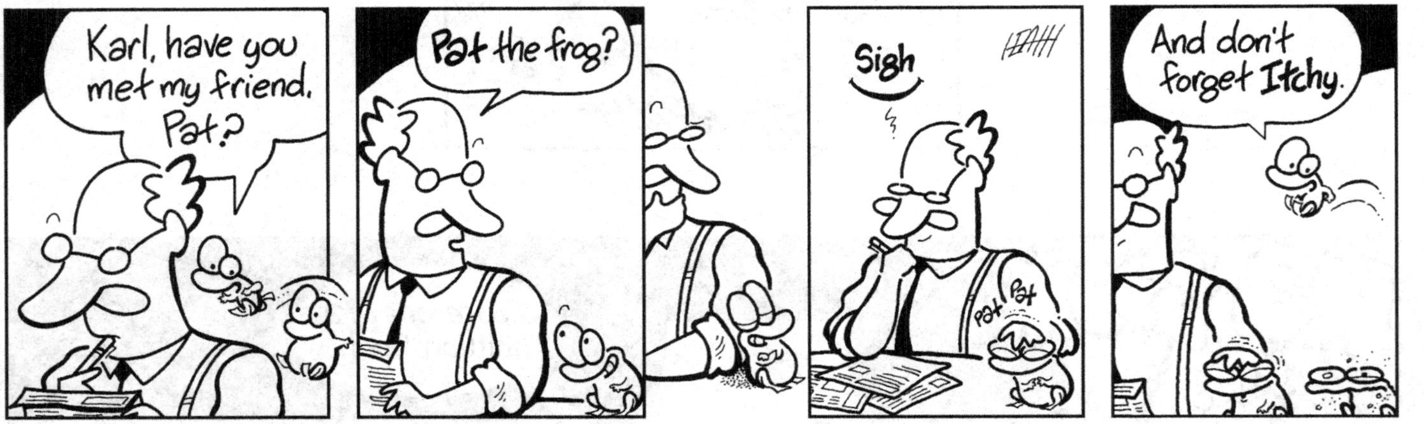
Karl, have you met my friend, Pat?
Pat the frog?
Sigh
Pat Pat
And don't forget Itchy.

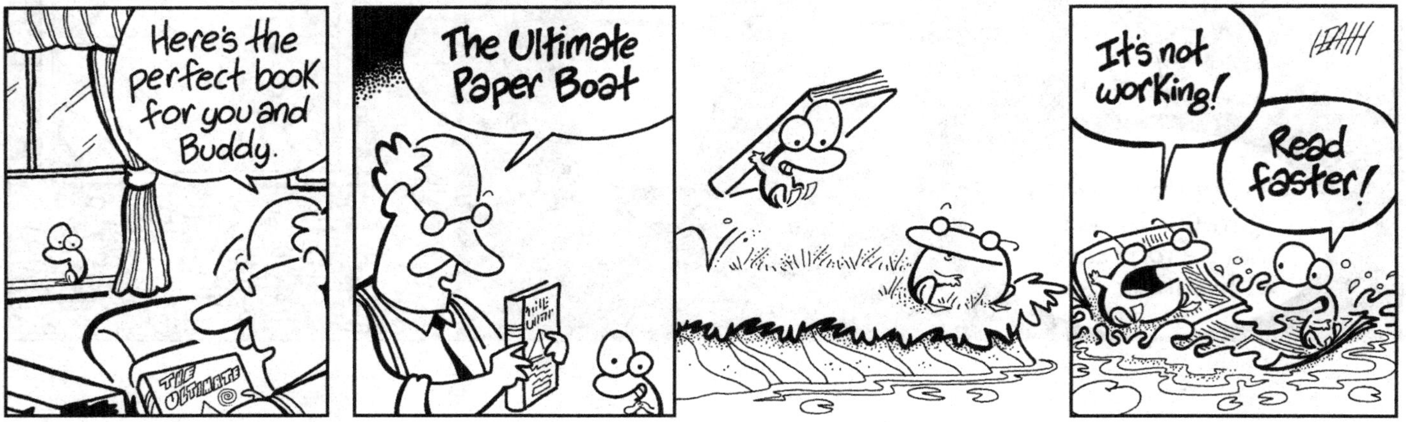
Here's the perfect book for you and Buddy.
The Ultimate Paper Boat
It's not working!
Read faster!

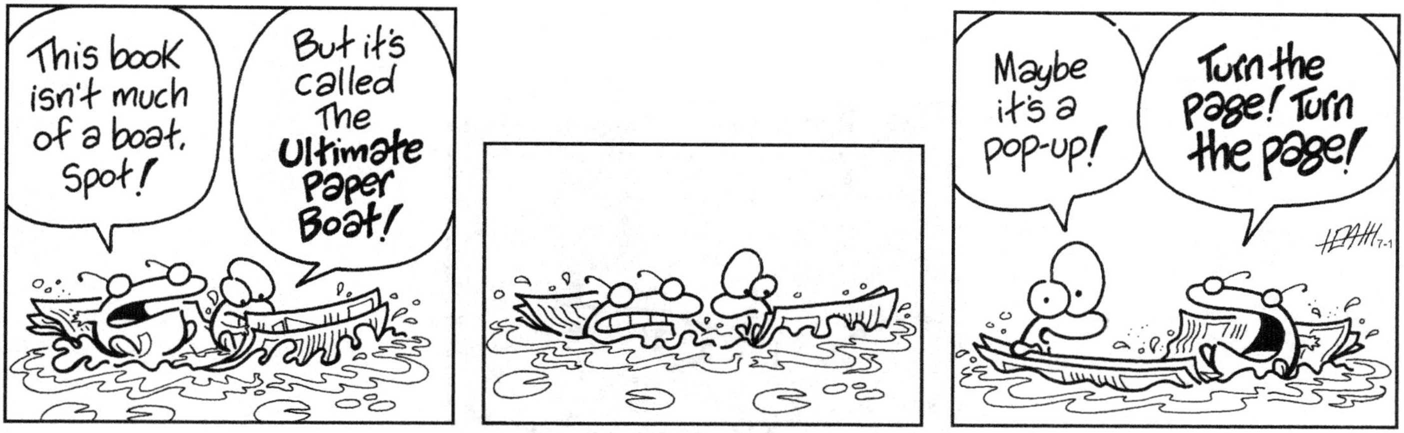
This book isn't much of a boat, Spot!
But it's called The **Ultimate Paper Boat!**
Maybe it's a pop-up!
Turn the page! Turn the page!

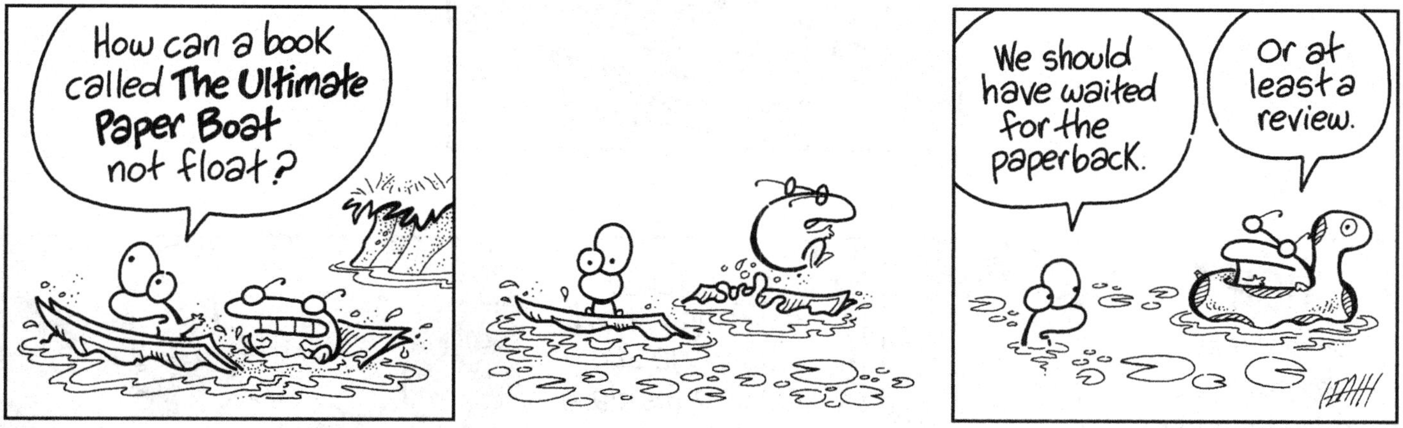
How can a book called **The Ultimate Paper Boat** not float?
We should have waited for the paperback.
Or at least a review.

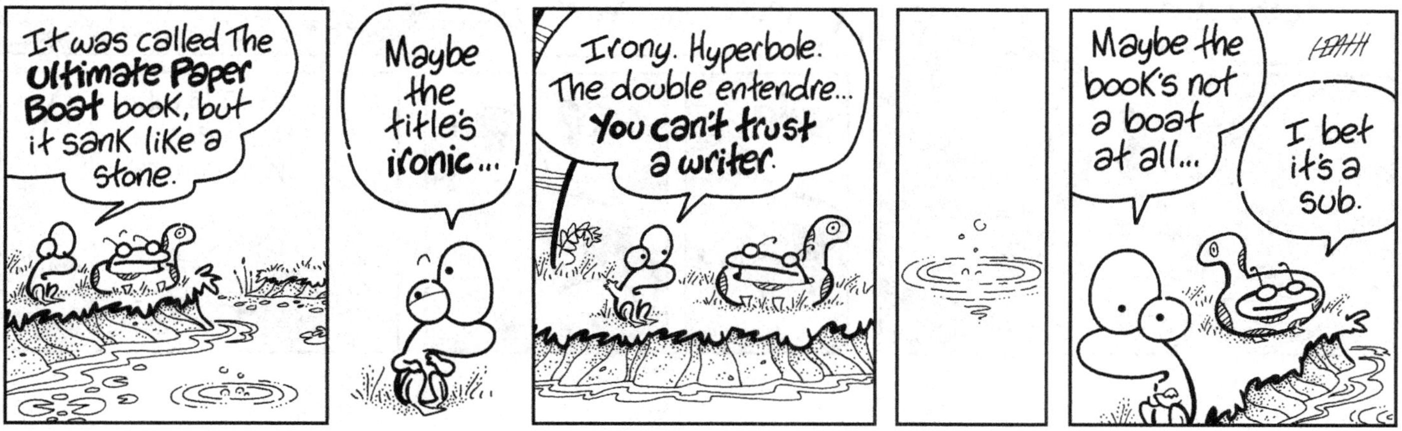
It was called The **Ultimate Paper Boat** book, but it sank like a stone.
Maybe the title's **ironic**...
Irony. Hyperbole. The double entendre... **You can't trust a writer.**
Maybe the book's not a boat at all...
I bet it's a sub.

The Frog by HEATH

Wait! Before you try to eat me, you should know that **toads taste bad!**

Instead of spitting me out, whaddaya say we skip the class-time and go straight to a lesson learned?

gulp

urp

This is why teachers need the summer off.

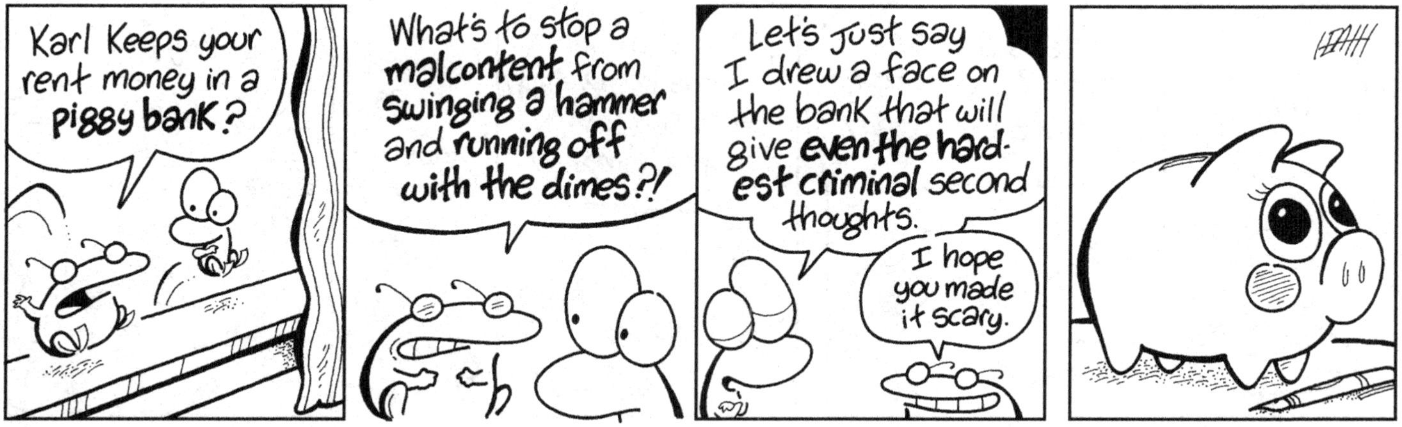

Karl Keeps your rent money in a piggy bank?
What's to stop a malcontent from swinging a hammer and running off with the dimes?!
Let's just say I drew a face on the bank that will give even the hard-est criminal second thoughts.
I hope you made it scary.

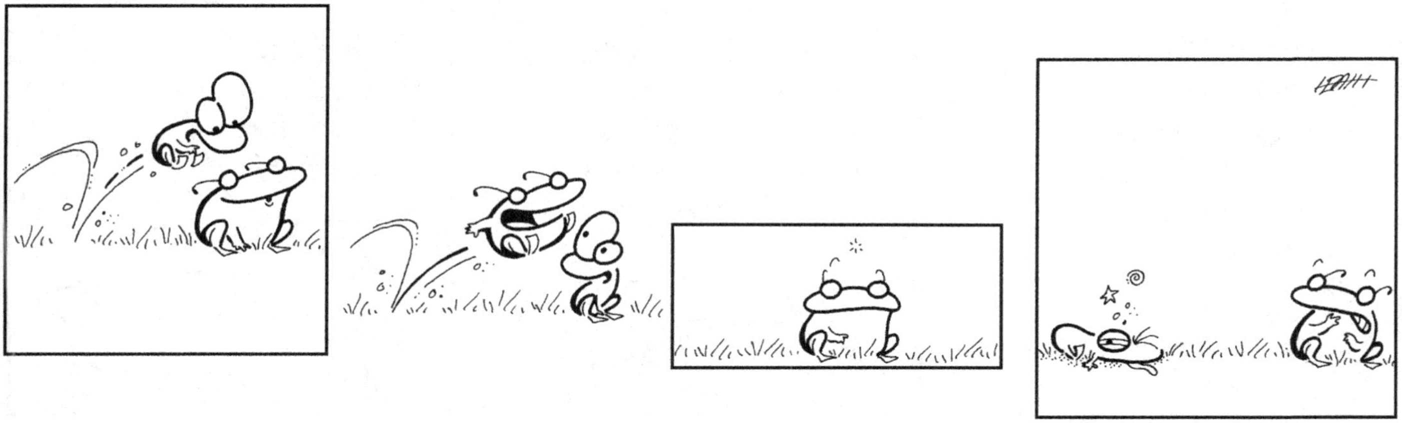

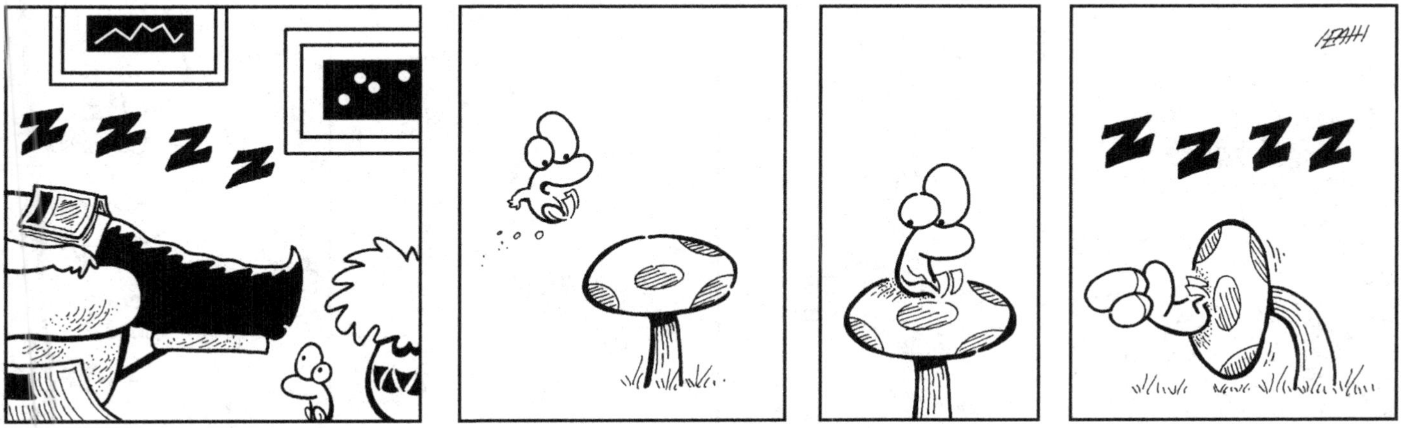

Z Z Z Z
Z Z Z Z

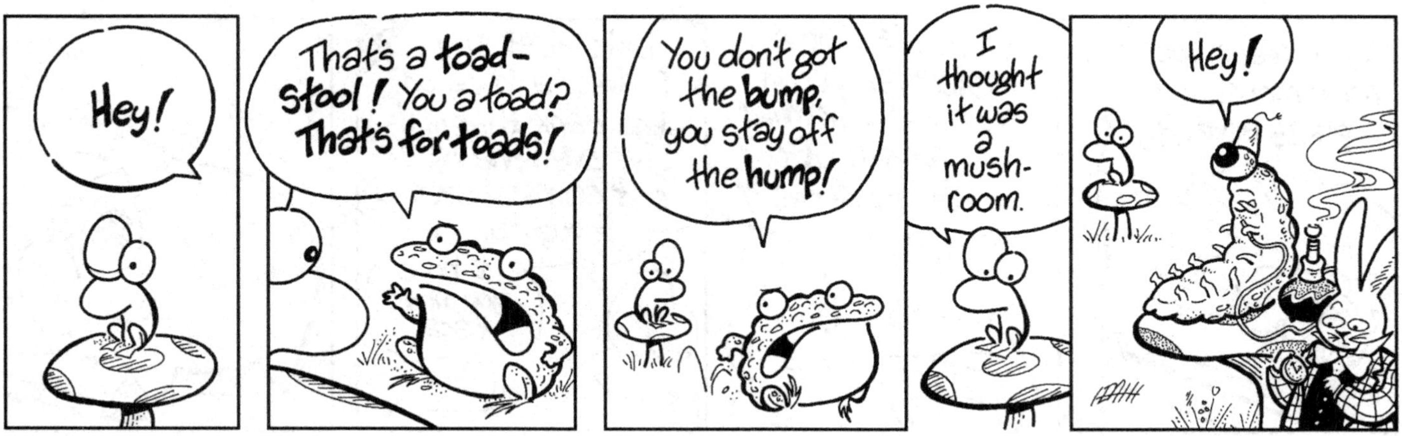
Hey!
That's a toad-stool! You a toad? That's for toads!
You don't got the bump, you stay off the hump!
I thought it was a mush-room.
Hey!

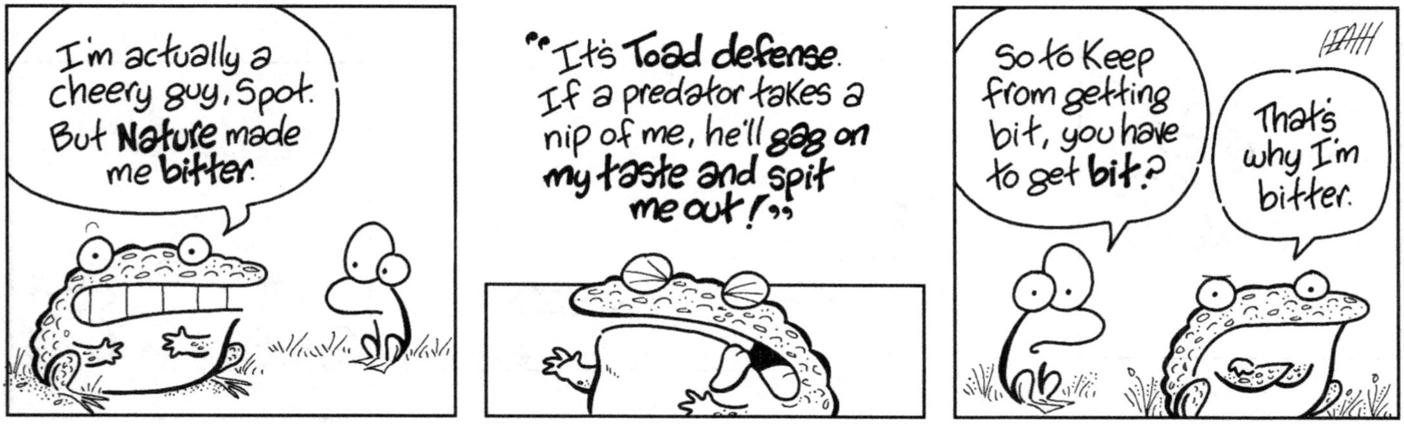
I'm actually a cheery guy, Spot. But Nature made me bitter.
"It's Toad defense. If a predator takes a nip of me, he'll gag on my taste and spit me out!"
So to Keep from getting bit, you have to get bit?
That's why I'm bitter.

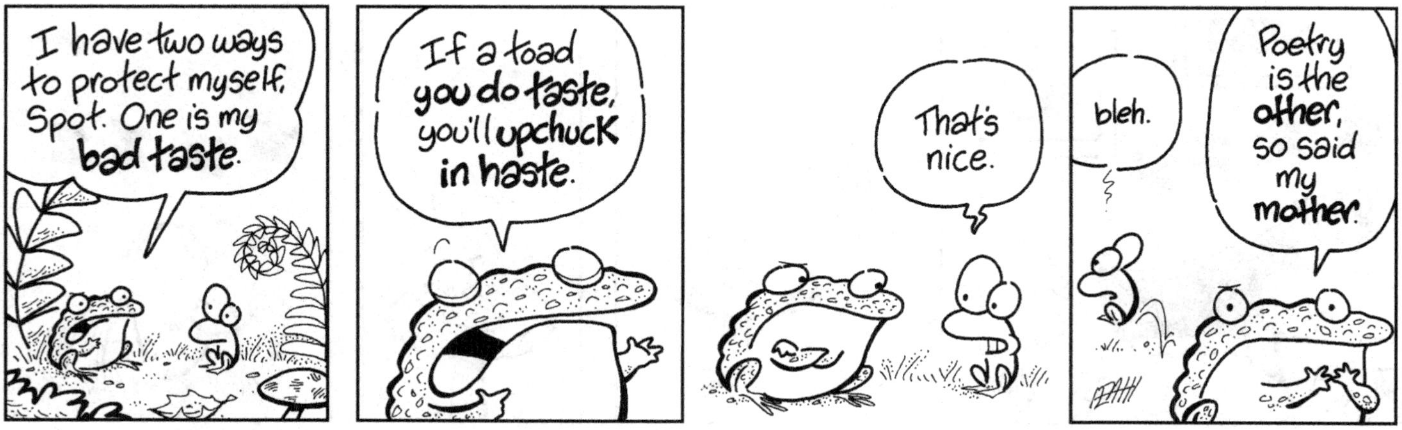
I have two ways to protect myself, Spot. One is my bad taste.
If a toad you do taste, you'll upchuck in haste.
That's nice.
bleh.
Poetry is the other, so said my mother.

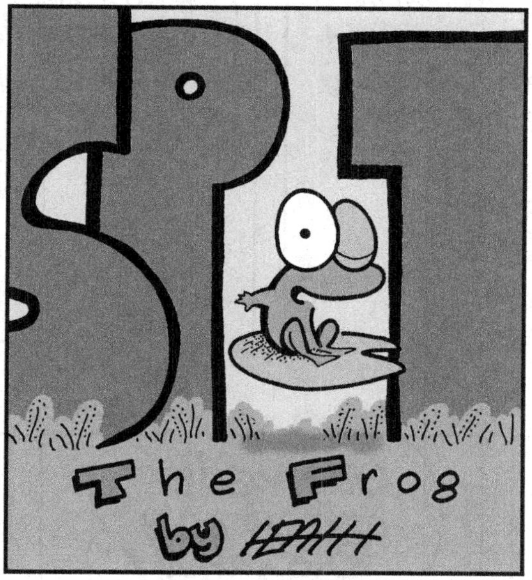
The Frog
by

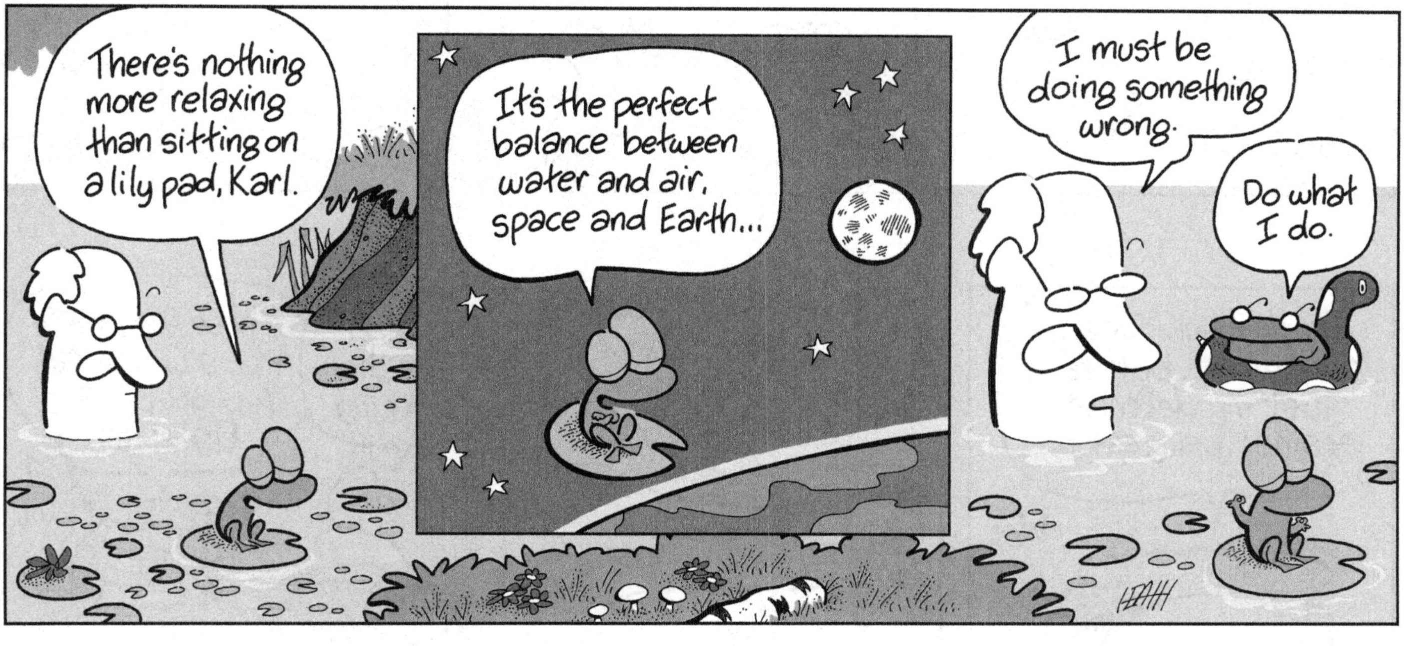
There's nothing more relaxing than sitting on a lily pad, Karl.
It's the perfect balance between water and air, space and Earth...
I must be doing something wrong.
Do what I do.

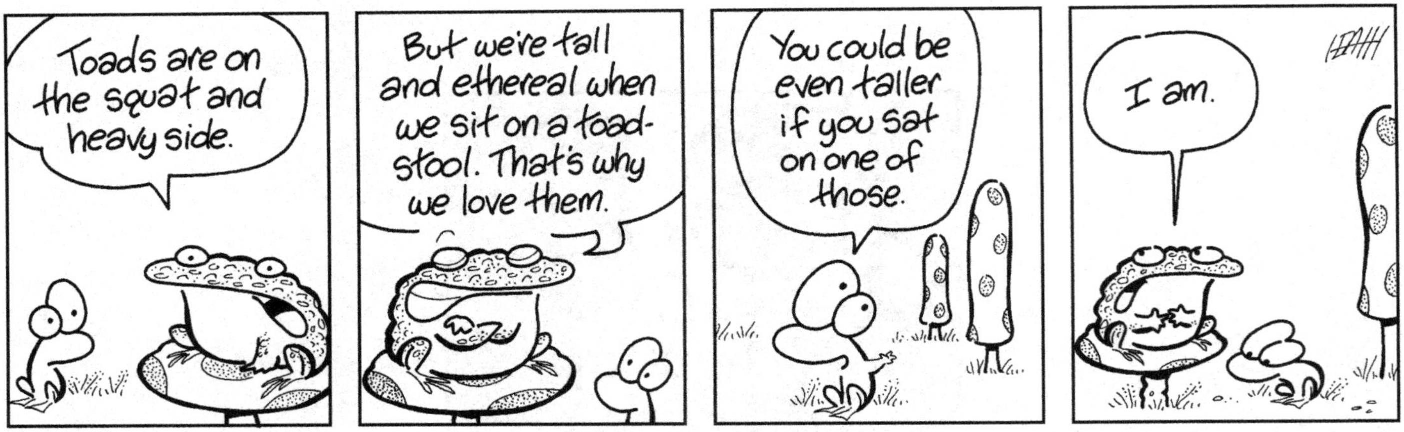
Toads are on the squat and heavy side.
But we're tall and ethereal when we sit on a toad-stool. That's why we love them.
You could be even taller if you sat on one of those.
I am.

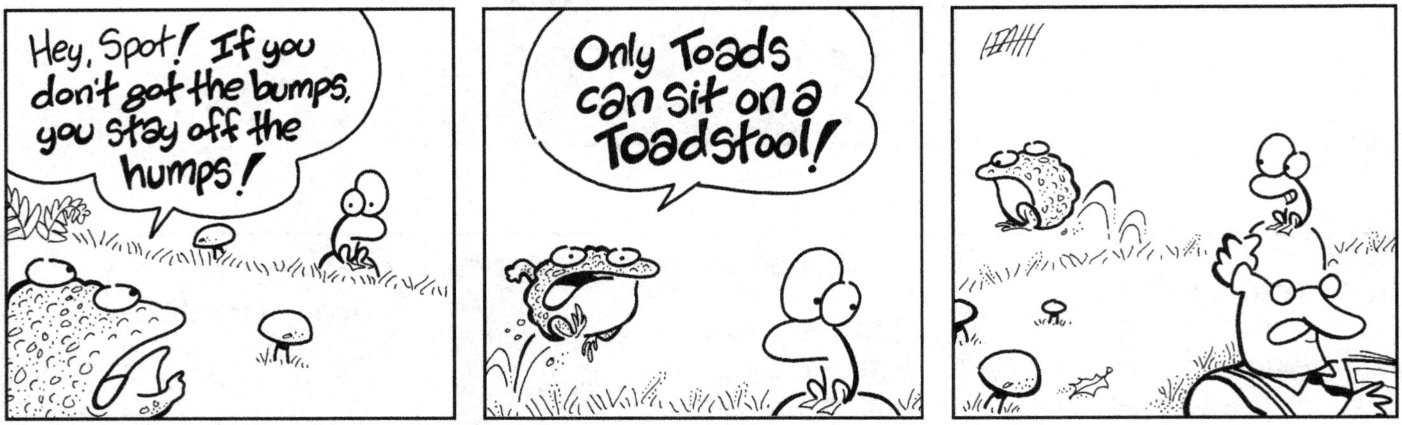
Hey, Spot! If you don't got the bumps, you stay off the humps!
Only Toads can sit on a Toadstool!

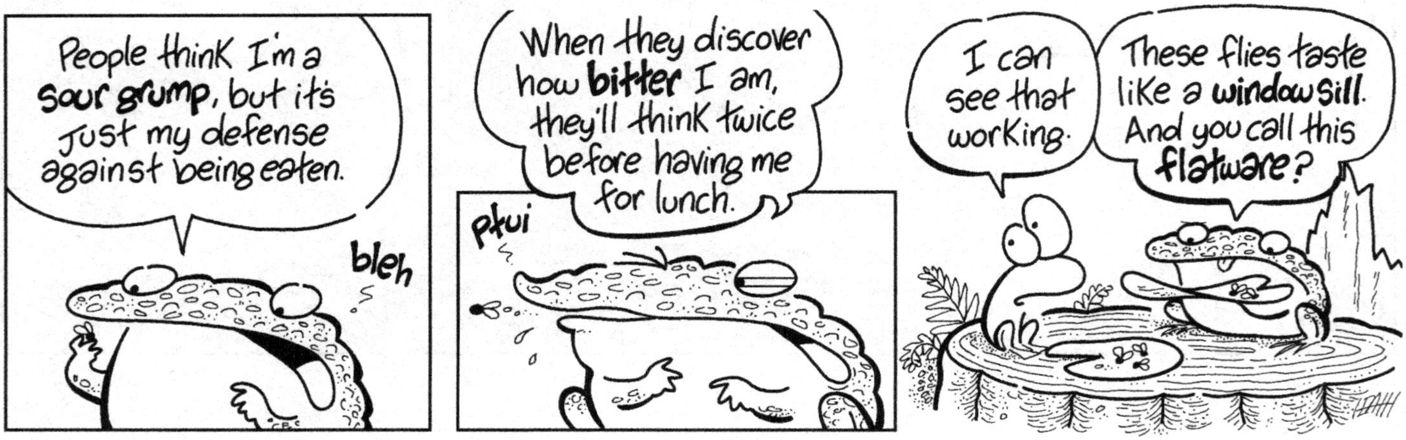
People think I'm a sour grump, but it's just my defense against being eaten.
bleh
When they discover how bitter I am, they'll think twice before having me for lunch.
ptui
I can see that working.
These flies taste like a window sill. And you call this flatware?

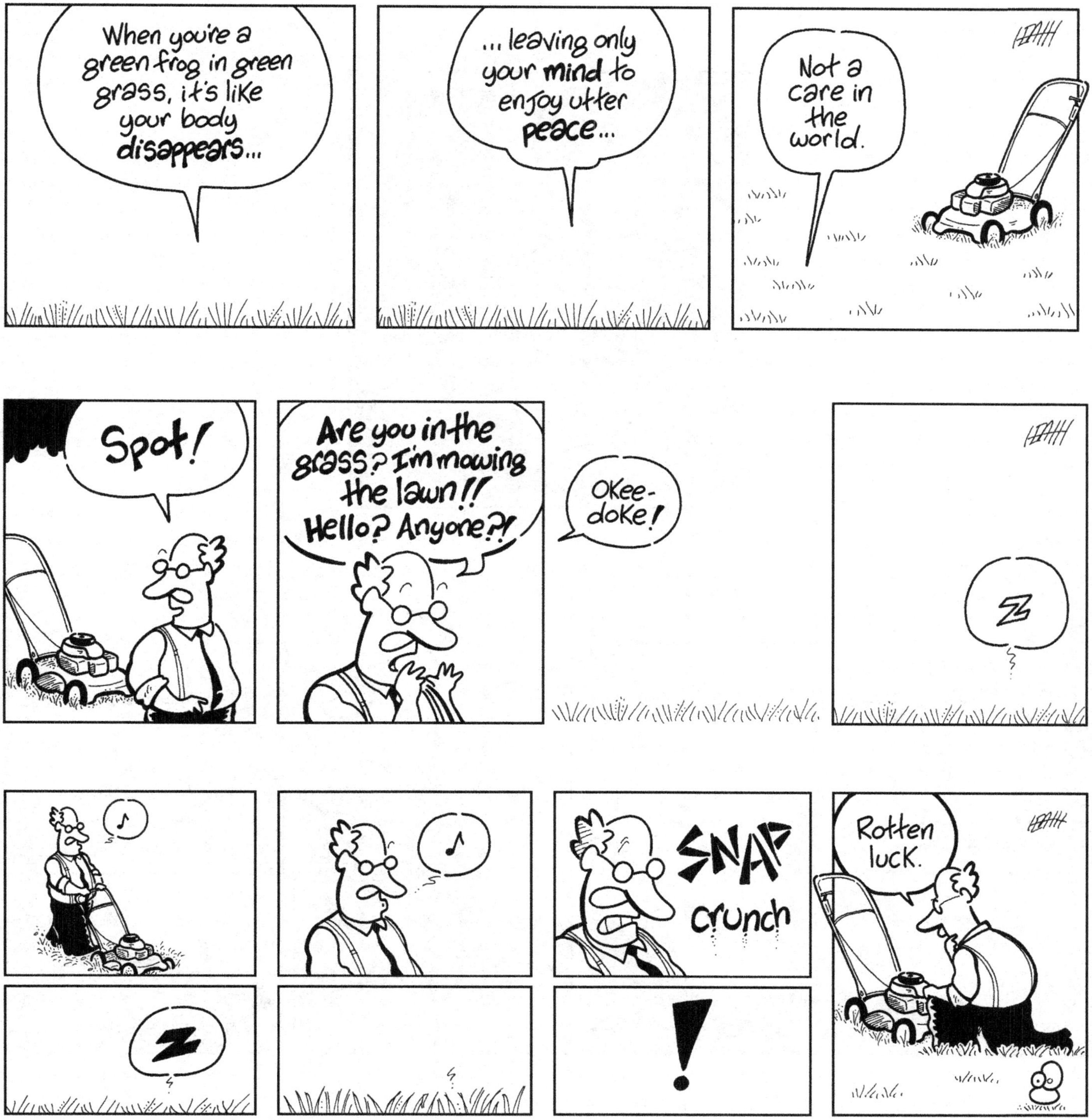
When you're a green frog in green grass, it's like your body disappears...
... leaving only your mind to enjoy utter peace...
Not a care in the world.
Spot!
Are you in the grass? I'm mowing the lawn!! Hello? Anyone?!
Okee-doke!
Z
♪
Z
♪
SNAP
crunch
!
Rotten luck.

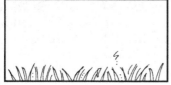

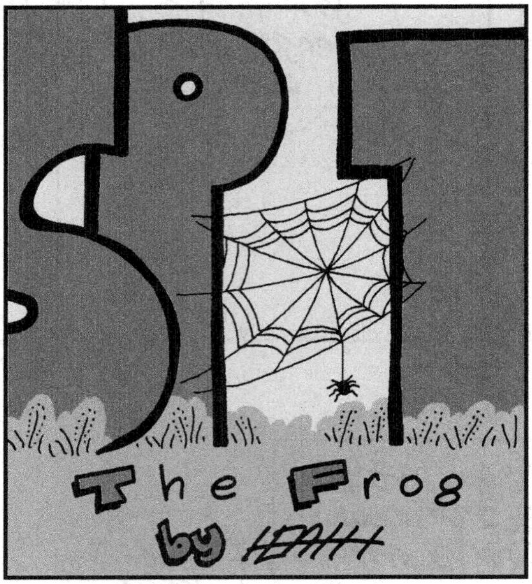
The Frog
by LEAHY

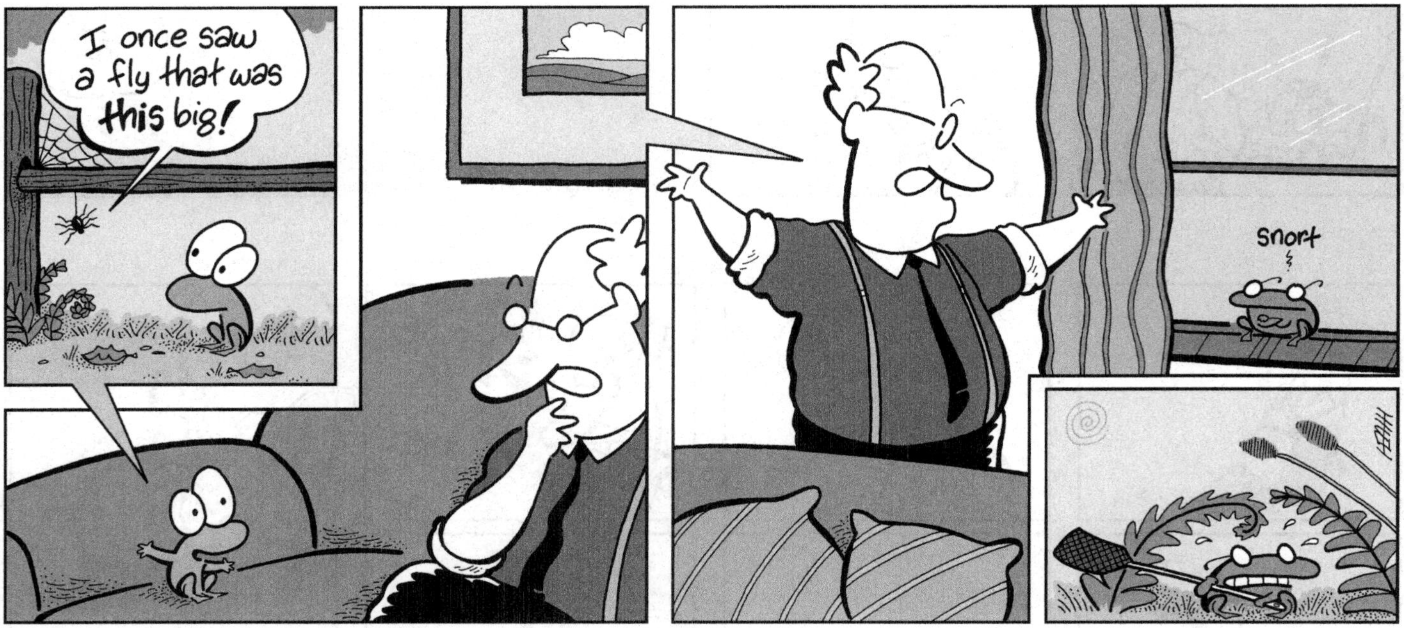
I once saw a fly that was **this** big!
snort

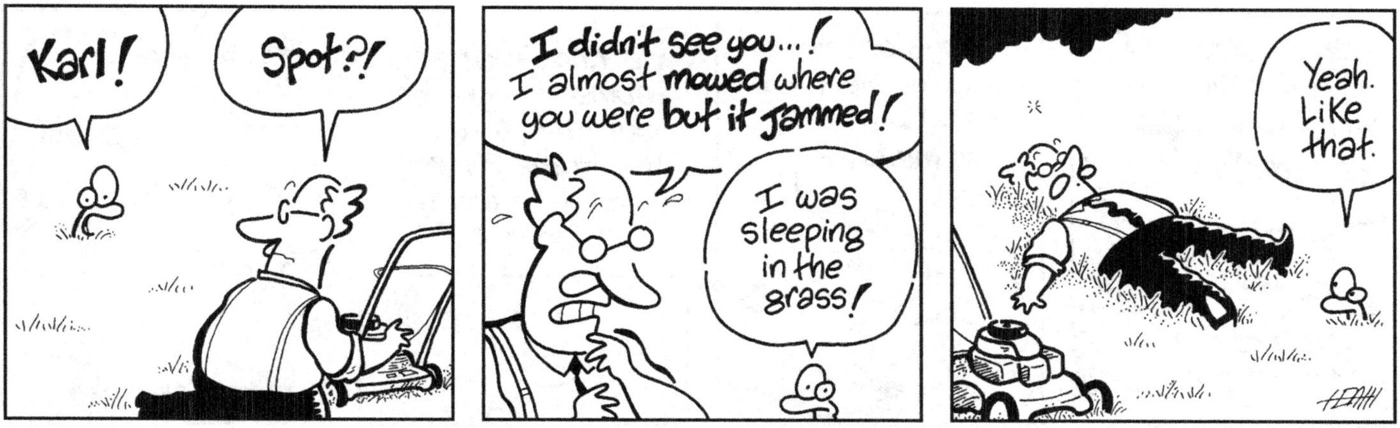
Karl!
Spot?!
I didn't see you...! I almost mowed where you were but it jammed!
I was sleeping in the grass!
Yeah. Like that.

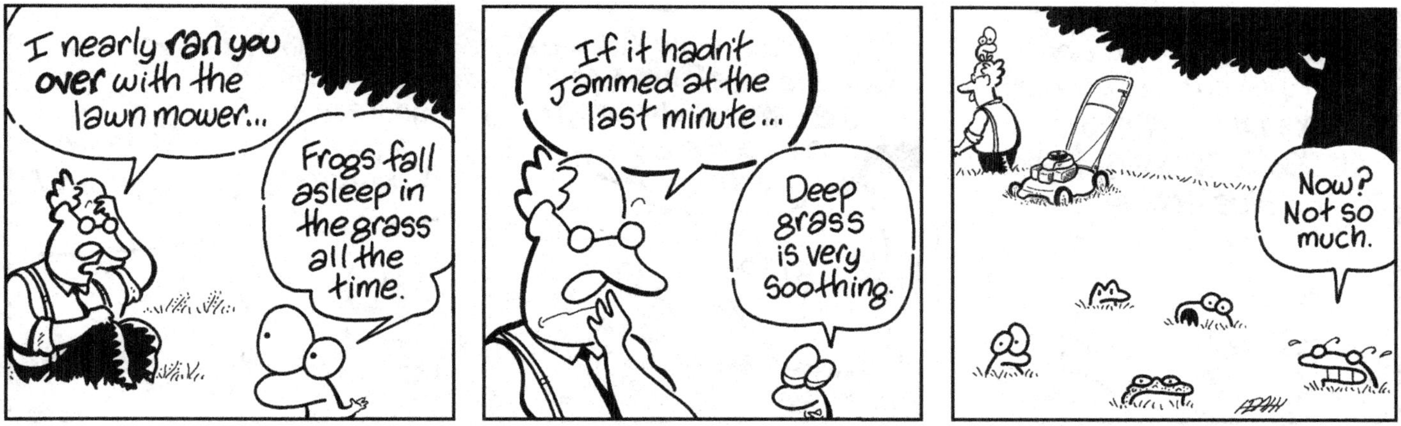
I nearly ran you over with the lawn mower...
Frogs fall asleep in the grass all the time.
If it hadn't jammed at the last minute...
Deep grass is very soothing.
Now? Not so much.

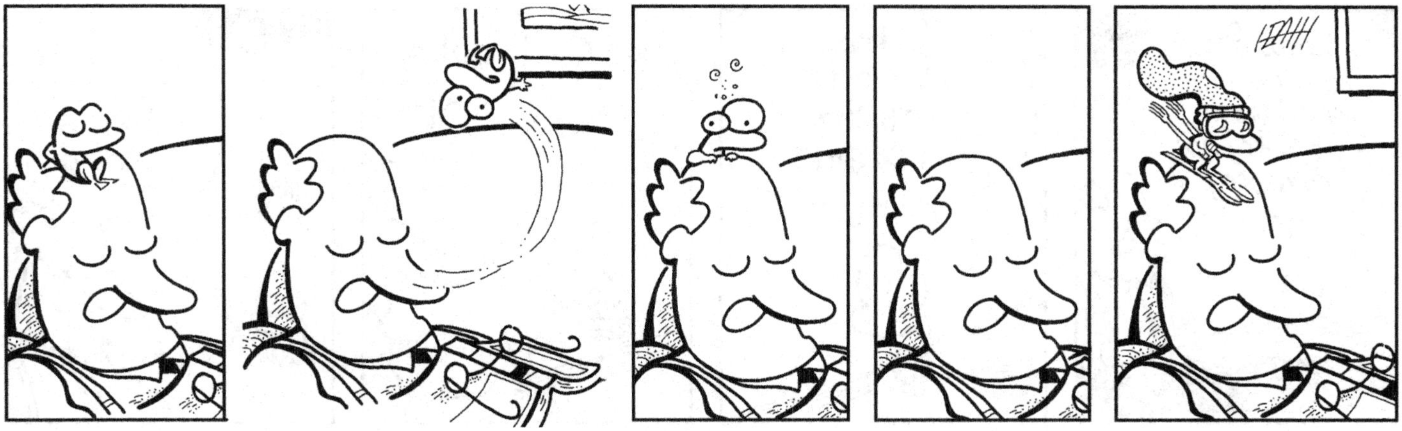

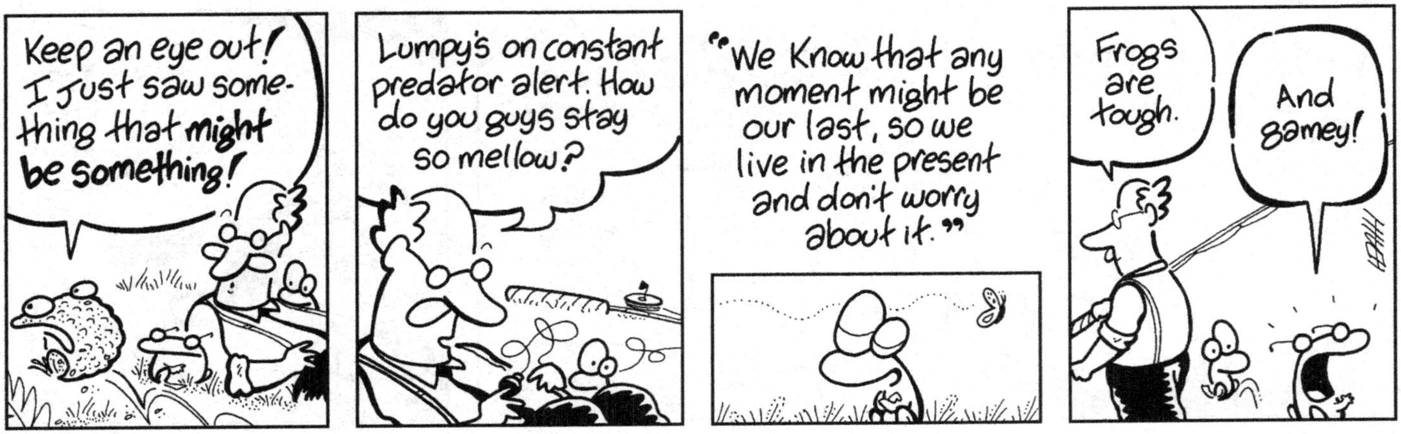
Keep an eye out! I just saw something that **might be something!**
Lumpy's on constant predator alert. How do you guys stay so mellow?
"We Know that any moment might be our last, so we live in the present and don't worry about it."
Frogs are tough.
And gamey!

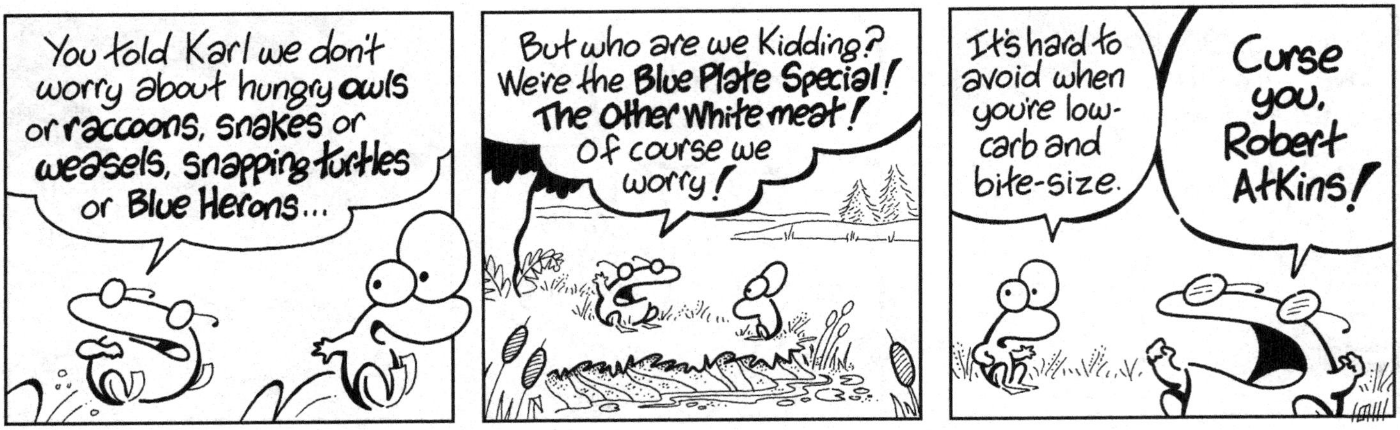
You told Karl we don't worry about hungry **owls** or **raccoons, snakes** or **weasels, snapping turtles** or **Blue Herons**...
But who are we Kidding? We're the **Blue Plate Special! The Other White meat!** Of course we worry!
It's hard to avoid when you're low-carb and bite-size.
Curse you, Robert Atkins!

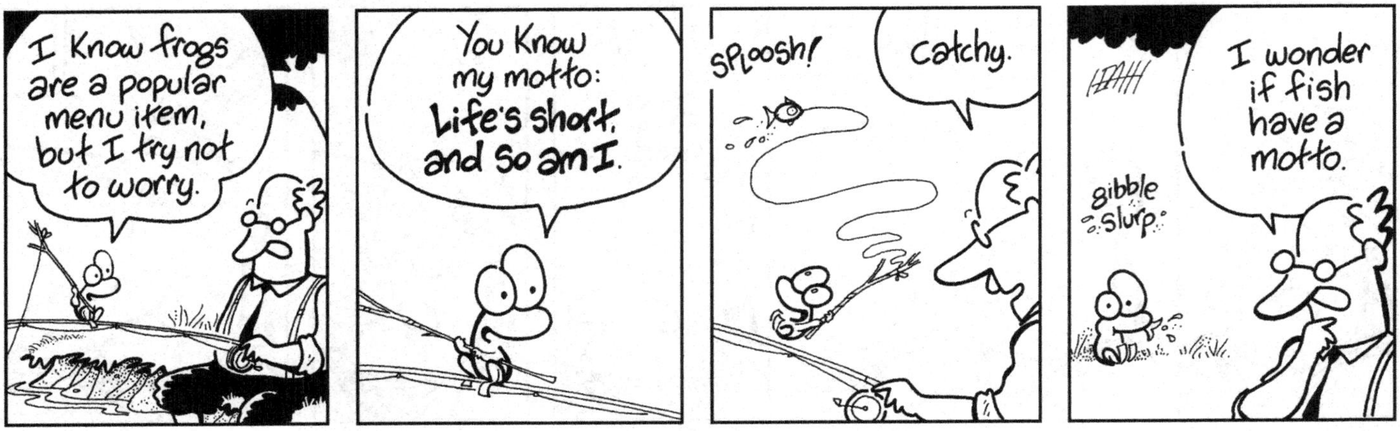
I Know frogs are a popular menu item, but I try not to worry.
You Know my motto: **Life's short, and so am I.**
SPLOOSH!
Catchy.
gibble slurp
I wonder if fish have a motto.

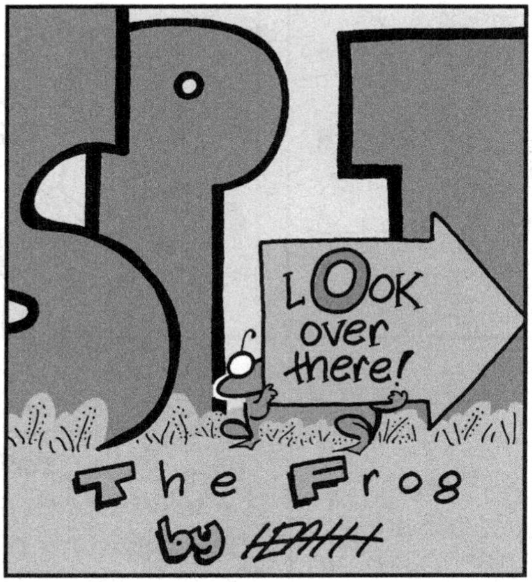
LOOK over there!
The Frog
by

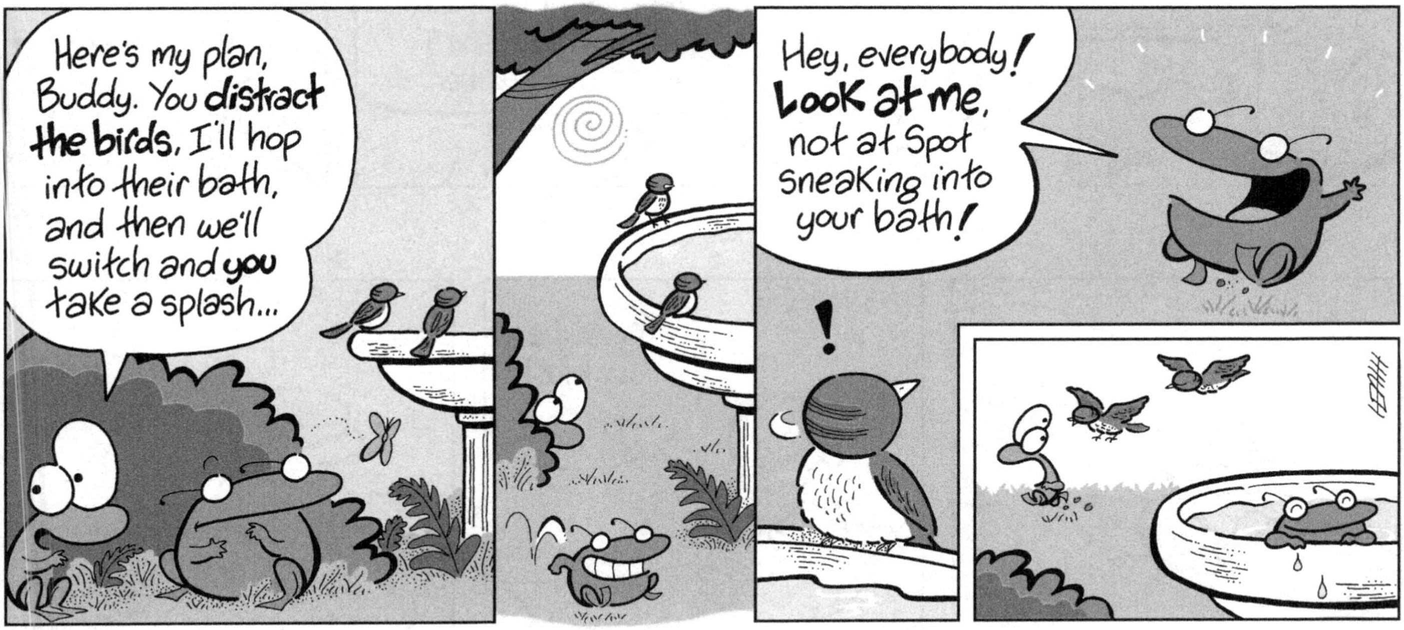
Here's my plan, Buddy. You **distract the birds**. I'll hop into their bath, and then we'll switch and **you** take a splash...
Hey, everybody! **Look at me**, not at Spot sneaking into your bath!
!

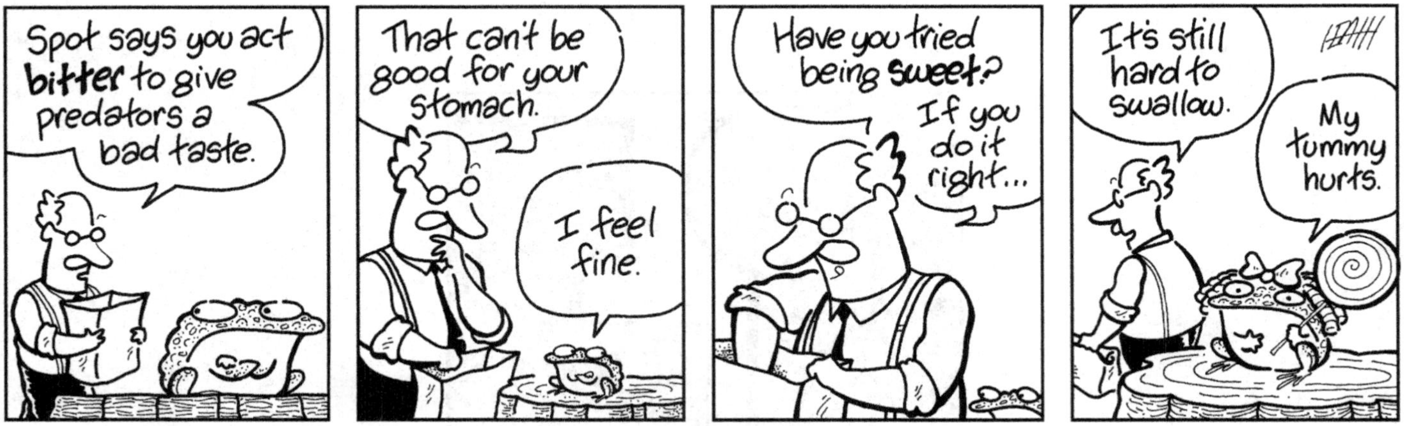
Spot says you act bitter to give predators a bad taste.
That can't be good for your stomach.
I feel fine.
Have you tried being sweet?
If you do it right...
It's still hard to swallow.
My tummy hurts.

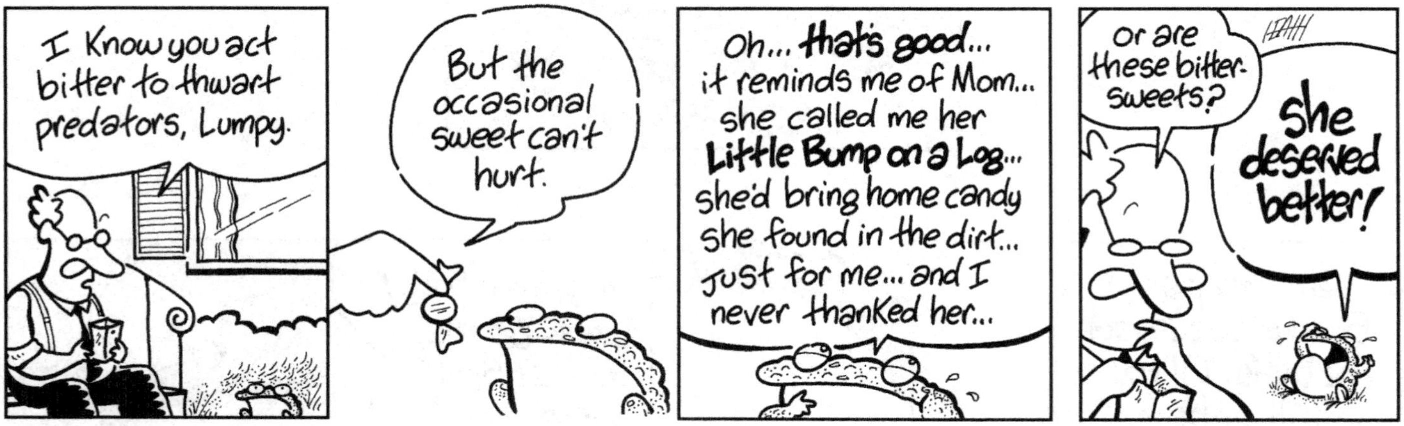
I Know you act bitter to thwart predators, Lumpy.
But the occasional sweet can't hurt.
Oh... that's good... it reminds me of Mom... she called me her Little Bump on a Log... she'd bring home candy she found in the dirt... just for me... and I never thanked her...
Or are these bitter-sweets?
She deserved better!

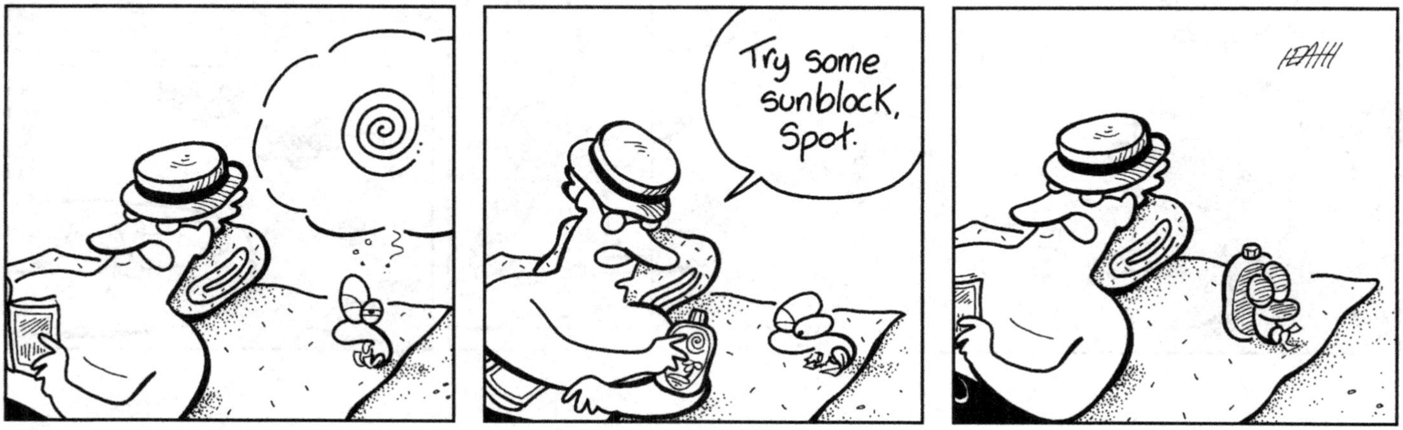
Try some sunblock, Spot.

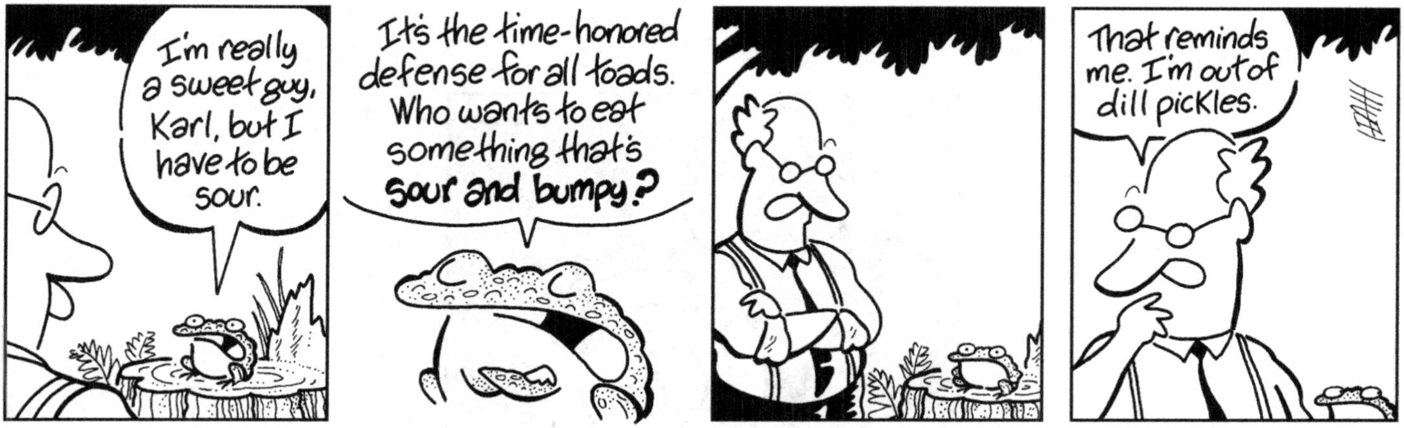
I'm really a sweet guy, Karl, but I have to be sour.
It's the time-honored defense for all toads. Who wants to eat something that's **sour and bumpy?**
That reminds me. I'm out of dill pickles.

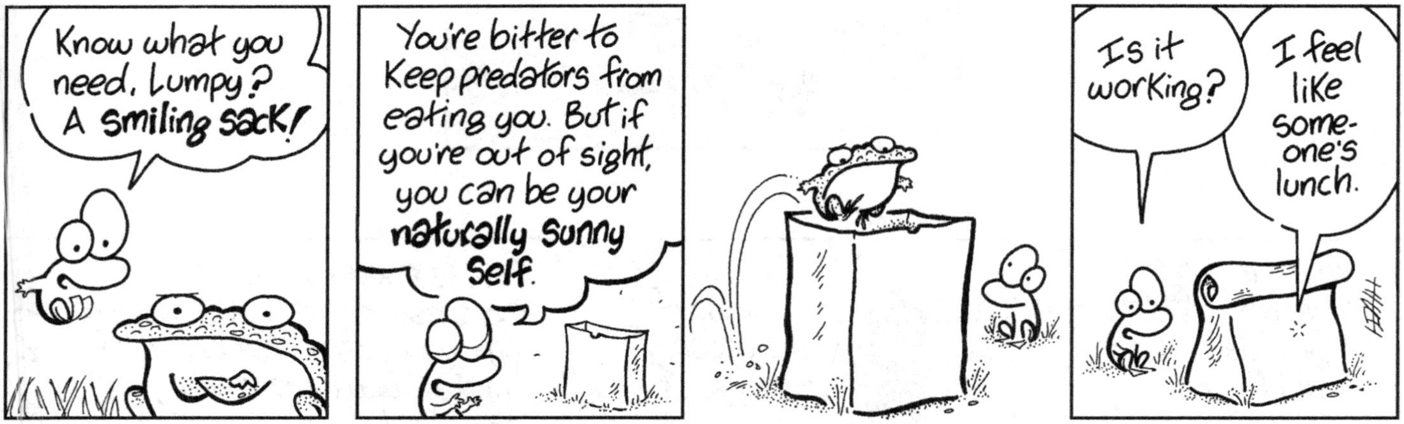
Know what you need, Lumpy? A **smiling sack!**
You're bitter to keep predators from eating you. But if you're out of sight, you can be your **naturally sunny self.**
Is it working?
I feel like some-one's lunch.

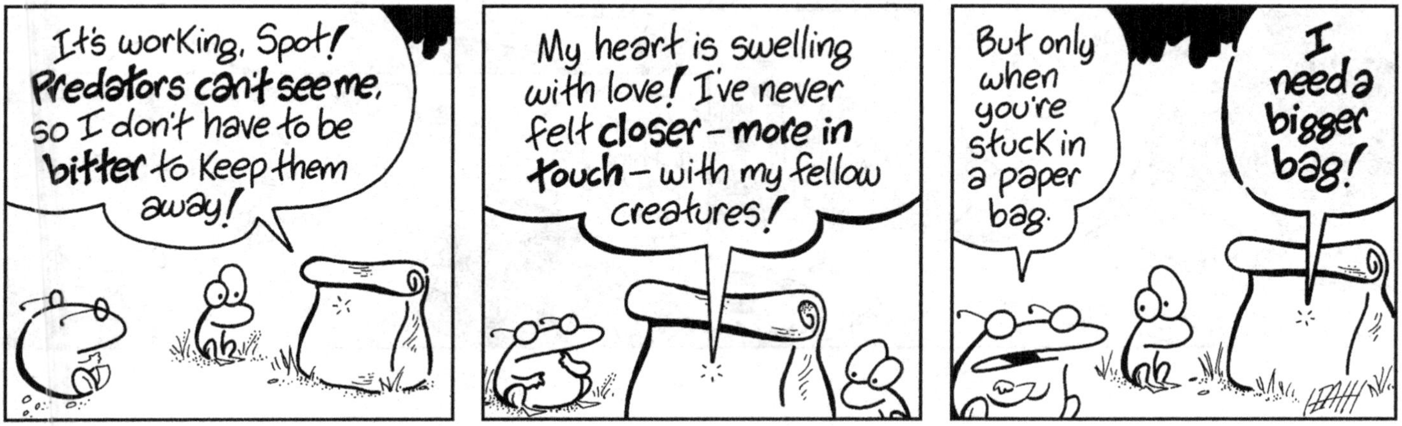
It's working, Spot! **Predators can't see me,** so I don't have to be **bitter** to keep them away!
My heart is swelling with love! I've never felt **closer – more in touch** – with my fellow creatures!
But only when you're stuck in a paper bag.
I need a bigger bag!

The Frog
by LEAH

You're in time for High Tide, Karl!

You're thinking of the ocean.

This is **pond** High Tide. It's too small to see, but if you put your nose **close to the water**, you'll eventually feel it.

Spot! I think I'm getting wet!

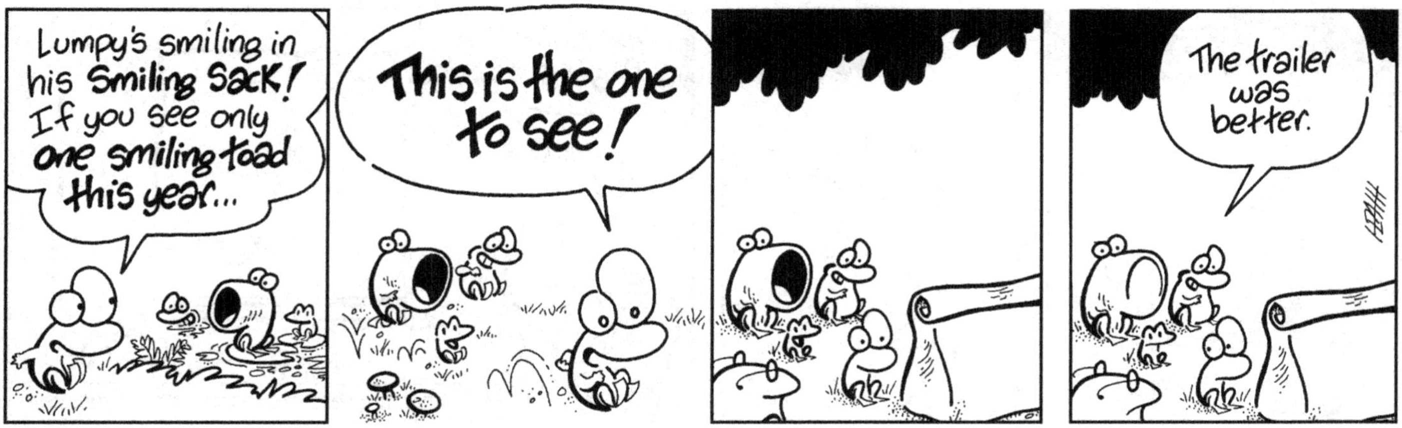
Lumpy's smiling in his Smiling Sack! If you see only one smiling toad this year...
This is the one to see!
The trailer was better.

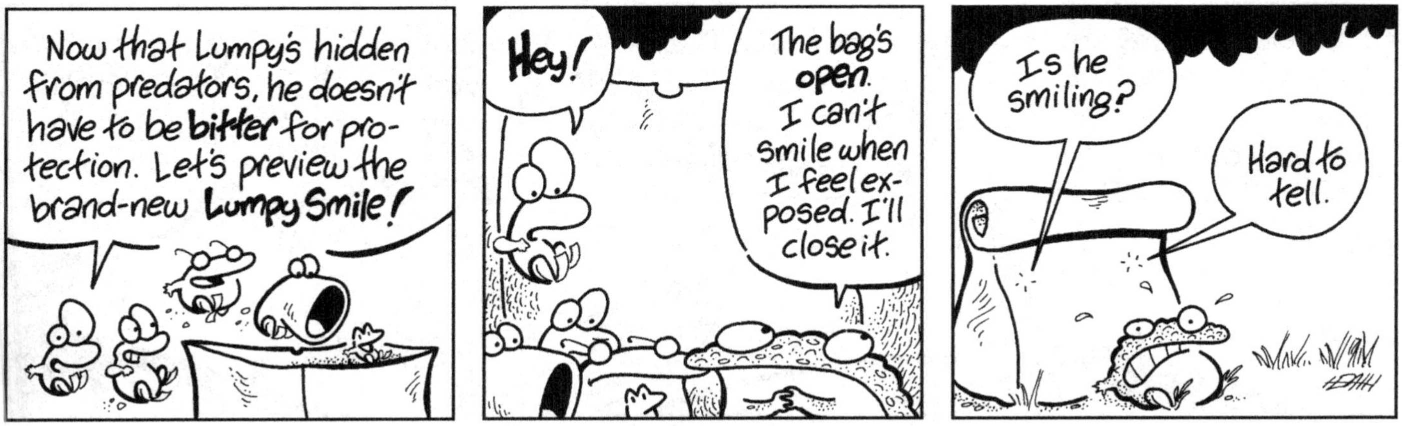
Now that Lumpy's hidden from predators, he doesn't have to be bitter for protection. Let's preview the brand-new Lumpy Smile!
Hey!
The bag's open. I can't smile when I feel exposed. I'll close it.
Is he smiling?
Hard to tell.

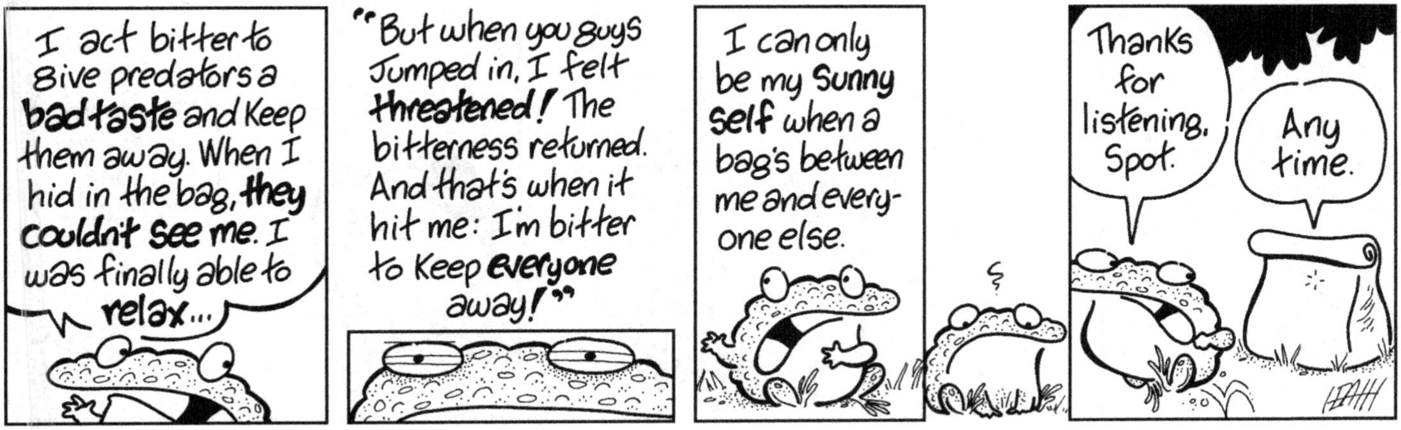
I act bitter to give predators a bad taste and keep them away. When I hid in the bag, they couldn't see me. I was finally able to relax...
"But when you guys jumped in, I felt threatened! The bitterness returned. And that's when it hit me: I'm bitter to keep everyone away!"
I can only be my sunny self when a bag's between me and everyone else.
Thanks for listening, Spot.
Any time.

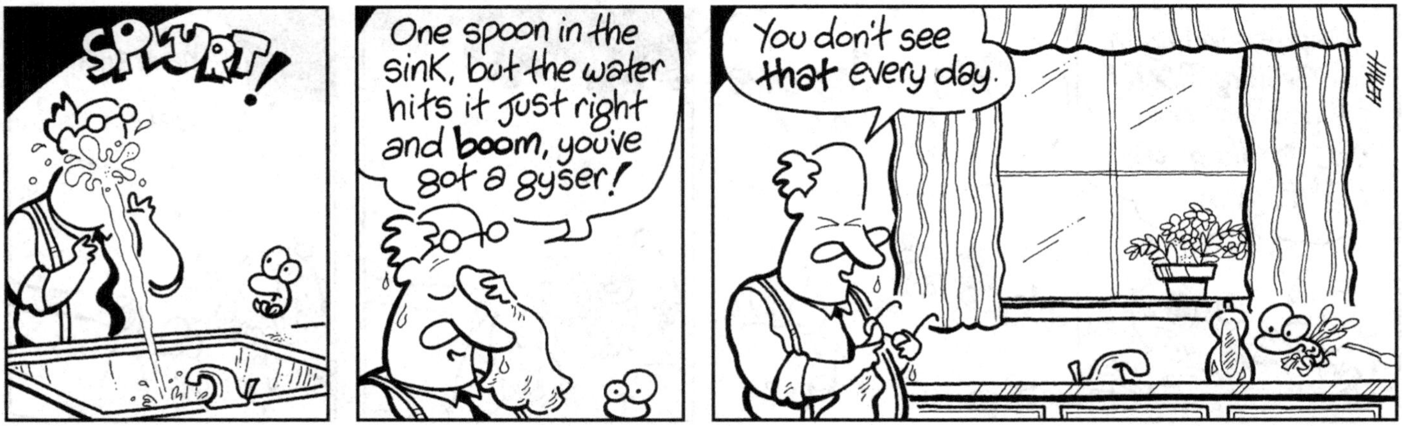
SPLURT!
One spoon in the sink, but the water hits it just right and boom, you've got a gyser!
You don't see that every day.

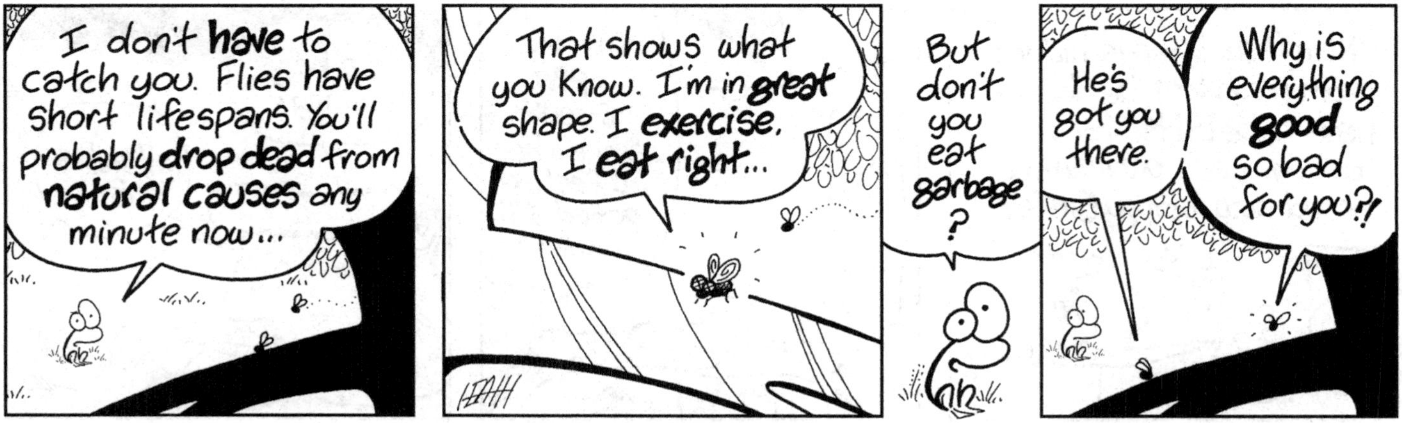
I don't have to catch you. Flies have short lifespans. You'll probably drop dead from natural causes any minute now...
That shows what you know. I'm in great shape. I exercise. I eat right...
But don't you eat garbage?
He's got you there.
Why is everything good so bad for you?!

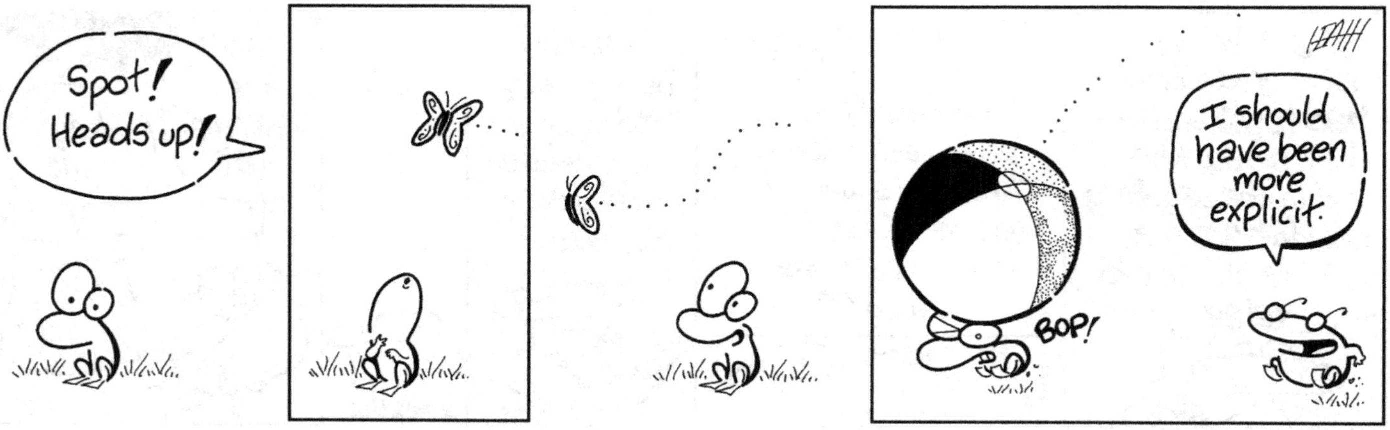
Spot! Heads up!
BOP!
I should have been more explicit.

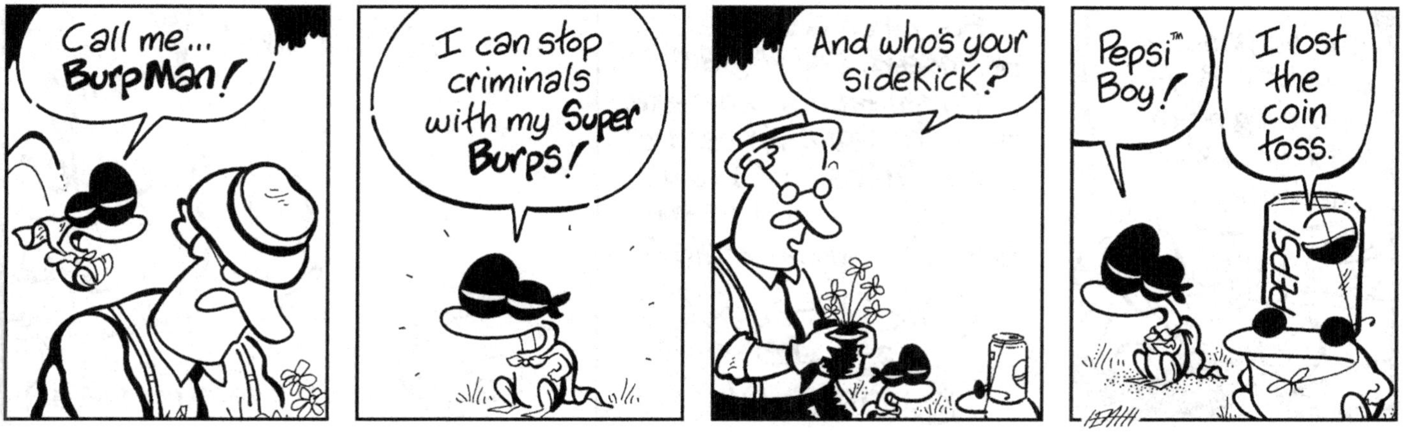
Call me... BurpMan!
I can stop criminals with my Super Burps!
And who's your sideKick?
Pepsi™ Boy!
I lost the coin toss.

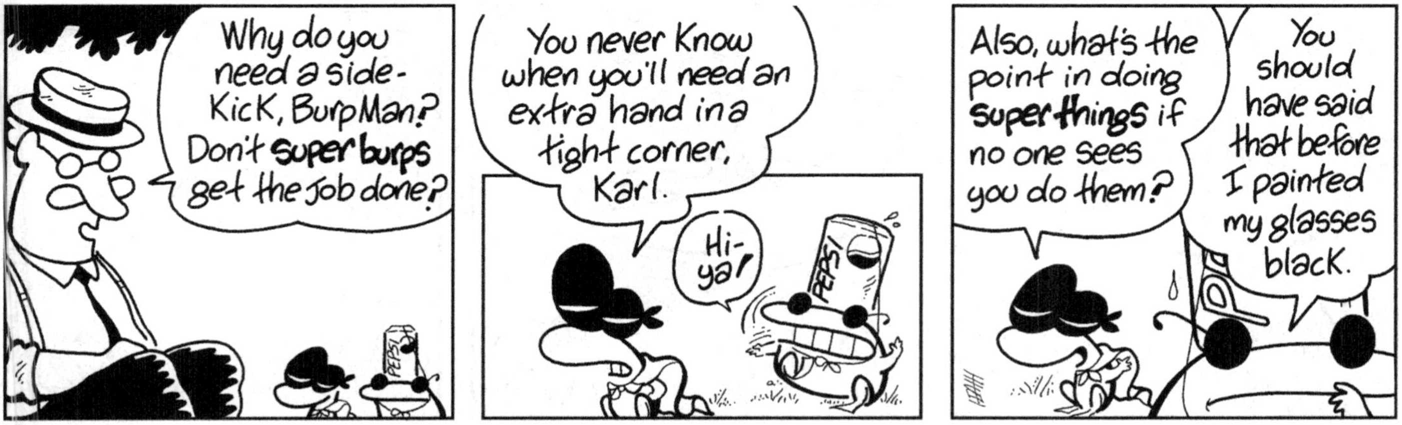
Why do you need a side-Kick, BurpMan? Don't super burps get the job done?
You never Know when you'll need an extra hand in a tight corner, Karl.
Hi-ya!
Also, what's the point in doing super things if no one sees you do them?
You should have said that before I painted my glasses black.

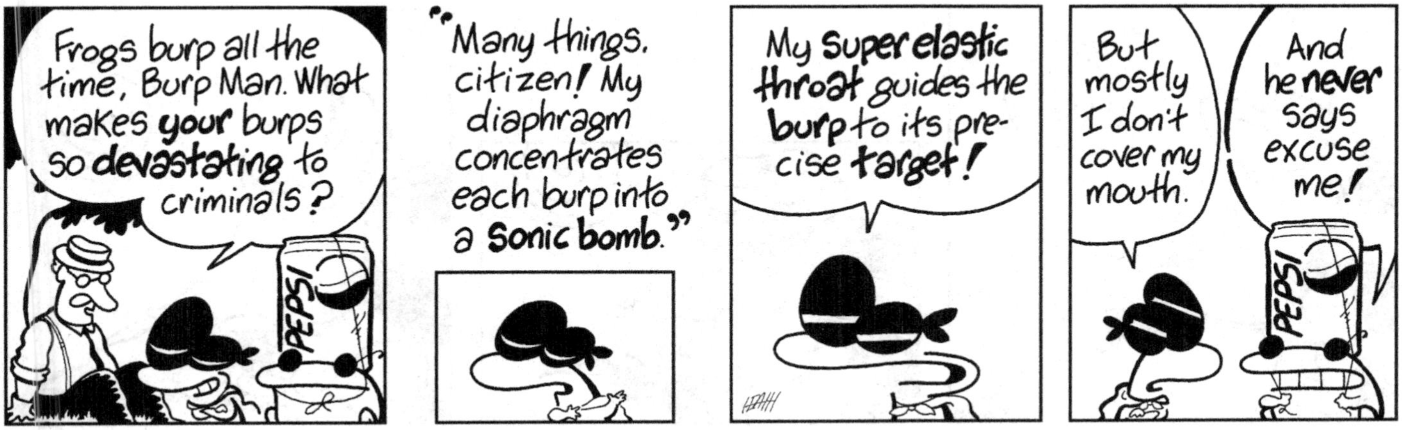
Frogs burp all the time, Burp Man. What makes your burps so devastating to criminals?
"Many things, citizen! My diaphragm concentrates each burp into a sonic bomb."
My super elastic throat guides the burp to its precise target!
But mostly I don't cover my mouth.
And he never says excuse me!

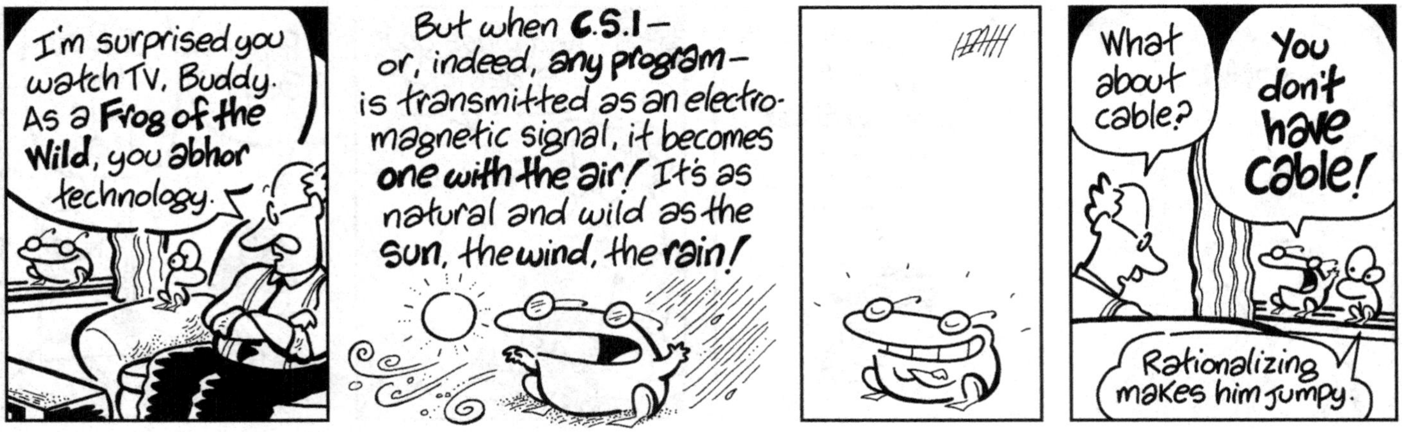
I'm surprised you watch TV, Buddy. As a Frog of the Wild, you abhor technology.
But when C.S.I — or, indeed, any program — is transmitted as an electro-magnetic signal, it becomes one with the air! It's as natural and wild as the sun, the wind, the rain!
What about cable?
You don't have cable!
Rationalizing makes him jumpy.

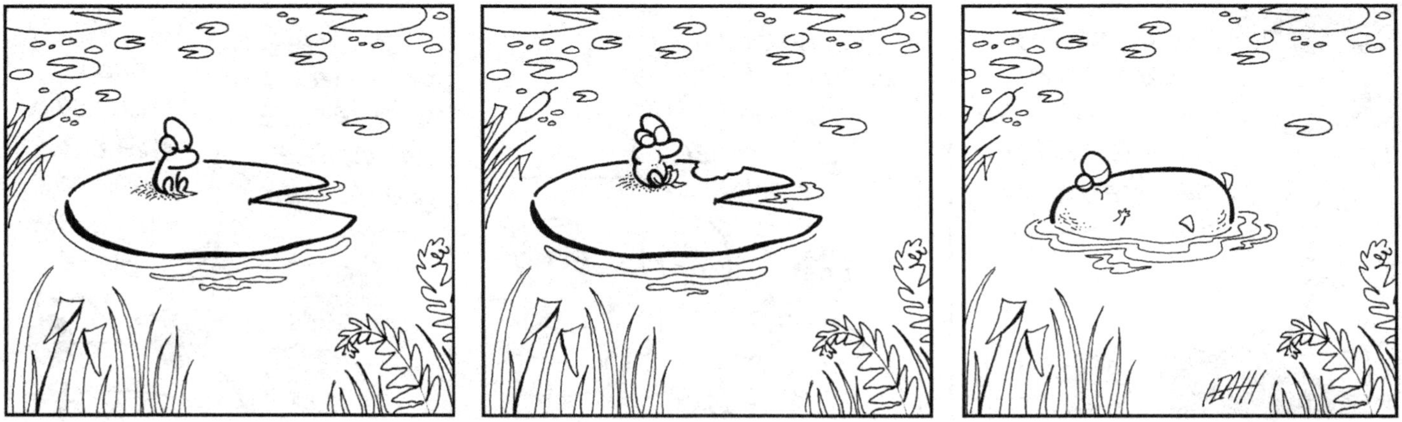

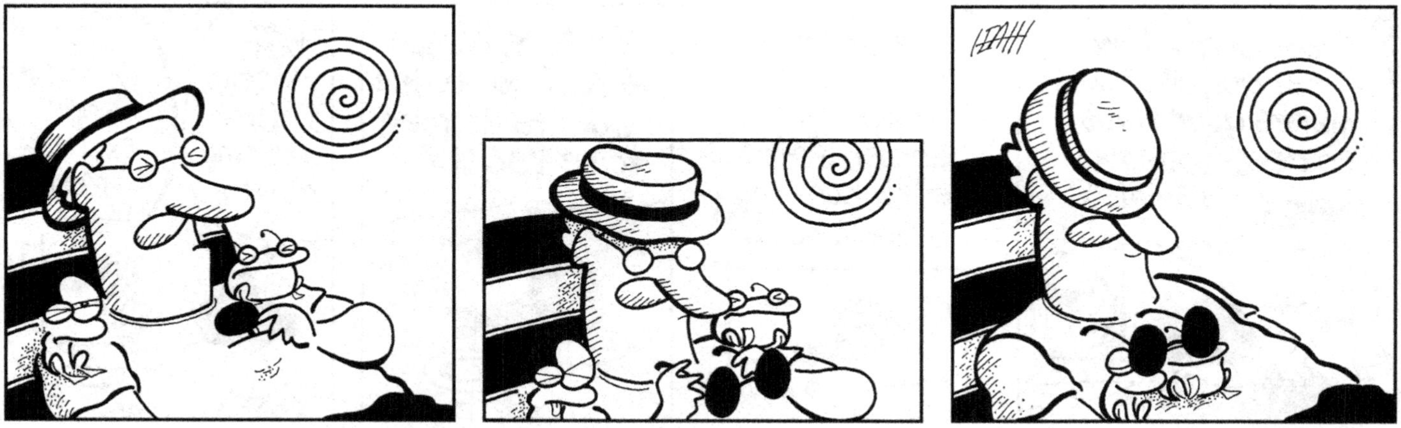

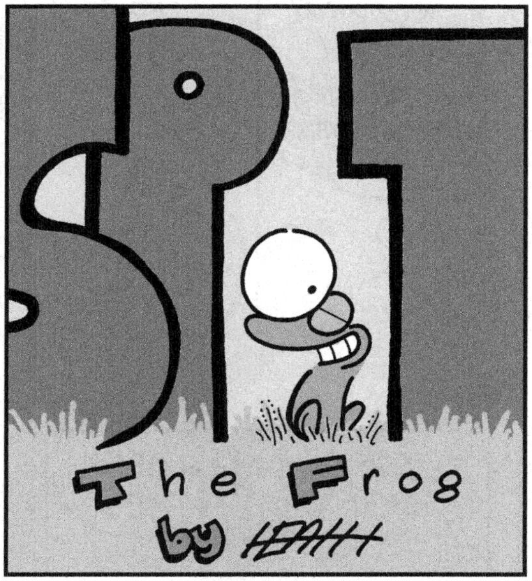
The Frog
by

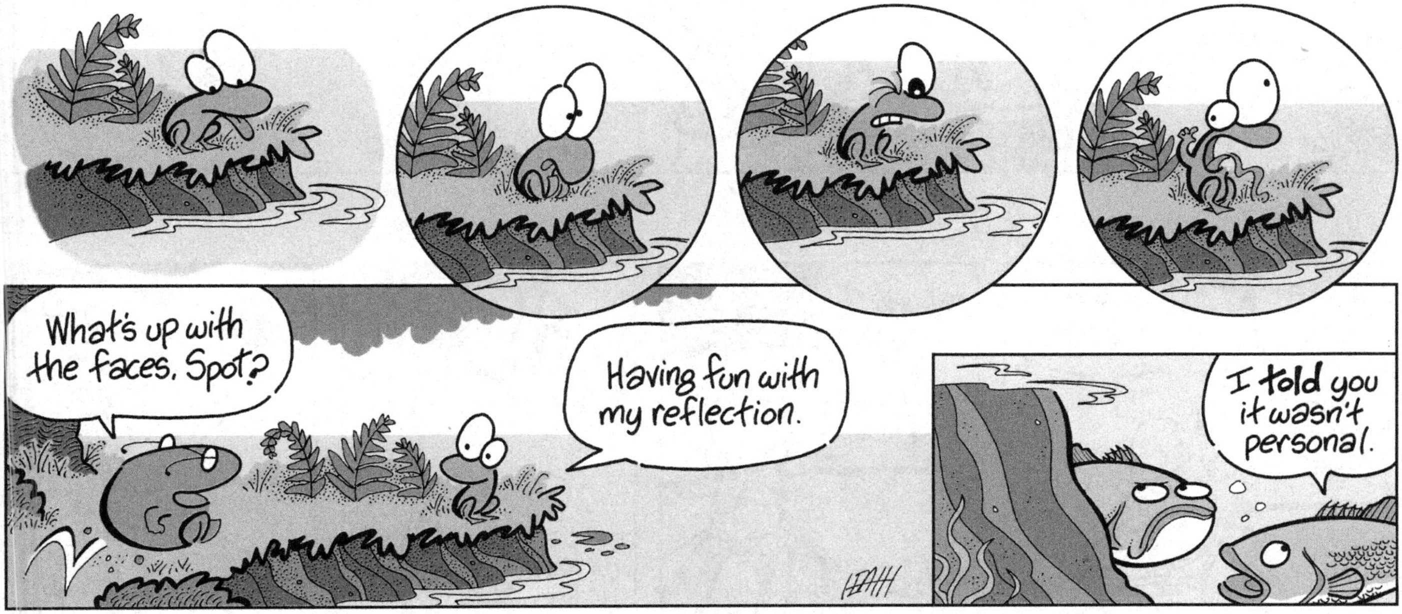
What's up with the faces, Spot?
Having fun with my reflection.
I **told** you it wasn't personal.

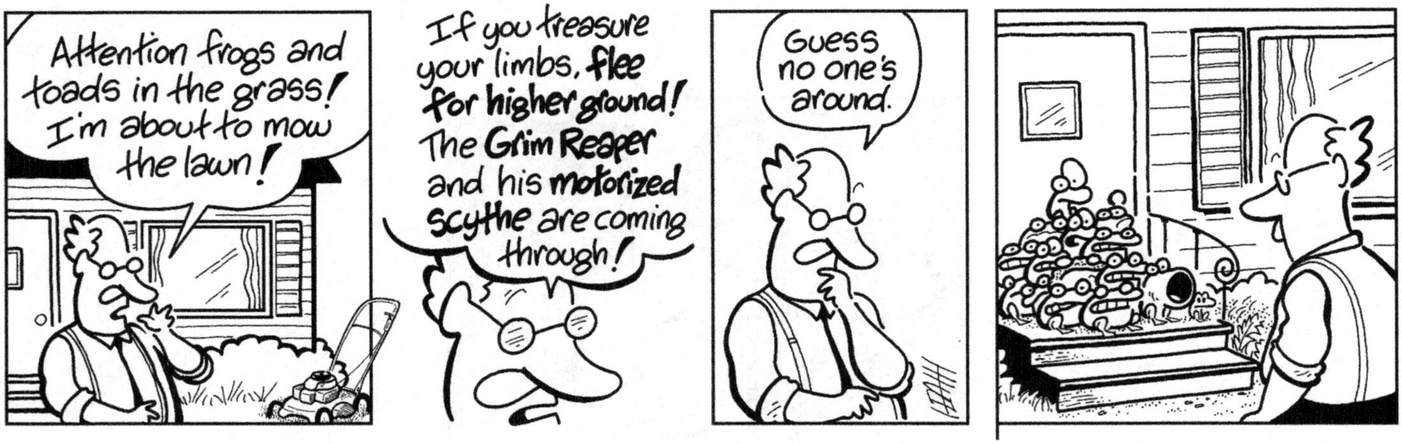
Attention frogs and toads in the grass! I'm about to mow the lawn!
If you treasure your limbs, **flee for higher ground!** The **Grim Reaper** and his **motorized scythe** are coming through!
Guess no one's around.

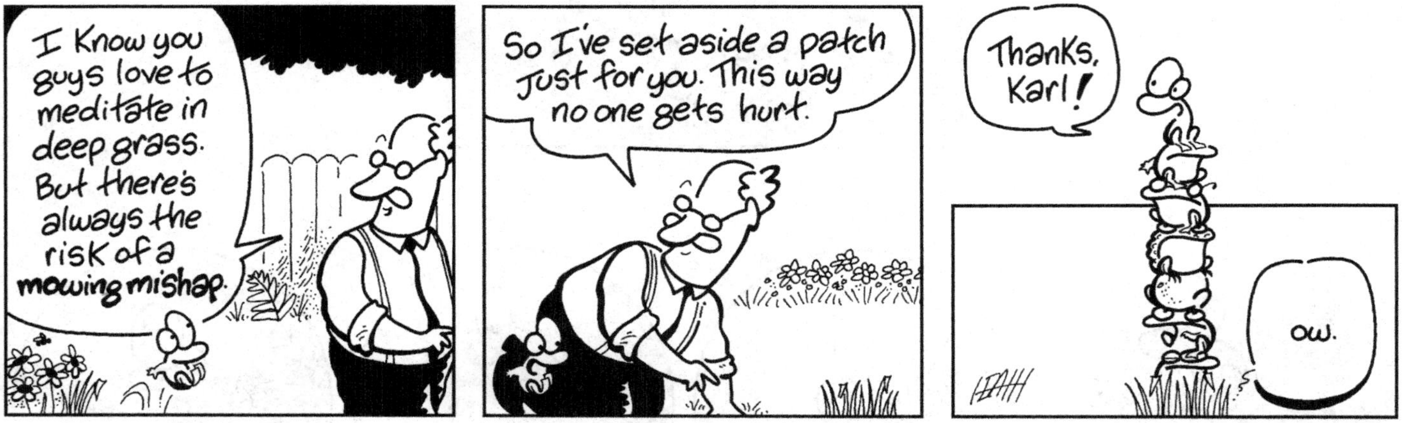
I Know you guys love to meditate in deep grass. But there's always the risk of a **mowing mishap**.
So I've set aside a patch just for you. This way no one gets hurt.
Thanks, Karl!
ow.

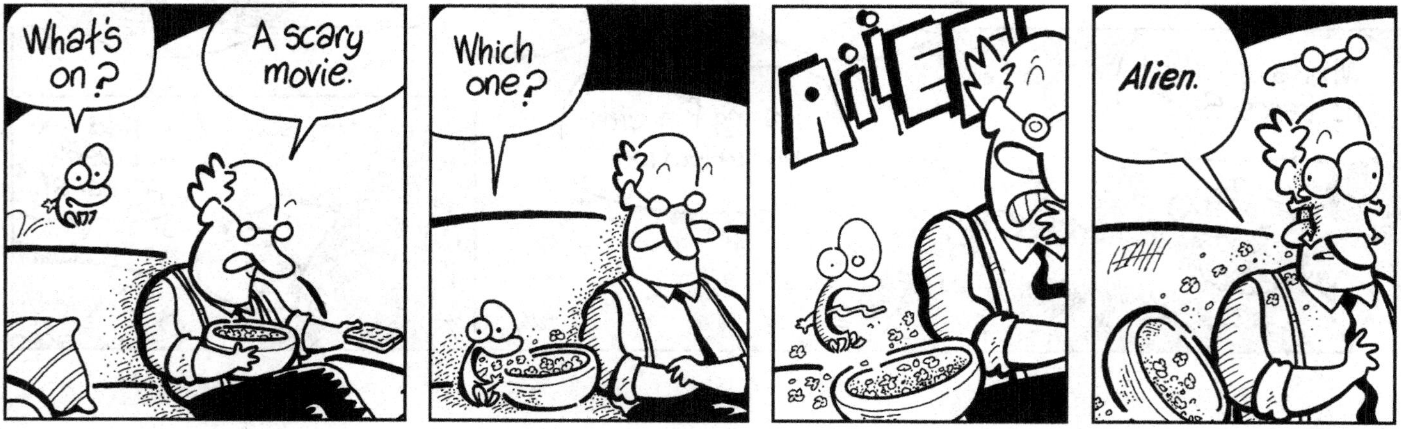
What's on?
A scary movie.
Which one?
AIEE
Alien.

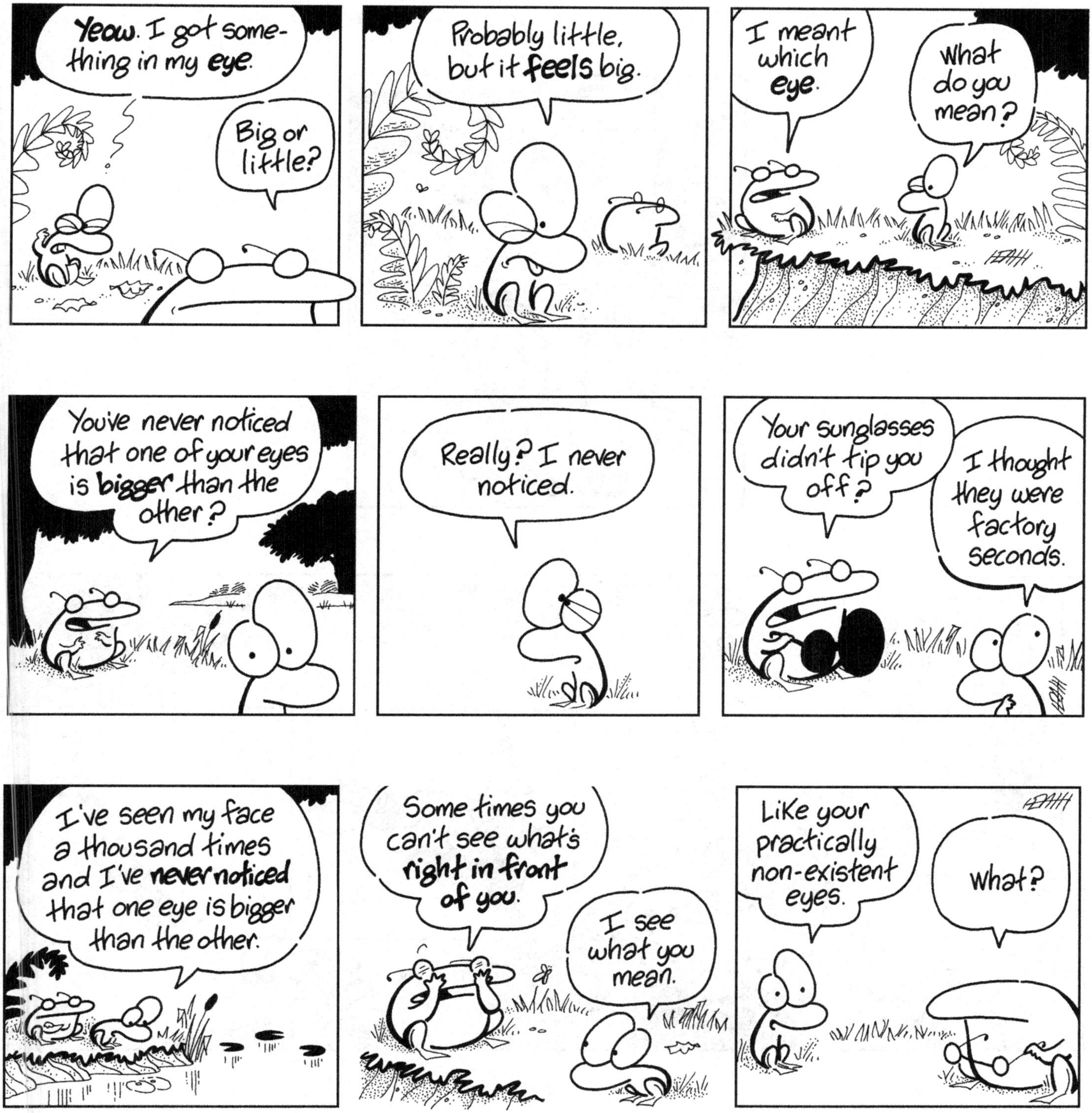

Yeow. I got something in my eye.
Big or little?
Probably little, but it feels big.
I meant which eye.
What do you mean?
You've never noticed that one of your eyes is bigger than the other?
Really? I never noticed.
Your sunglasses didn't tip you off?
I thought they were factory seconds.
I've seen my face a thousand times and I've never noticed that one eye is bigger than the other.
Some times you can't see what's right in front of you.
I see what you mean.
Like your practically non-existent eyes.
What?

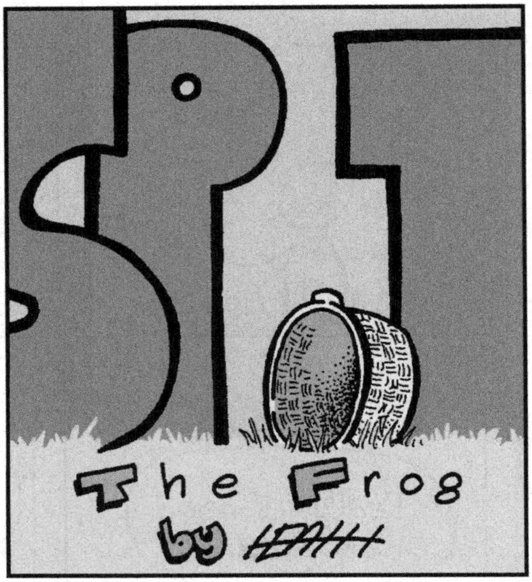

The Frog
by

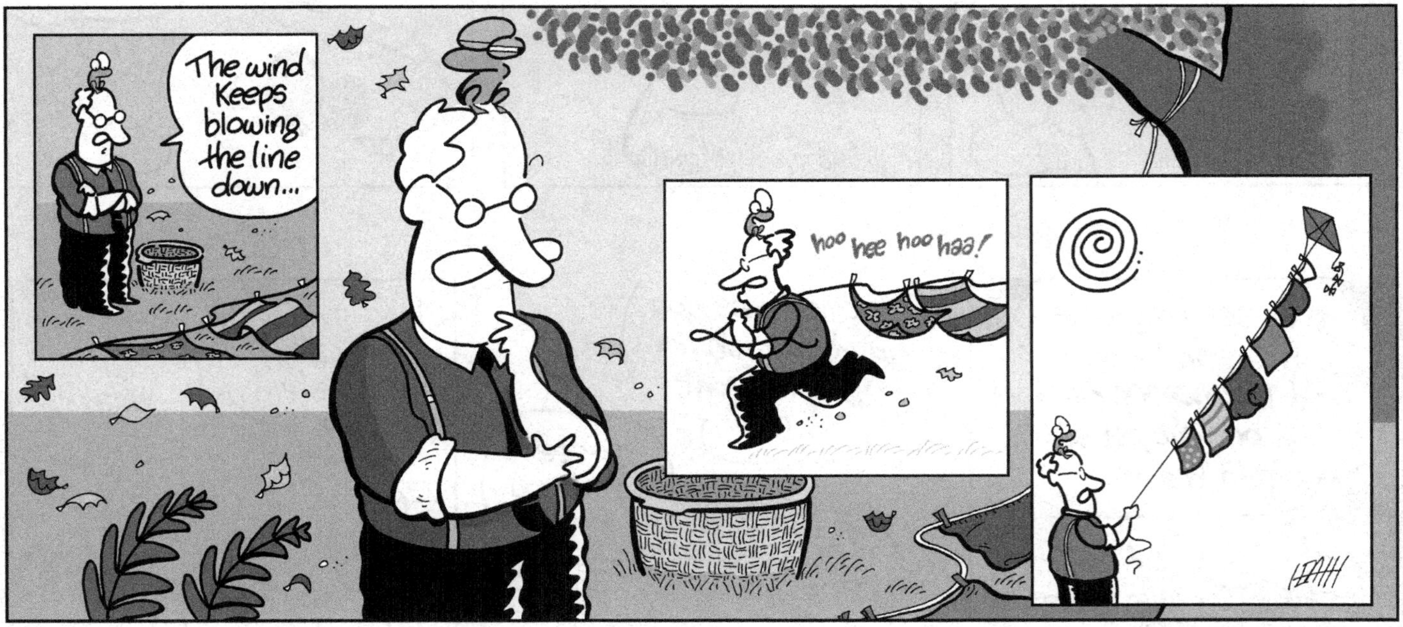

The wind Keeps blowing the line down...
hoo hee hoo haa!

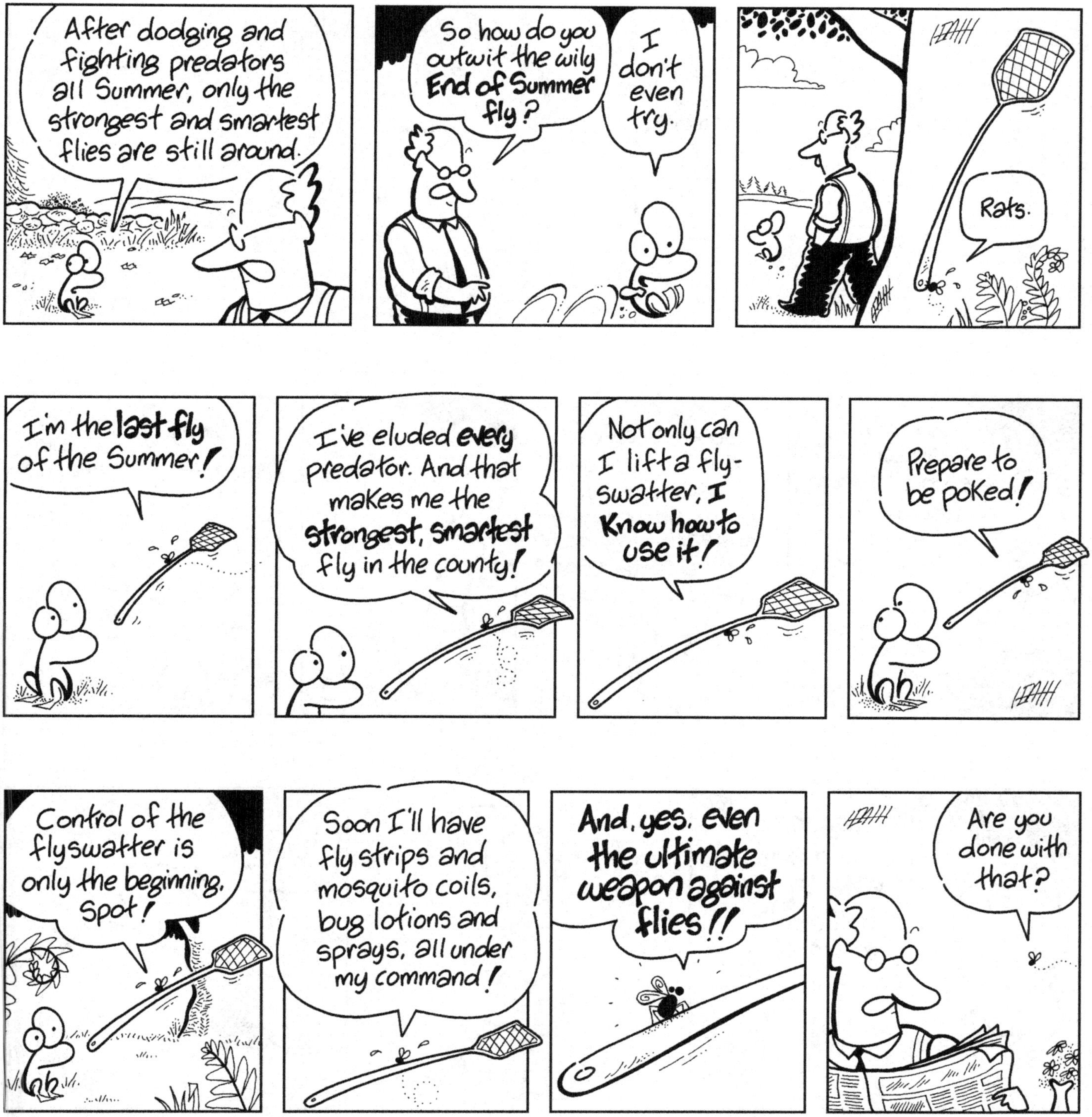
After dodging and fighting predators all Summer, only the strongest and smartest flies are still around.
So how do you outwit the wily **End of Summer** fly?
I don't even try.
Rats.
I'm the **last fly** of the Summer!
I've eluded **every** predator. And that makes me the **strongest, smartest** fly in the county!
Not only can I lift a fly-swatter, **I Know how to use it!**
Prepare to be poked!
Control of the flyswatter is only the beginning, Spot!
Soon I'll have fly strips and mosquito coils, bug lotions and sprays, all under my command!
And, yes, even the ultimate weapon against flies!!
Are you done with that?

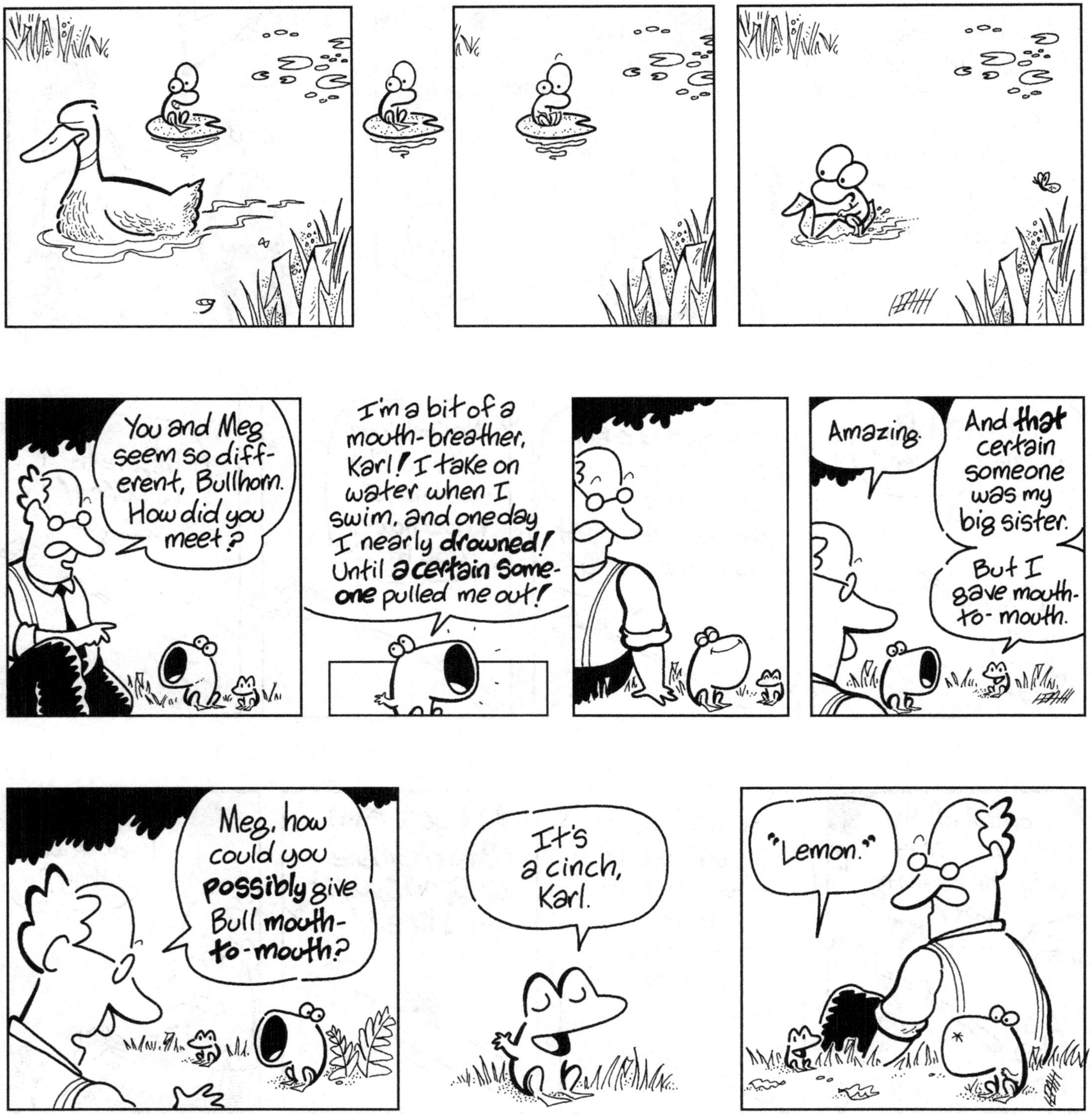
You and Meg seem so different, Bullhorn. How did you meet?
I'm a bit of a mouth-breather, Karl! I take on water when I swim, and one day I nearly **drowned**! Until **a certain someone** pulled me out!
Amazing.
And **that** certain someone was my big sister.
But I gave mouth-to-mouth.
Meg, how could you **possibly** give Bull **mouth-to-mouth**?
It's a cinch, Karl.
"Lemon."

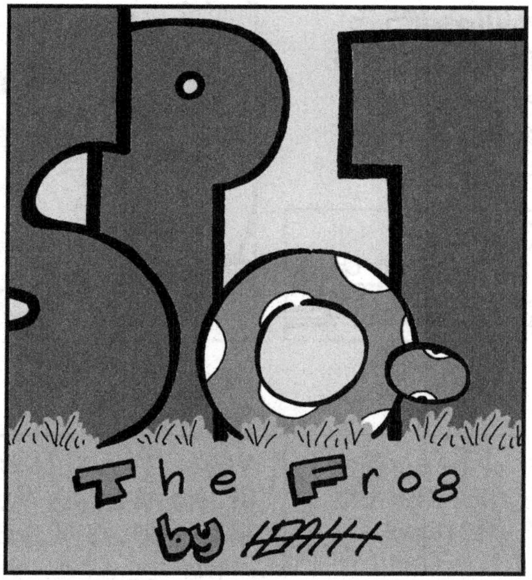
The Frog
by

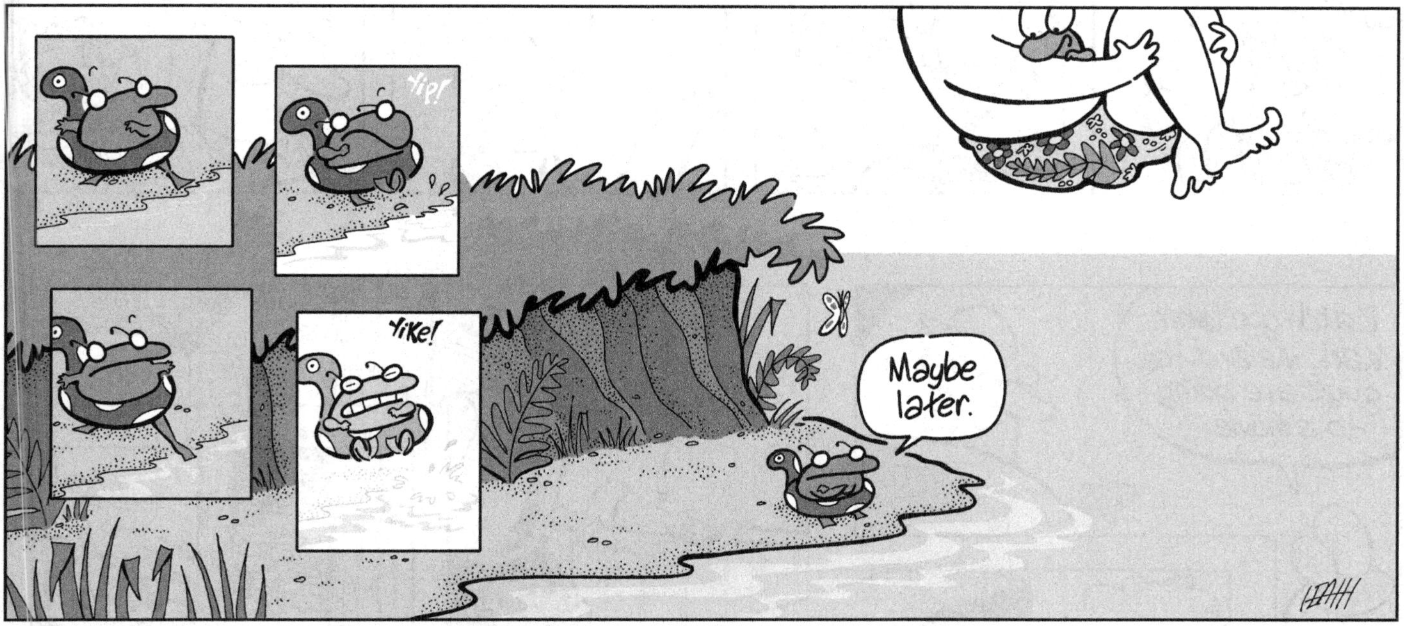
Yip!
Yike!
Maybe later.

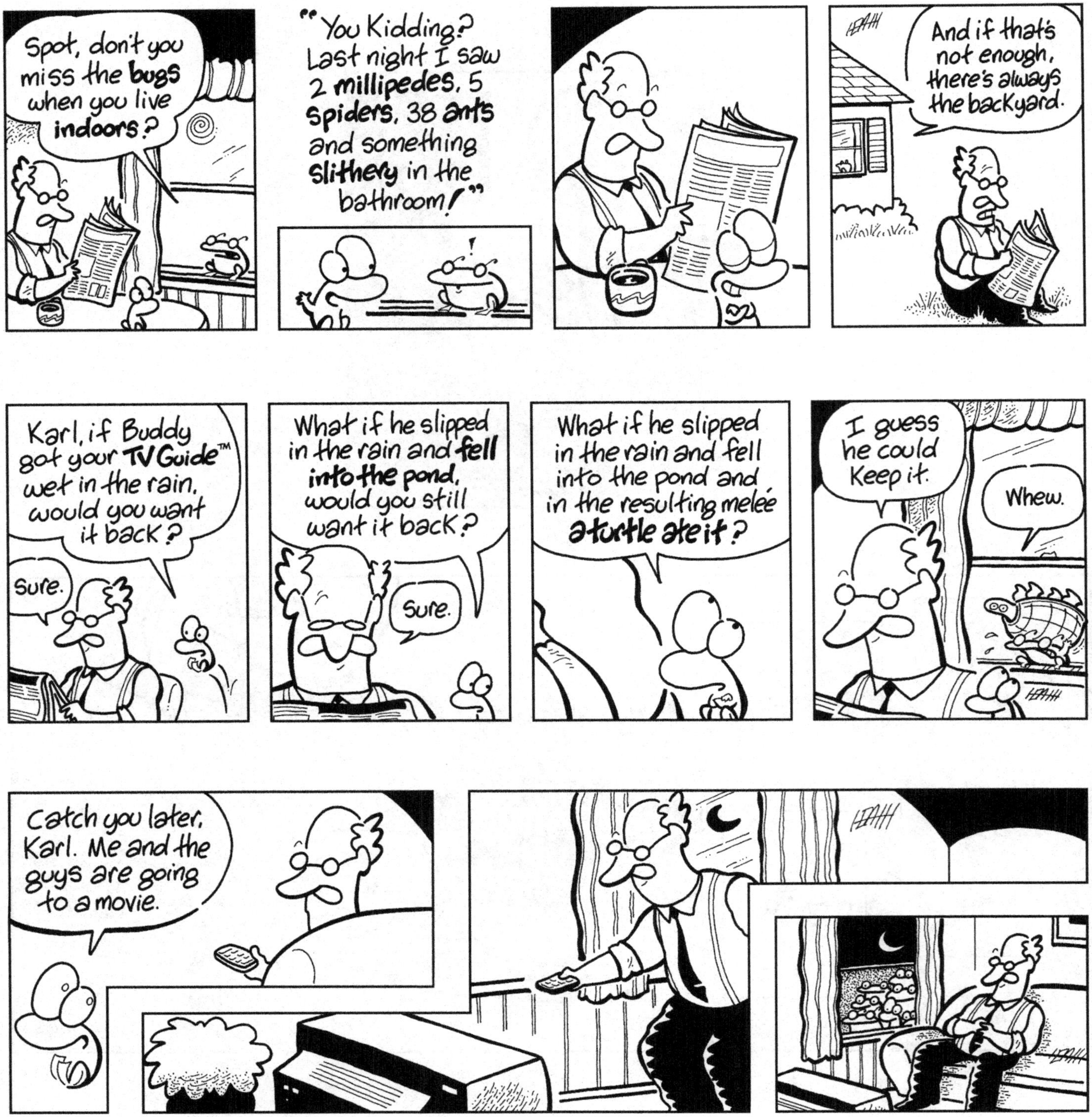
Spot, don't you miss the **bugs** when you live **indoors**?
"You Kidding? Last night I saw 2 **millipedes**, 5 **spiders**, 38 **ants** and something **slithery** in the bathroom!"
And if that's not enough, there's always the backyard.
Karl, if Buddy got your **TV Guide**™ wet in the rain, would you want it back?
Sure.
What if he slipped in the rain and **fell into the pond**, would you still want it back?
Sure.
What if he slipped in the rain and fell into the pond and in the resulting melée **a turtle ate it**?
I guess he could keep it.
Whew.
Catch you later, Karl. Me and the guys are going to a movie.

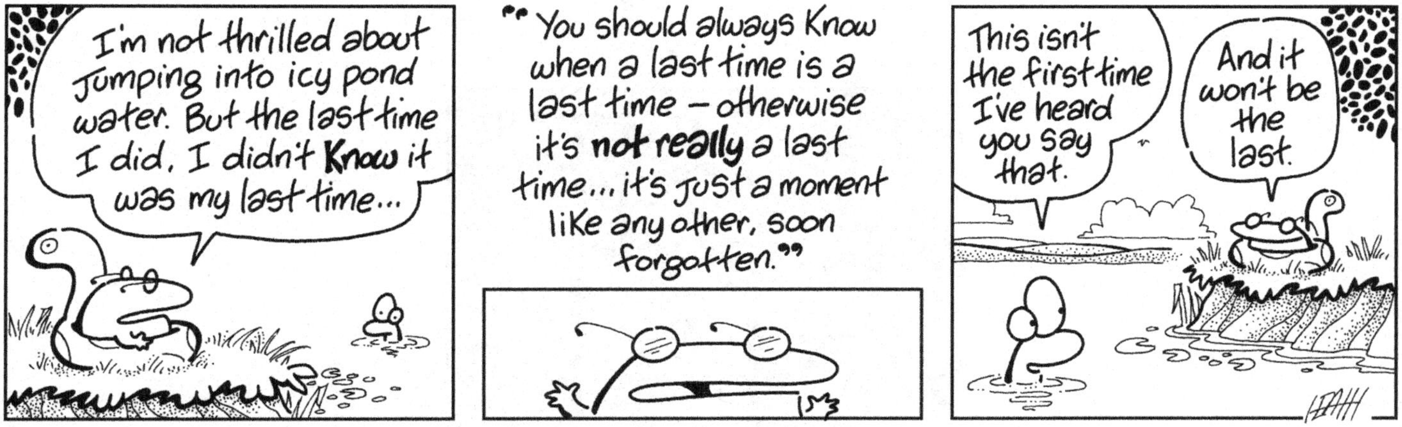
I'm not thrilled about jumping into icy pond water. But the last time I did, I didn't **know** it was my last time...
"You should always know when a last time is a last time – otherwise it's **not really** a last time... it's just a moment like any other, soon forgotten."
This isn't the first time I've heard you say that.
And it won't be the last.

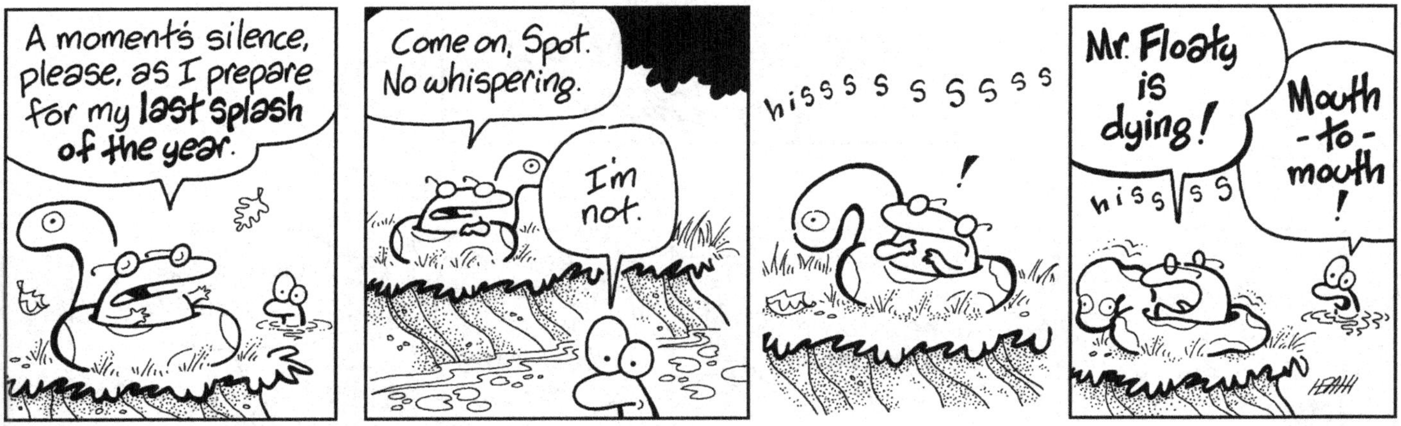
A moment's silence, please, as I prepare for my **last splash of the year.**
Come on, Spot. No whispering.
I'm not.
hisss s s s s s s s
!
Mr. Floaty is dying!
hiss s s s
Mouth -to- mouth!

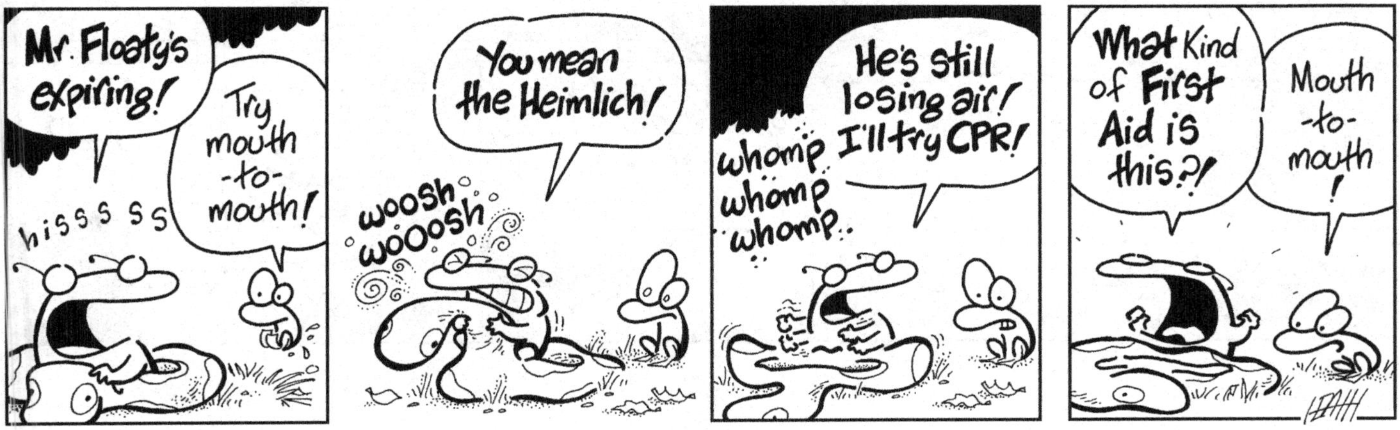
Mr. Floaty's expiring!
Try mouth -to- mouth!
hisss s s s
You mean the Heimlich!
woosh wooosh
He's still losing air! I'll try CPR!
whomp whomp whomp
What kind of **First Aid** is this?!
Mouth -to- mouth!

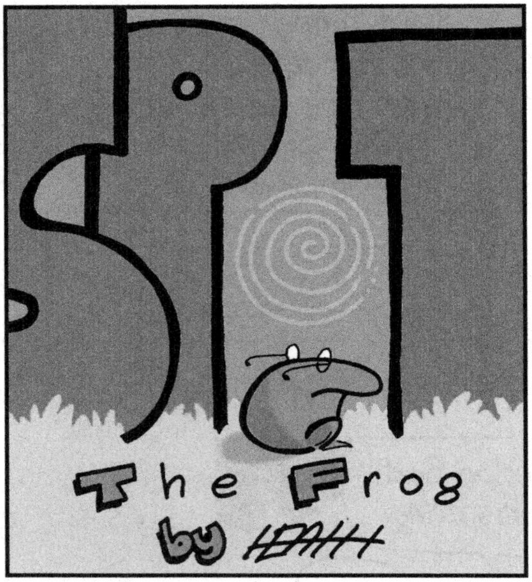
SPIT
The Frog
by HEATH

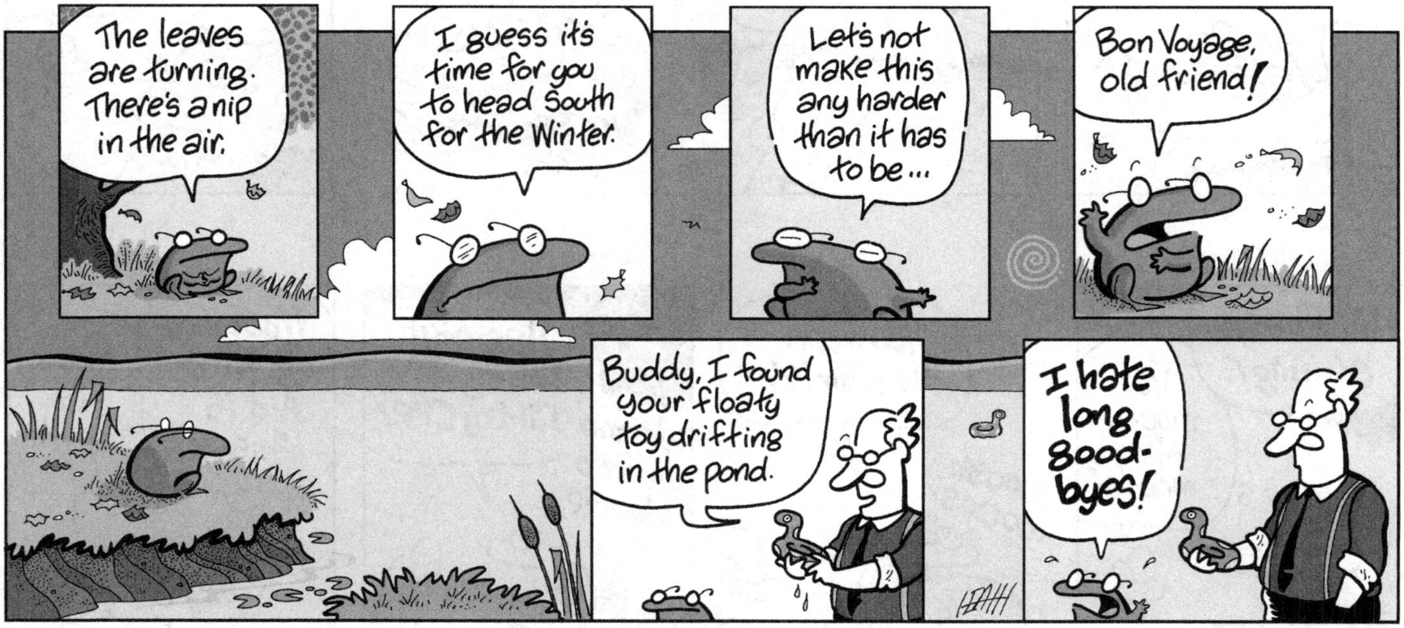
The leaves are turning. There's a nip in the air.
I guess it's time for you to head South for the Winter.
Let's not make this any harder than it has to be...
Bon Voyage, old friend!
Buddy, I found your floaty toy drifting in the pond.
I hate long good-byes!
HEATH

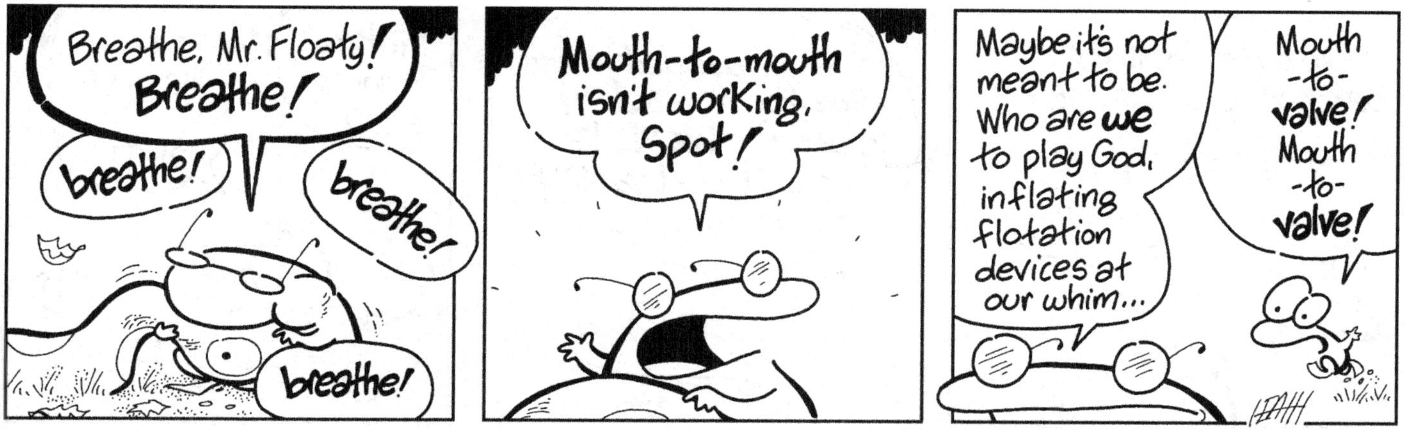
Breathe, Mr. Floaty! Breathe!
breathe!
breathe!
breathe!
Mouth-to-mouth isn't working, Spot!
Maybe it's not meant to be. Who are we to play God, inflating flotation devices at our whim...
Mouth -to- valve! Mouth -to- valve!

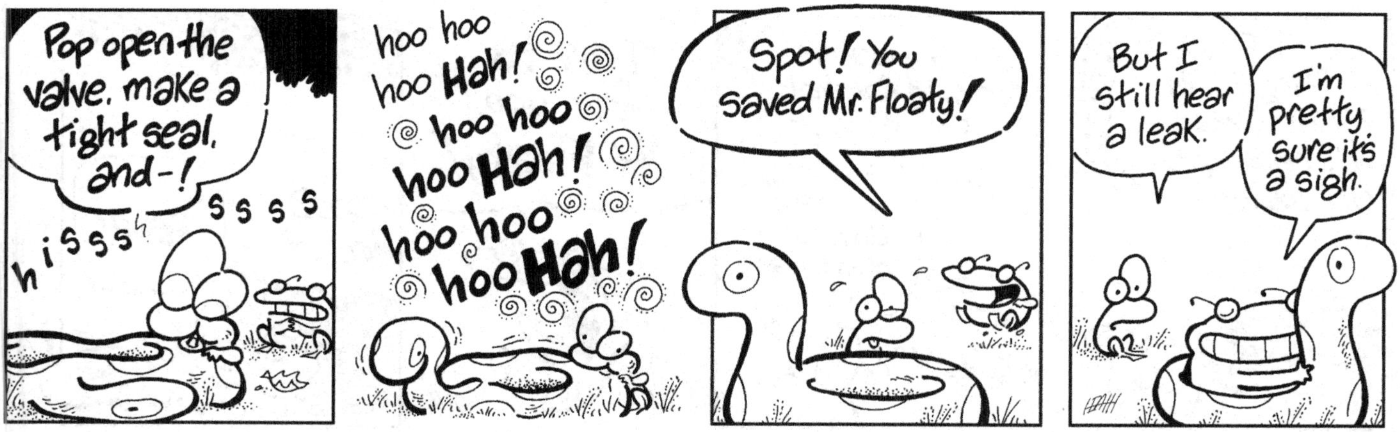
Pop open the valve, make a tight seal, and-!
hissss ssss
hoo hoo hoo Hah! hoo hoo hoo Hah! hoo hoo hoo Hah!
Spot! You saved Mr. Floaty!
But I still hear a leak.
I'm pretty sure it's a sigh.

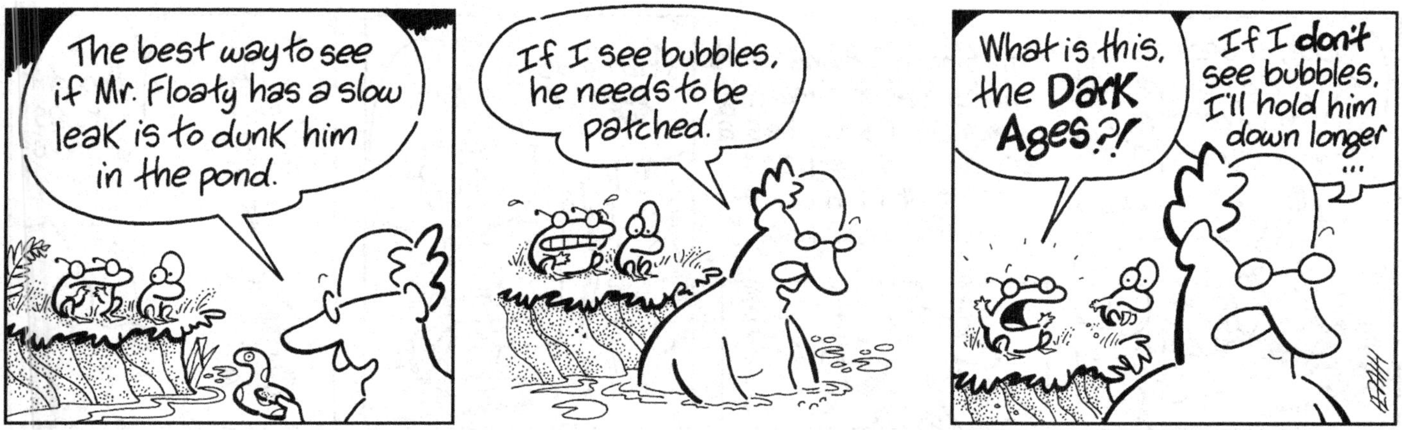
The best way to see if Mr. Floaty has a slow leak is to dunk him in the pond.
If I see bubbles, he needs to be patched.
What is this, the Dark Ages?!
If I don't see bubbles, I'll hold him down longer ...

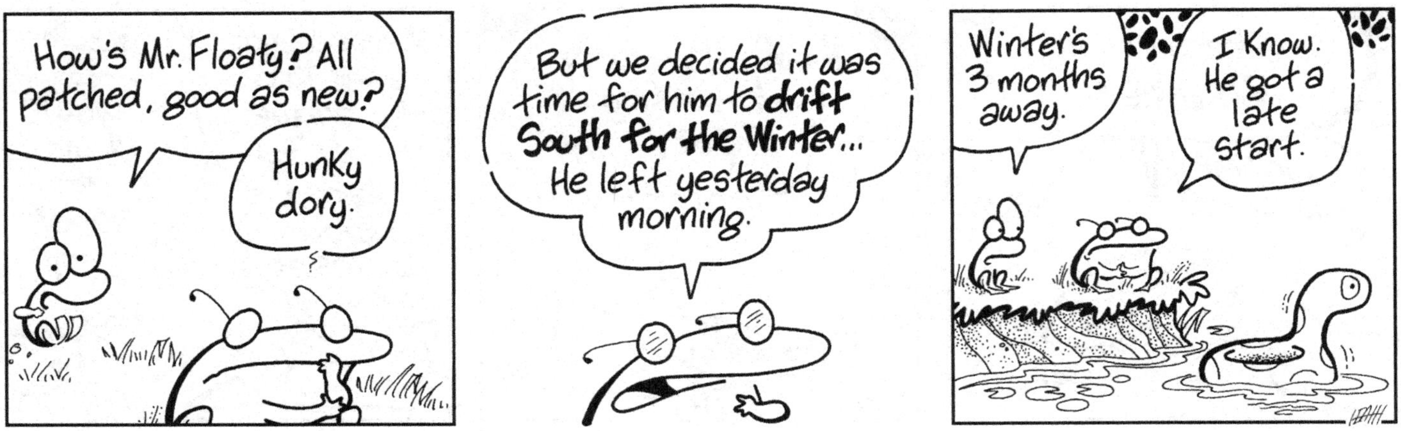
How's Mr. Floaty? All patched, good as new?
Hunky dory.
But we decided it was time for him to **drift South for the Winter**... He left yesterday morning.
Winter's 3 months away.
I Know. He got a late start.

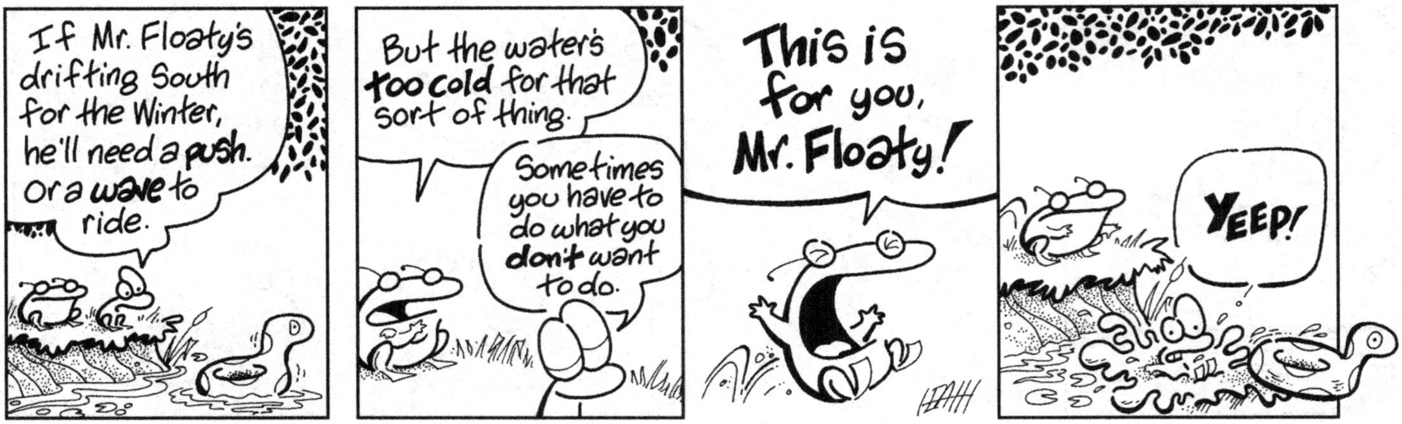
If Mr. Floaty's drifting South for the Winter, he'll need a **push**. Or a **wave** to ride.
But the water's **too cold** for that sort of thing.
Sometimes you have to do what you **don't** want to do.
This is for you, Mr. Floaty!
YEEP!

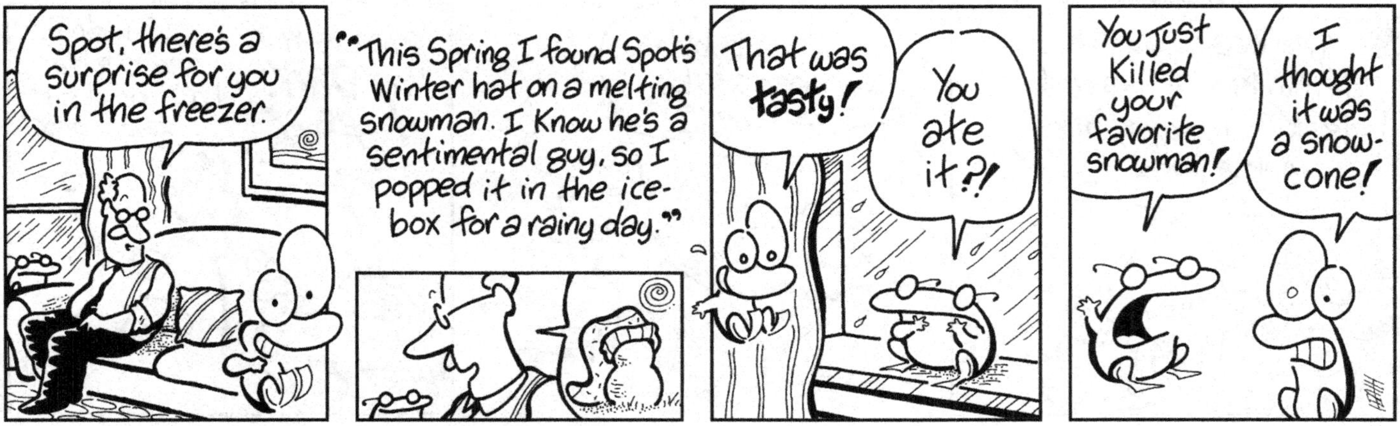
Spot, there's a surprise for you in the freezer.
"This Spring I found Spot's Winter hat on a melting snowman. I Know he's a sentimental guy, so I popped it in the ice-box for a rainy day."
That was **tasty**!
You ate it?!
You just Killed your favorite snowman!
I thought it was a snow-cone!

SPI The Frog by HEATH

When I was a kid, we used the hose to make water balloons. No one stayed dry.

I could get some balloons. How's that sound?

Besides redundant.

Throw me at Buddy!

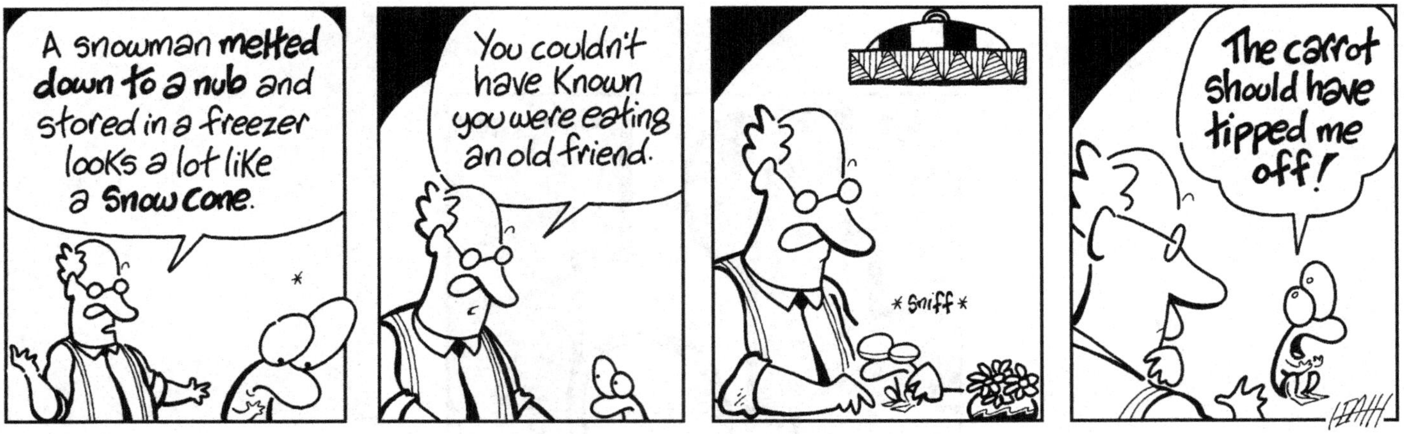
A snowman **melted down to a nub** and stored in a freezer looks a lot like a **snow cone**.
You couldn't have known you were eating an old friend.
sniff
The carrot should have tipped me off!

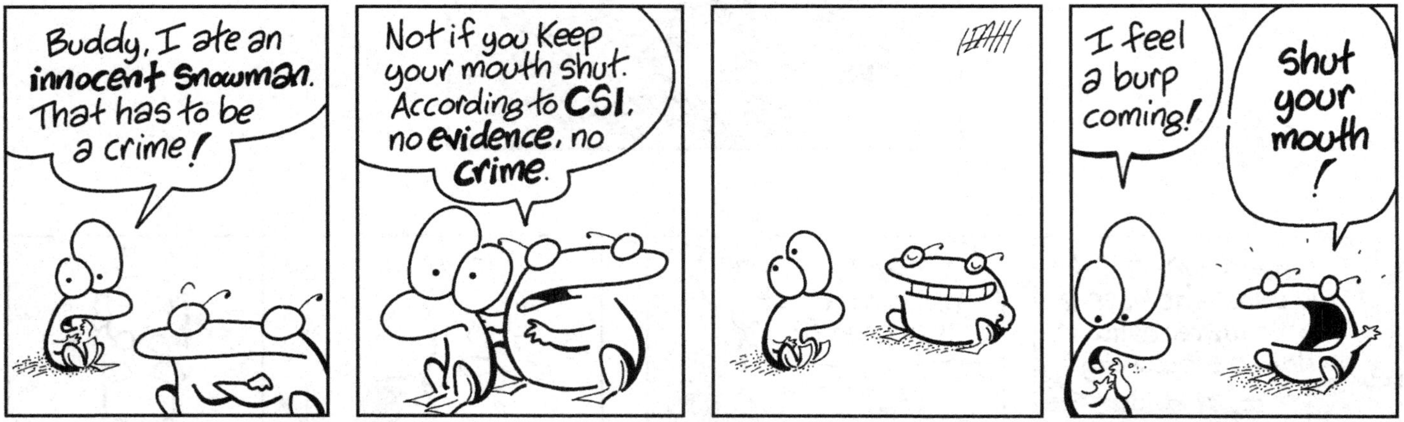
Buddy, I ate an **innocent snowman**. That has to be a crime!
Not if you keep your mouth shut. According to **CSI**, no **evidence**, no **crime**.
I feel a burp coming!
Shut your mouth!

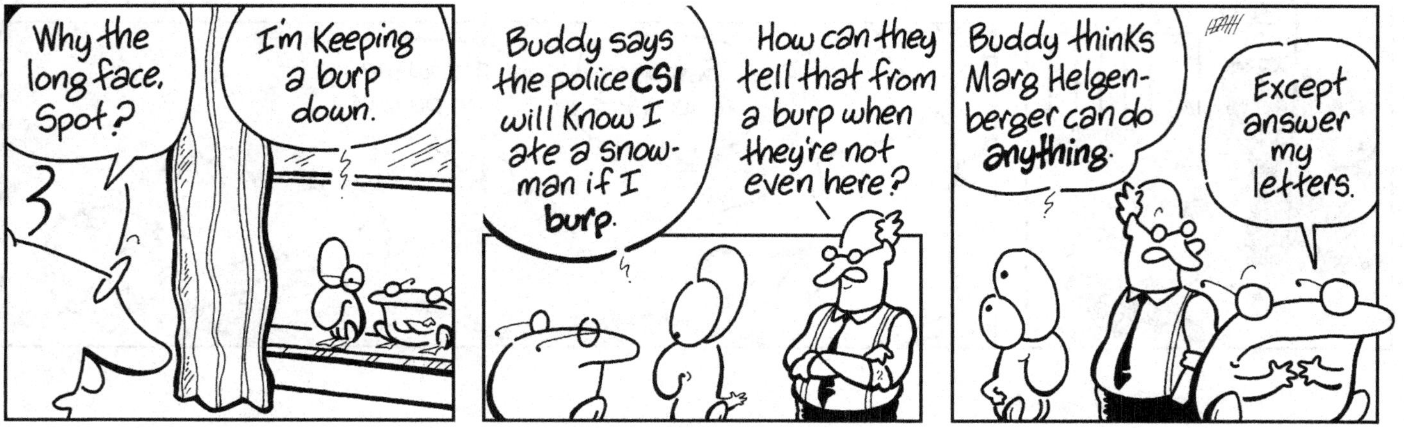
Why the long face, Spot?
I'm keeping a burp down.
Buddy says the police CSI will know I ate a snowman if I **burp**.
How can they tell that from a burp when they're not even here?
Buddy thinks Marg Helgenberger can do **anything**.
Except answer my letters.

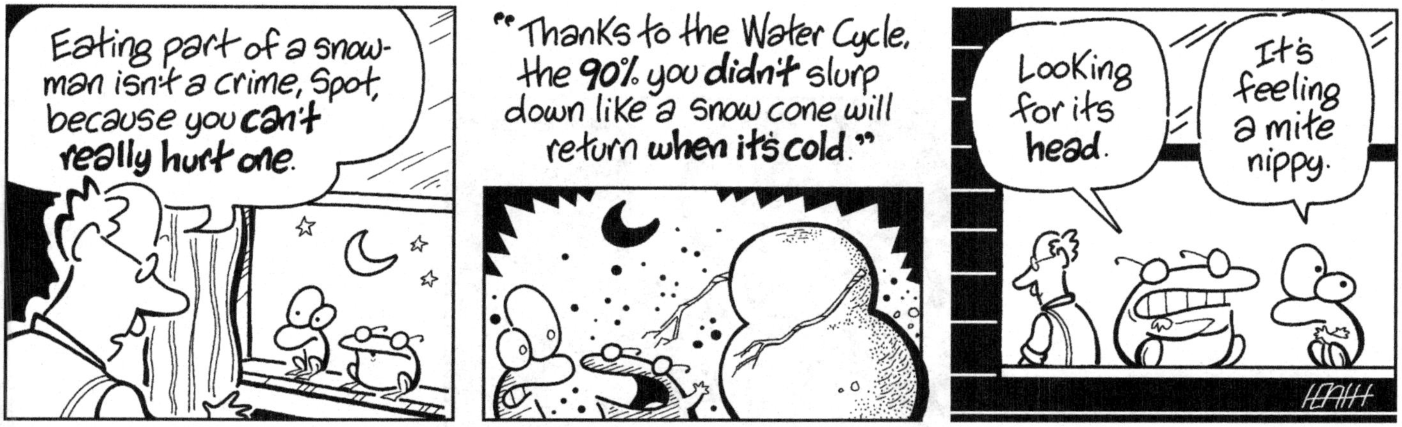
Eating part of a snowman isn't a crime, Spot, because you **can't really hurt one**.
"Thanks to the Water Cycle, the **90%** you **didn't** slurp down like a snow cone will return **when it's cold**."
Looking for its **head**.
It's feeling a mite nippy.

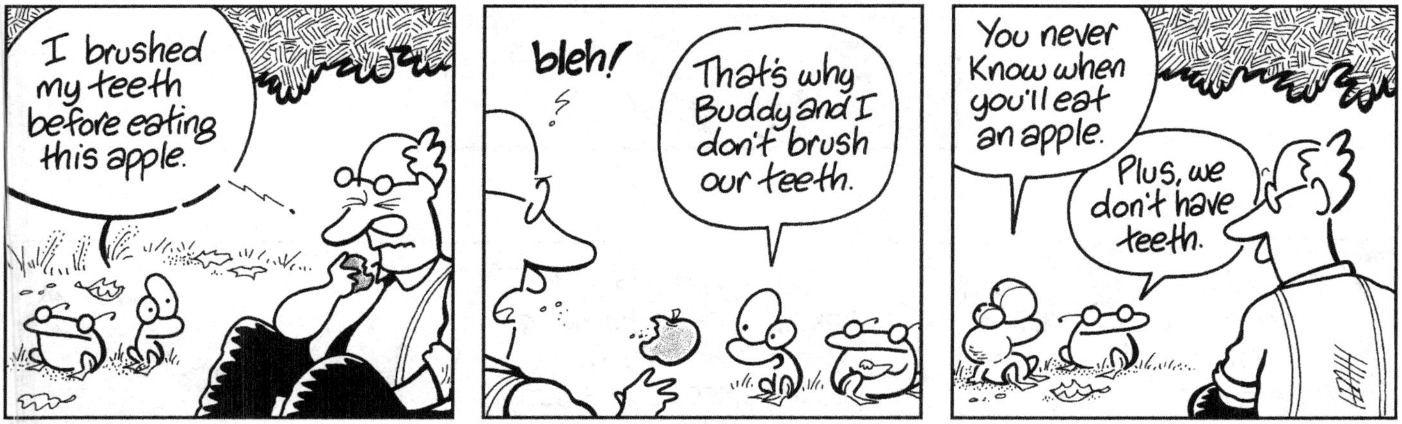
I brushed my teeth before eating this apple.
bleh!
That's why Buddy and I don't brush our teeth.
You never know when you'll eat an apple.
Plus, we don't have teeth.

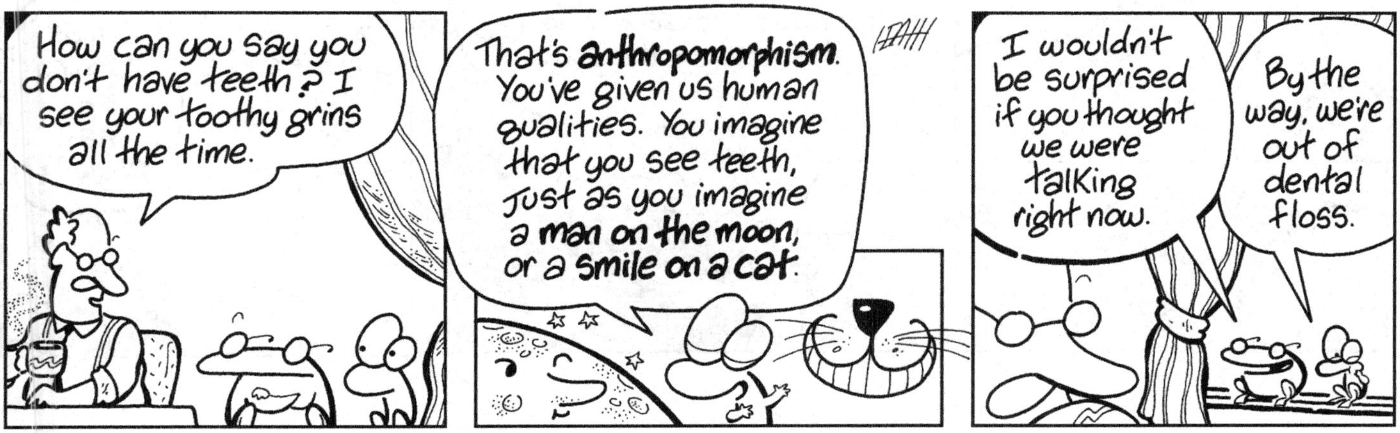
How can you say you don't have teeth? I see your toothy grins all the time.
That's **anthropomorphism**. You've given us human qualities. You imagine that you see teeth, just as you imagine a **man on the moon**, or a **smile on a cat**.
I wouldn't be surprised if you thought we were talking right now.
By the way, we're out of dental floss.

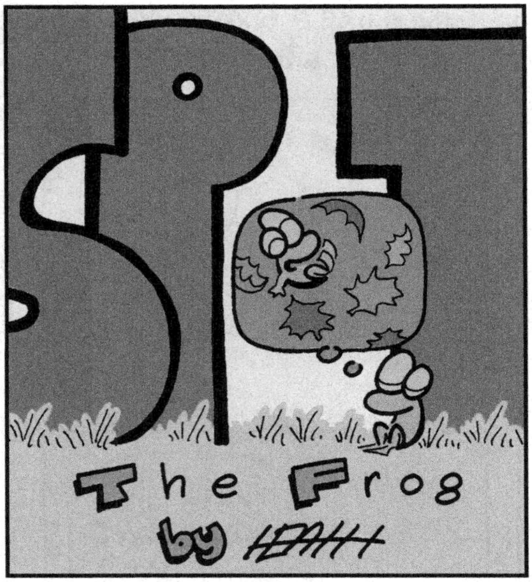
The Frog
by

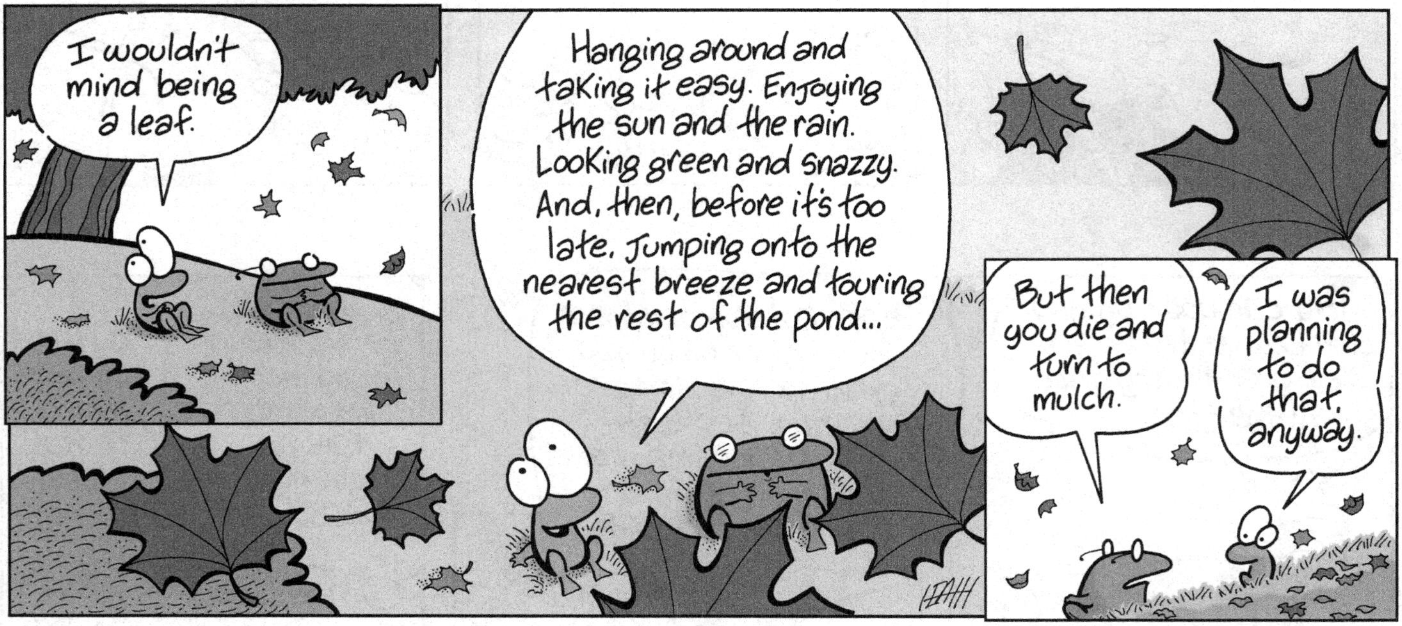
I wouldn't mind being a leaf.
Hanging around and taking it easy. Enjoying the sun and the rain. Looking green and snazzy. And, then, before it's too late, jumping onto the nearest breeze and touring the rest of the pond...
But then you die and turn to mulch.
I was planning to do that, anyway.

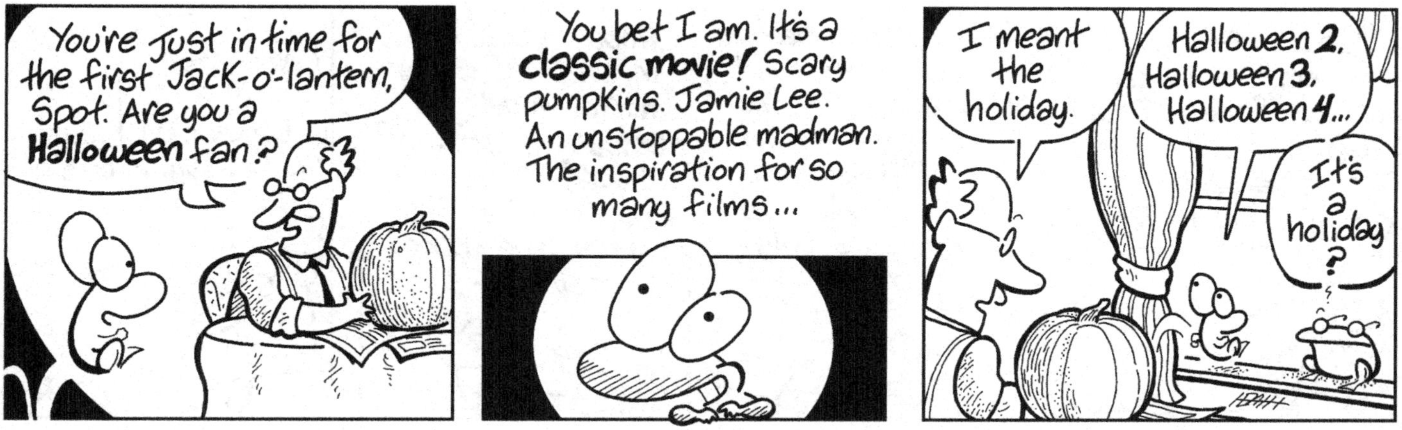
You're just in time for the first Jack-o'-lantern, Spot. Are you a **Halloween** fan?
You bet I am. It's a **classic movie!** Scary pumpkins. Jamie Lee. An unstoppable madman. The inspiration for so many films...
I meant the holiday.
Halloween **2**, Halloween **3**, Halloween **4**...
It's a holiday?

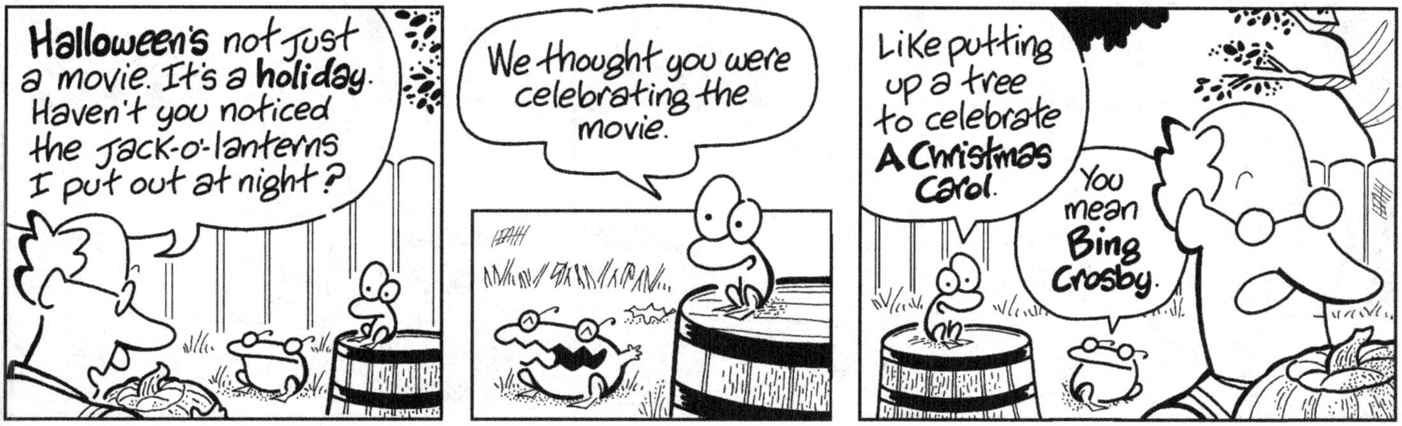
Halloween's not just a movie. It's a **holiday**. Haven't you noticed the jack-o'-lanterns I put out at night?
We thought you were celebrating the movie.
Like putting up a tree to celebrate **A Christmas Carol**.
You mean **Bing Crosby**.

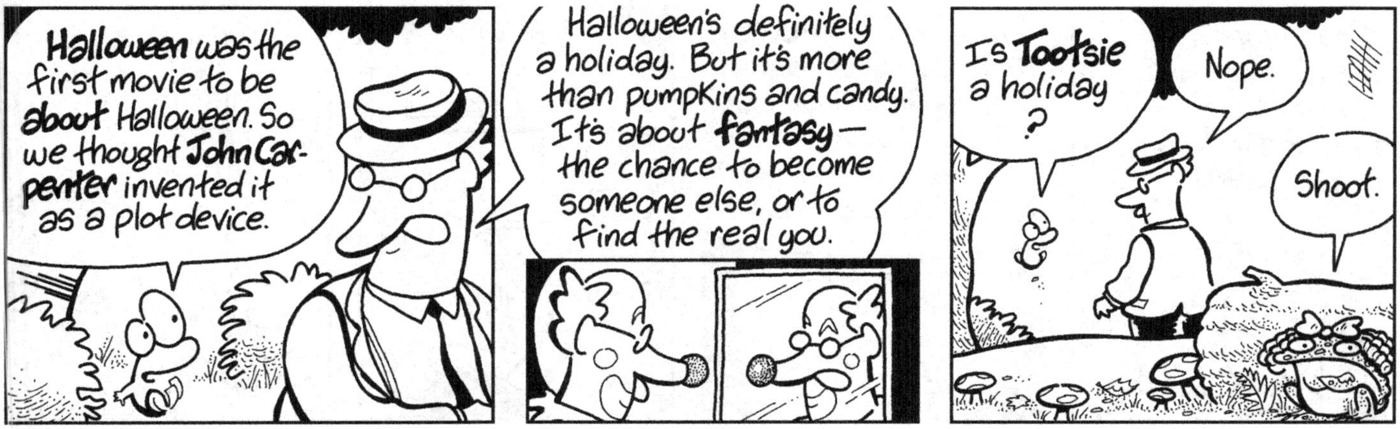
Halloween was the first movie to be **about** Halloween. So we thought **John Carpenter** invented it as a plot device.
Halloween's definitely a holiday. But it's more than pumpkins and candy. It's about **fantasy** — the chance to become someone else, or to find the real you.
Is **Tootsie** a holiday?
Nope.
Shoot.

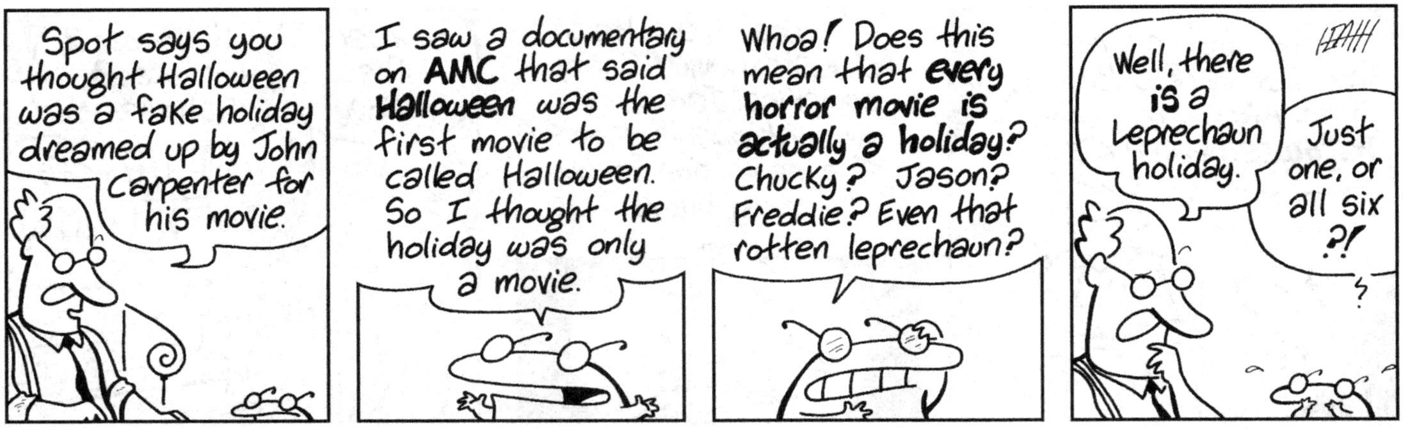
Spot says you thought Halloween was a fake holiday dreamed up by John Carpenter for his movie.
I saw a documentary on **AMC** that said **Halloween** was the first movie to be called Halloween. So I thought the holiday was only a movie.
Whoa! Does this mean that **every horror movie is actually a holiday?** Chucky? Jason? Freddie? Even that rotten leprechaun?
Well, there **is** a Leprechaun holiday.
Just one, or all six ?!

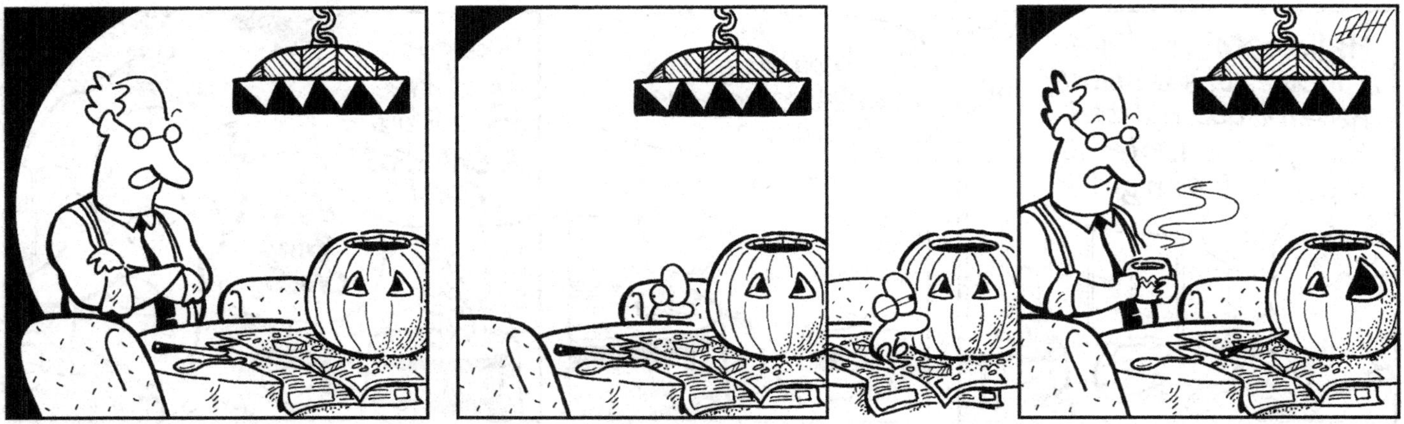

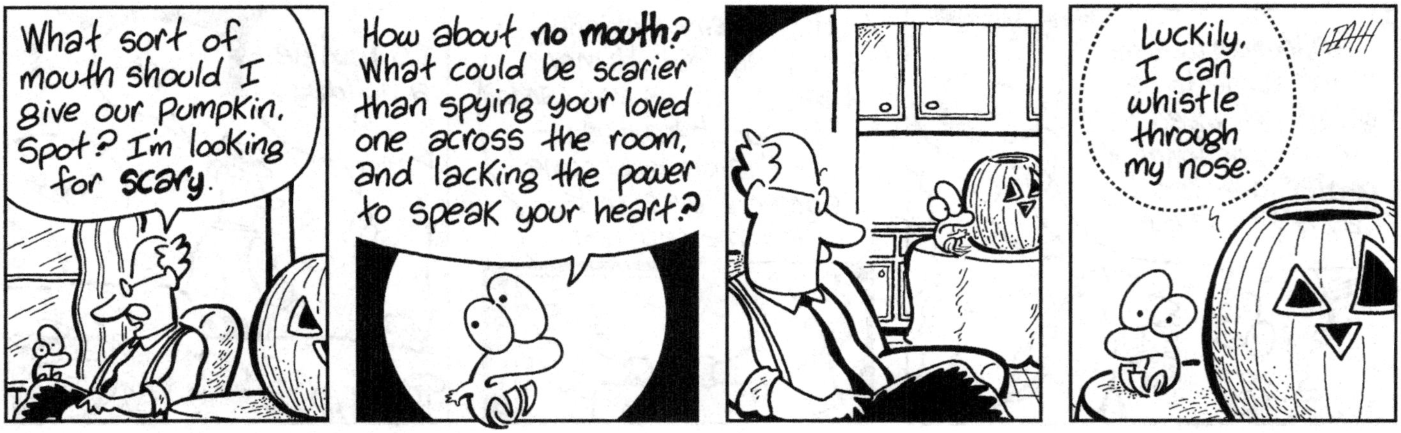
What sort of mouth should I give our pumpkin, Spot? I'm looking for **scary**.
How about **no mouth?** What could be scarier than spying your loved one across the room, and lacking the power to speak your heart?
Luckily, I can whistle through my nose.

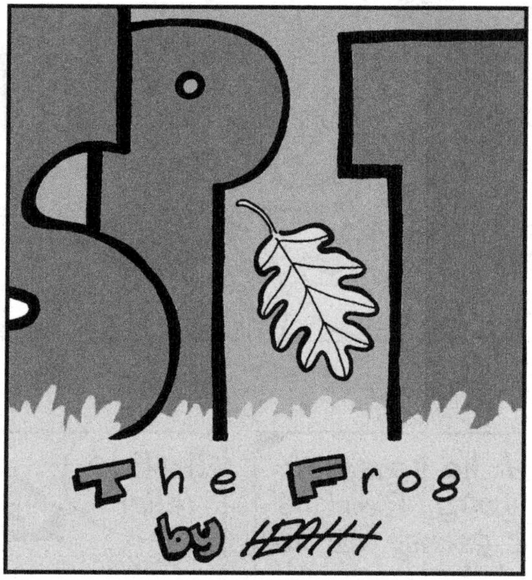
The Frog
by HEATH

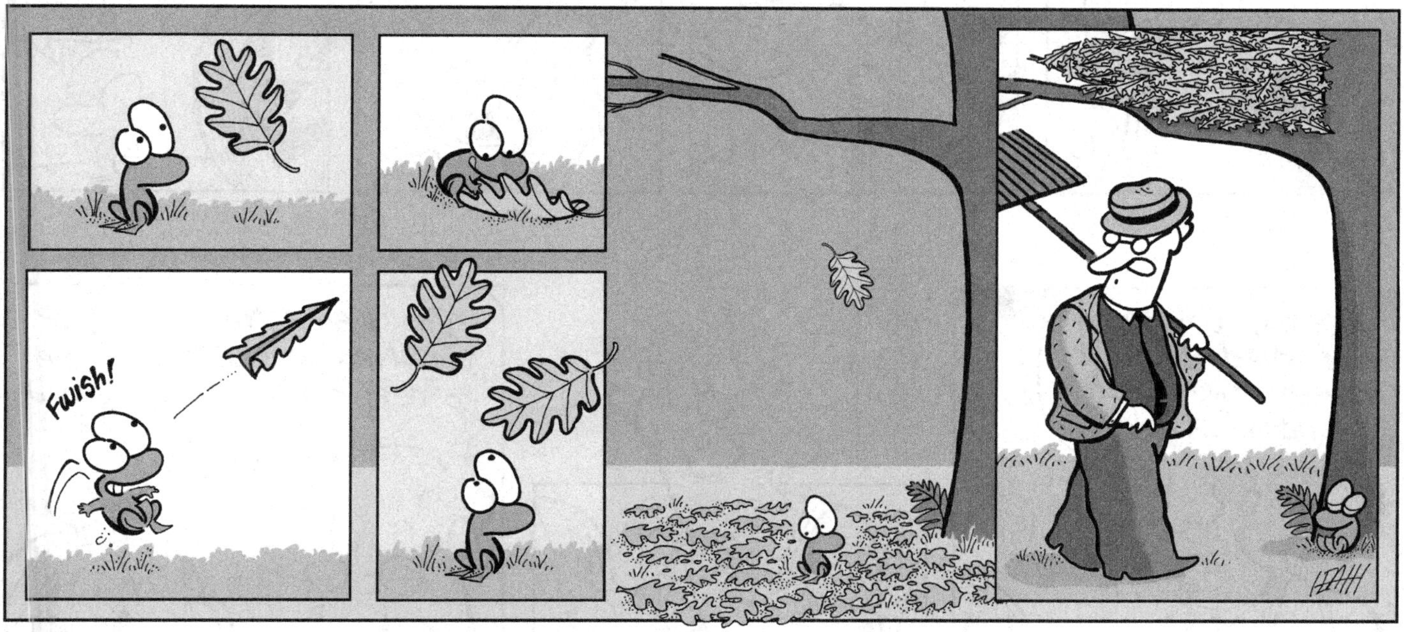
FWISH!

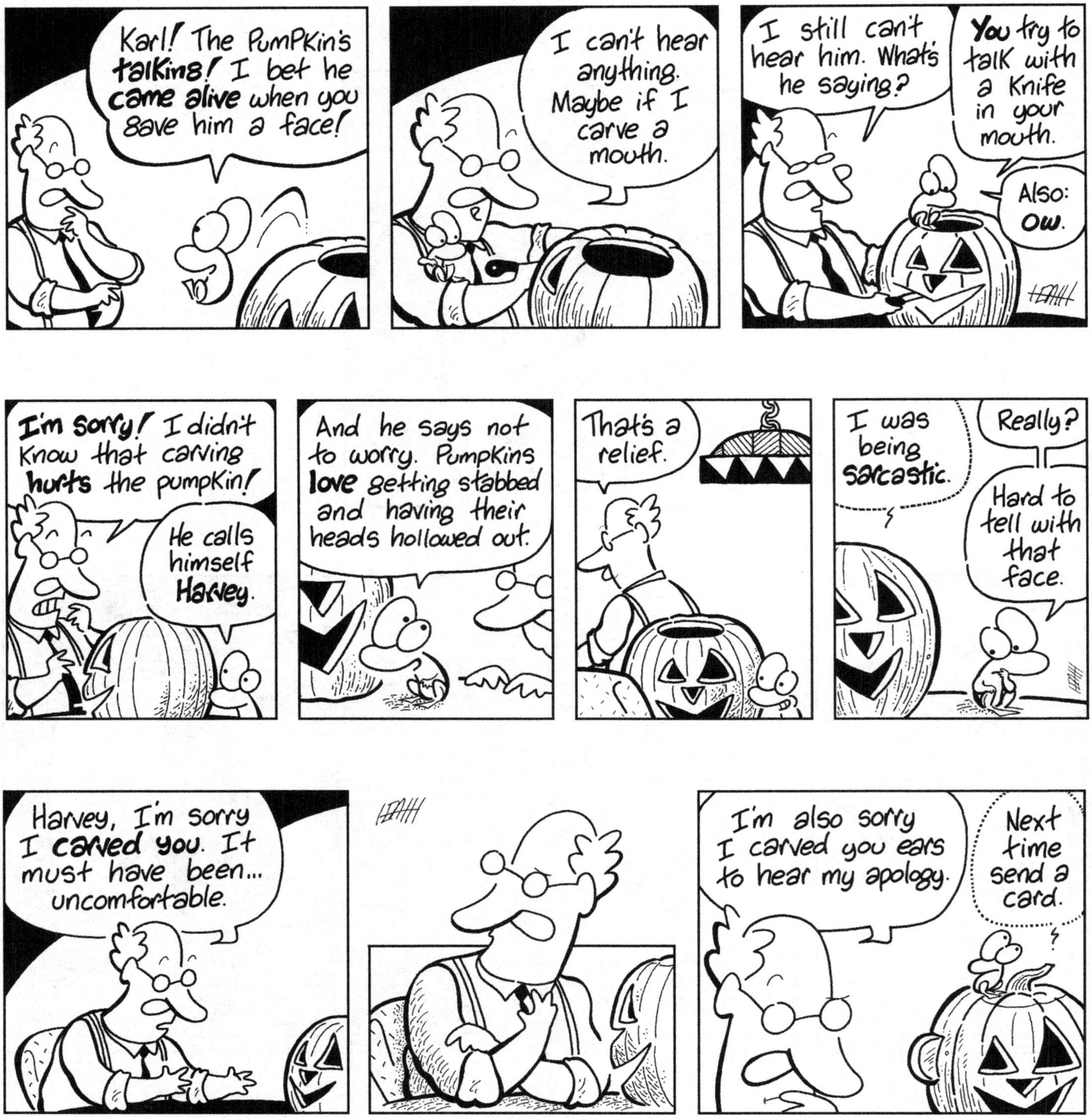
Karl! The Pumpkin's talking! I bet he came alive when you gave him a face!
I can't hear anything. Maybe if I carve a mouth.
I still can't hear him. What's he saying?
You try to talk with a Knife in your mouth.
Also: OW.
I'm sorry! I didn't know that carving hurts the pumpkin!
He calls himself Harvey.
And he says not to worry. Pumpkins love getting stabbed and having their heads hollowed out.
That's a relief.
I was being sarcastic.
Really?
Hard to tell with that face.
Harvey, I'm sorry I carved you. It must have been... uncomfortable.
I'm also sorry I carved you ears to hear my apology.
Next time send a card.

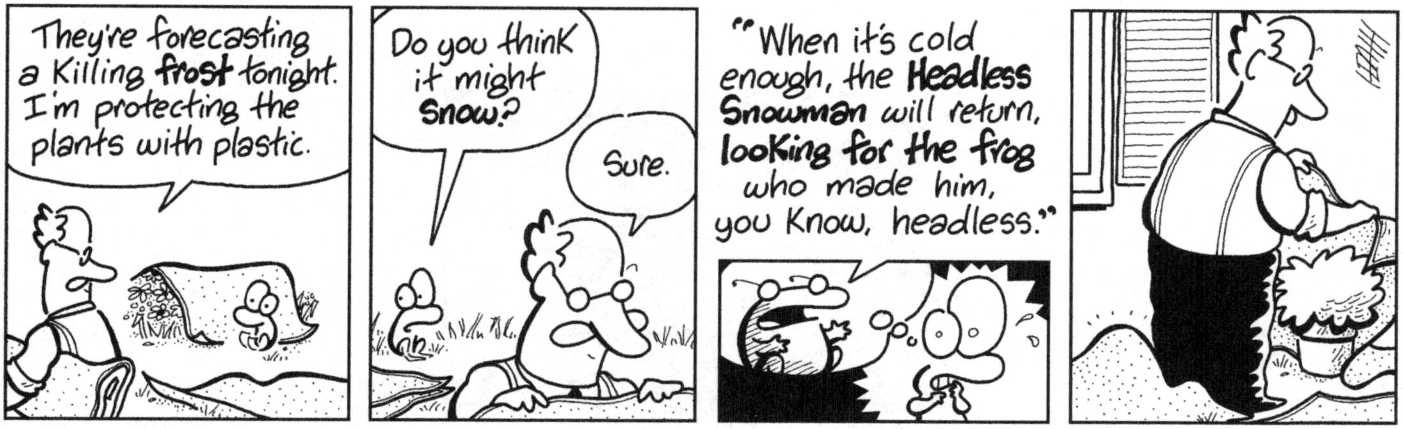
They're forecasting a Killing **frost** tonight. I'm protecting the plants with plastic.
Do you think it might **snow?**
Sure.
"When it's cold enough, the **Headless Snowman** will return, **looking for the frog** who made him, you Know, headless."

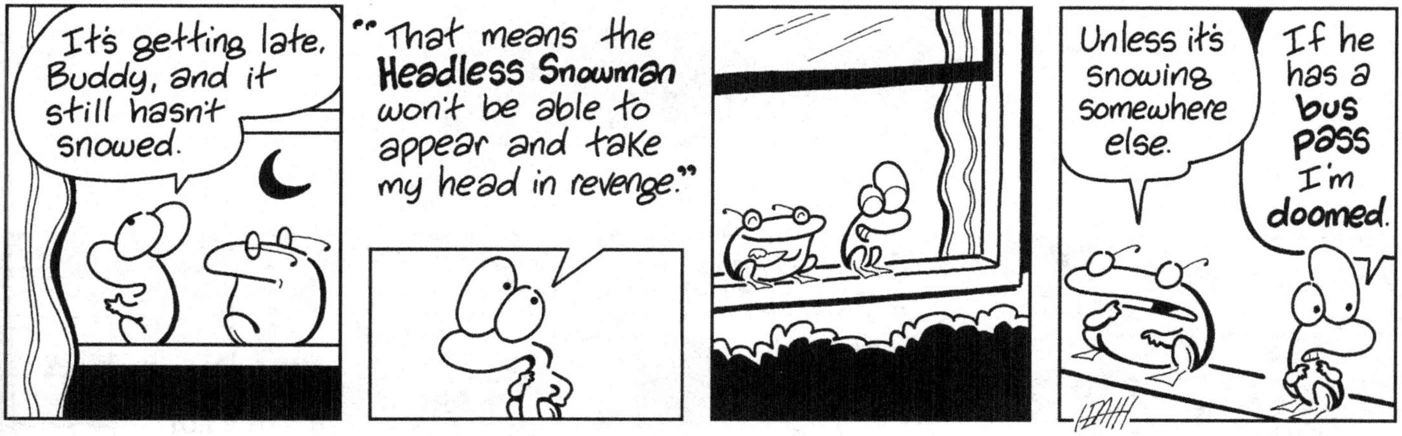
It's getting late, Buddy, and it still hasn't snowed.
"That means the **Headless Snowman** won't be able to appear and take my head in revenge."
Unless it's snowing somewhere else.
If he has a **bus pass** I'm **doomed**.

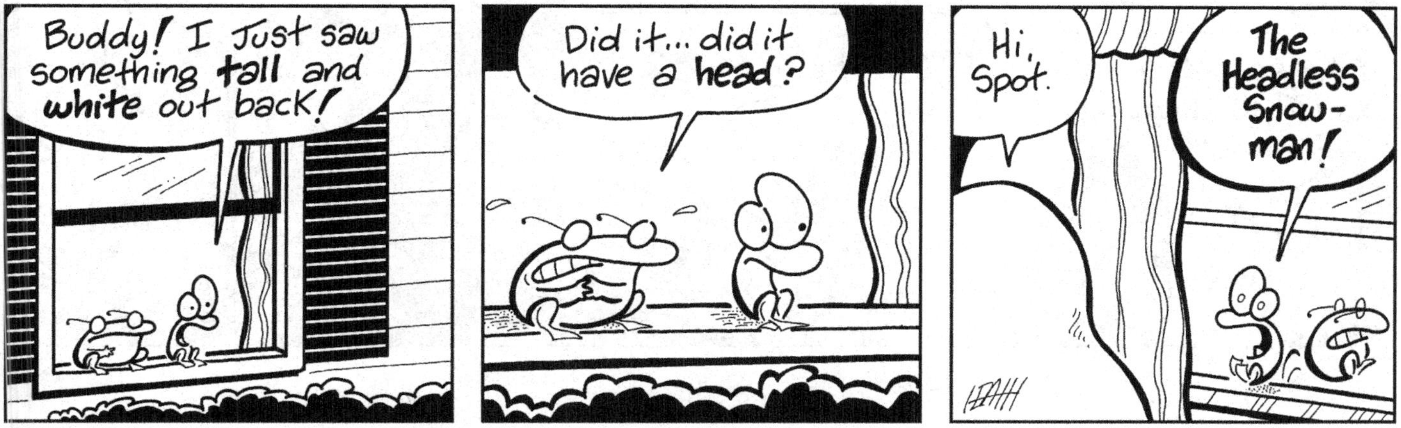
Buddy! I Just saw something **tall** and **white** out back!
Did it... did it have a **head**?
Hi, Spot.
The Headless Snow-man!

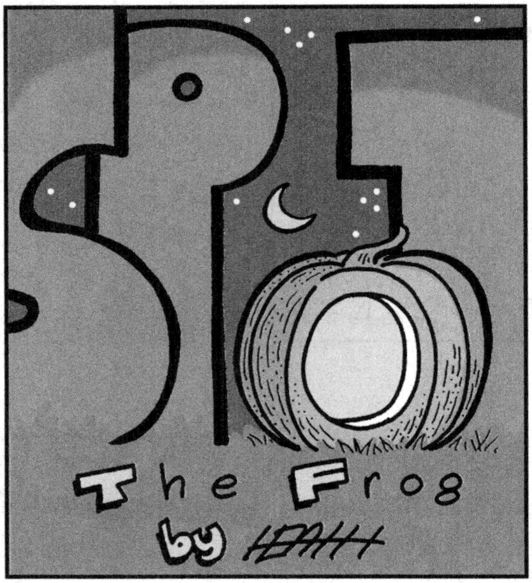
The Frog
by

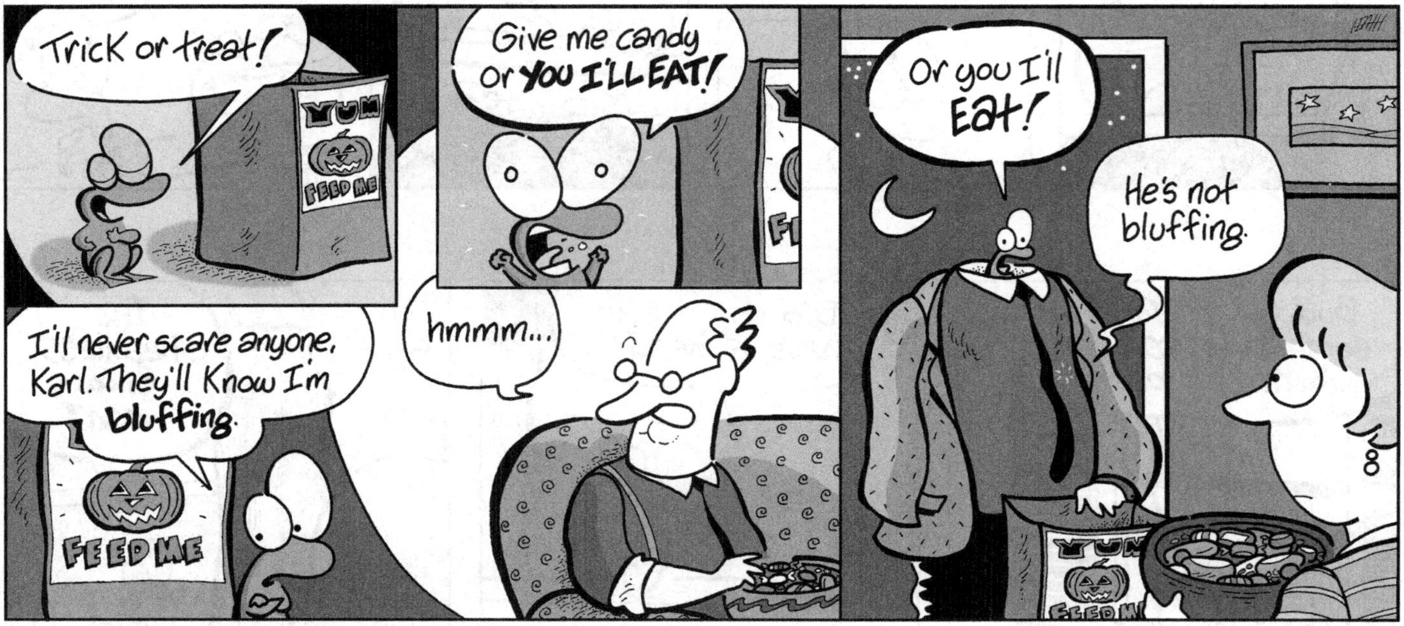
Trick or treat!
YUM
FEED ME
Give me candy or YOU I'LL EAT!
I'll never scare anyone, Karl. They'll Know I'm bluffing.
FEED ME
hmmm...
Or you I'll Eat!
He's not bluffing.
YUM

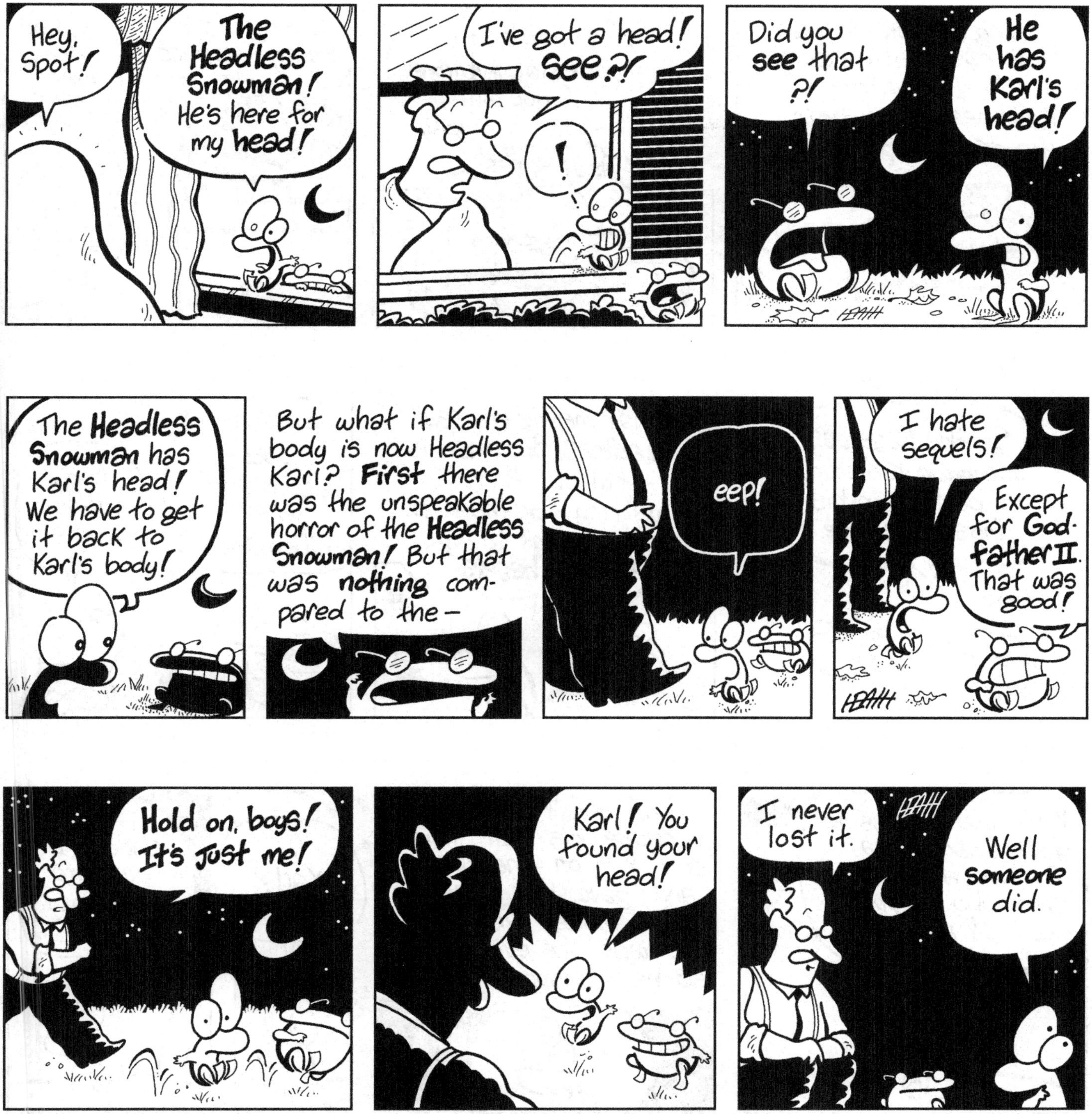
Hey, Spot!
The Headless Snowman! He's here for my head!
I've got a head! see?!
!
Did you see that?!
He has Karl's head!
The Headless Snowman has Karl's head! We have to get it back to Karl's body!
But what if Karl's body is now Headless Karl? First there was the unspeakable horror of the Headless Snowman! But that was nothing compared to the–
eep!
I hate sequels!
Except for Godfather II. That was good!
Hold on, boys! It's just me!
Karl! You found your head!
I never lost it.
Well someone did.

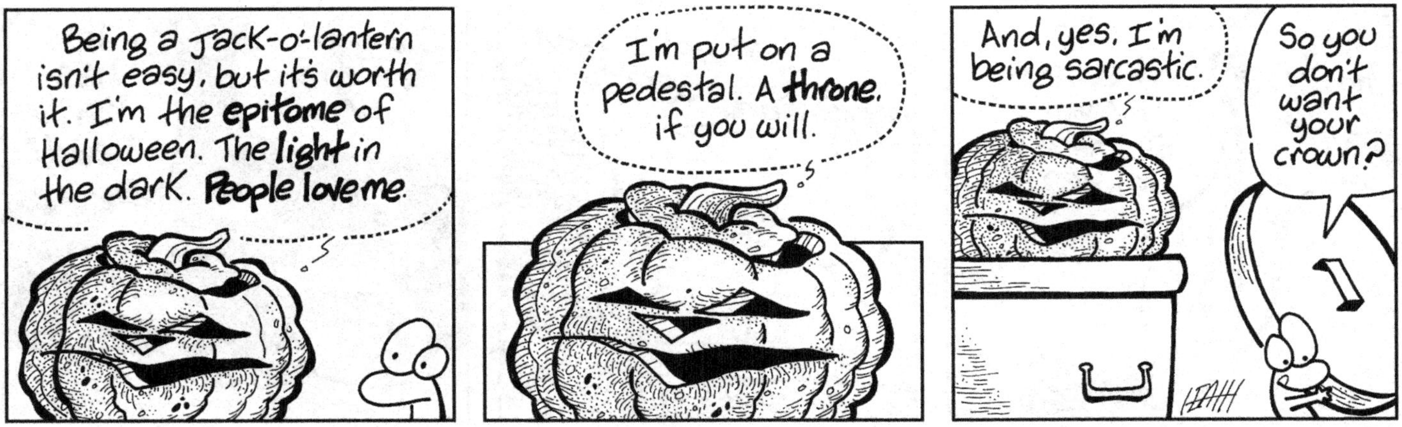
Being a Jack-o-lantern isn't easy, but it's worth it. I'm the epitome of Halloween. The light in the dark. People love me.
I'm put on a pedestal. A throne, if you will.
And, yes, I'm being sarcastic.
So you don't want your crown?

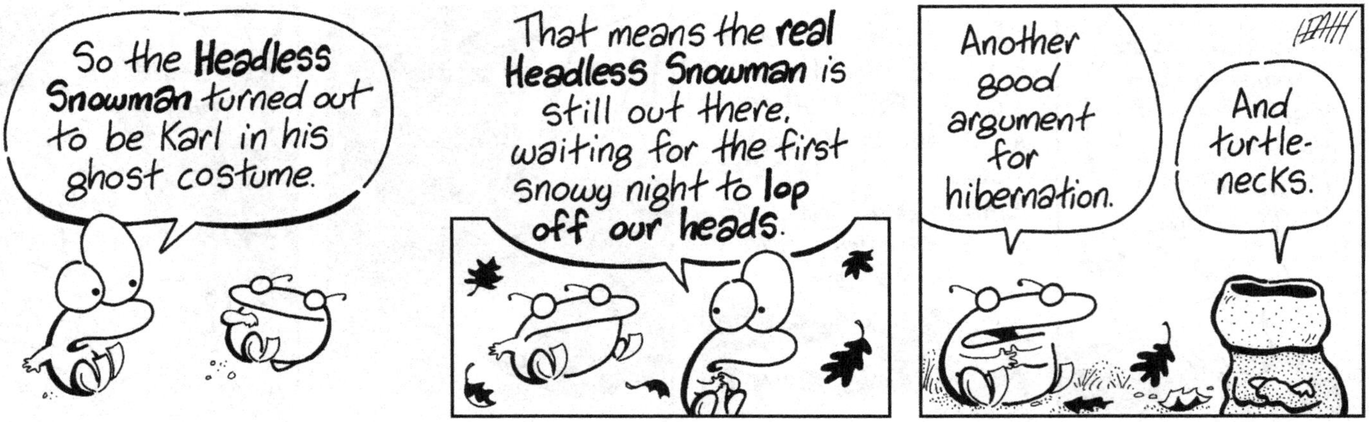
So the Headless Snowman turned out to be Karl in his ghost costume.
That means the real Headless Snowman is still out there, waiting for the first snowy night to lop off our heads.
Another good argument for hibernation.
And turtle-necks.

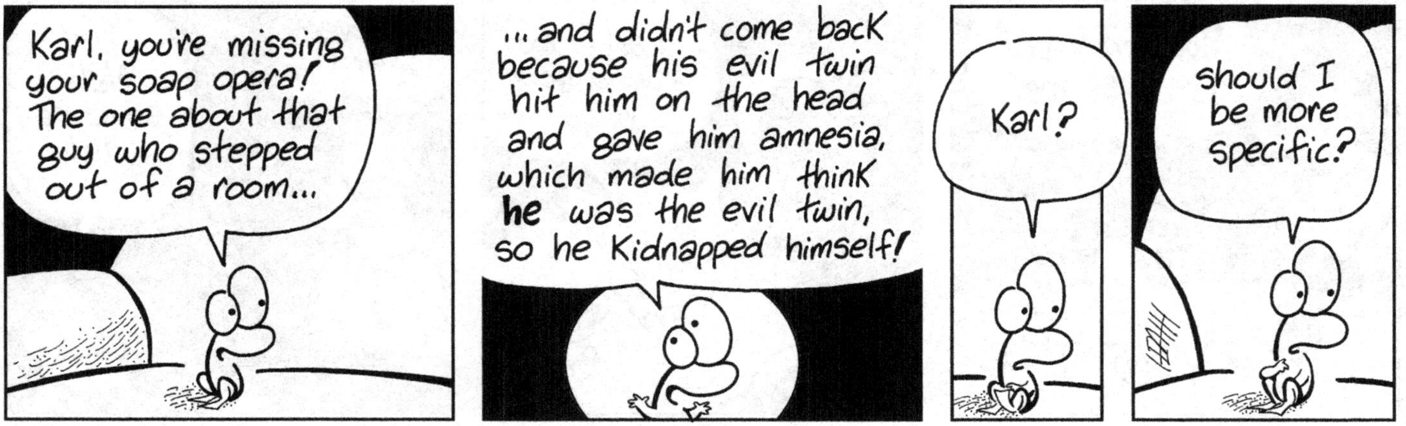
Karl, you're missing your soap opera! The one about that guy who stepped out of a room...
...and didn't come back because his evil twin hit him on the head and gave him amnesia, which made him think he was the evil twin, so he kidnapped himself!
Karl?
Should I be more specific?

SPLT

The Frog

by HEATH

Either you're right, Buddy, and your hat flew to Winnipeg for the summer and it's flying back here for the winter...

Or **I'm** right, and the wind blew your hat away, and it's not likely to blow it back. We can't **both** be right.

Never doubt a **Frog** of the **Wild**...

It flew back this morning!

I stand corrected.

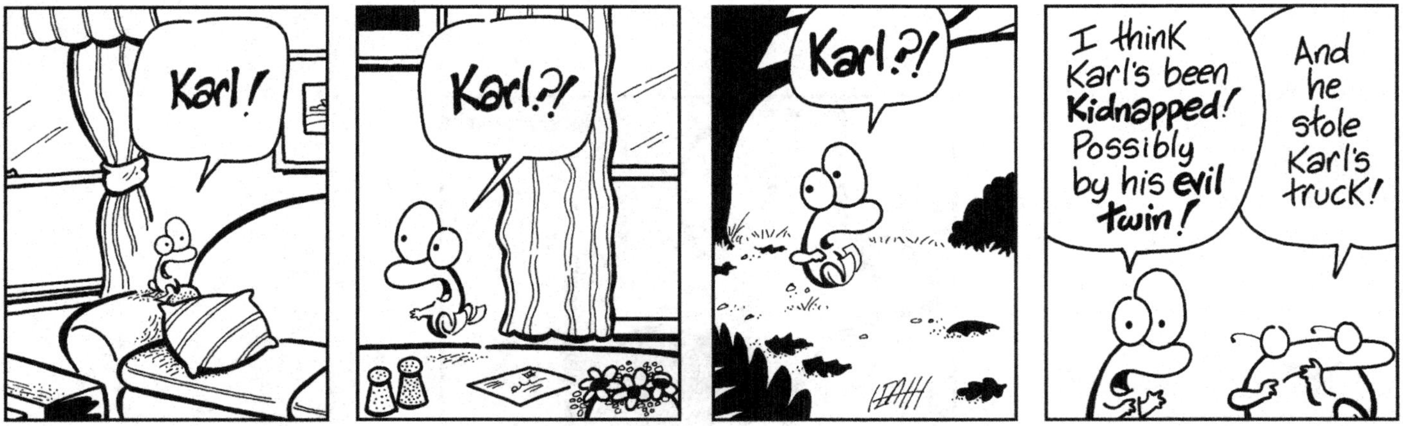
Karl!
Karl?!
Karl?!
I think Karl's been Kidnapped! Possibly by his evil twin!
And he stole Karl's truck!

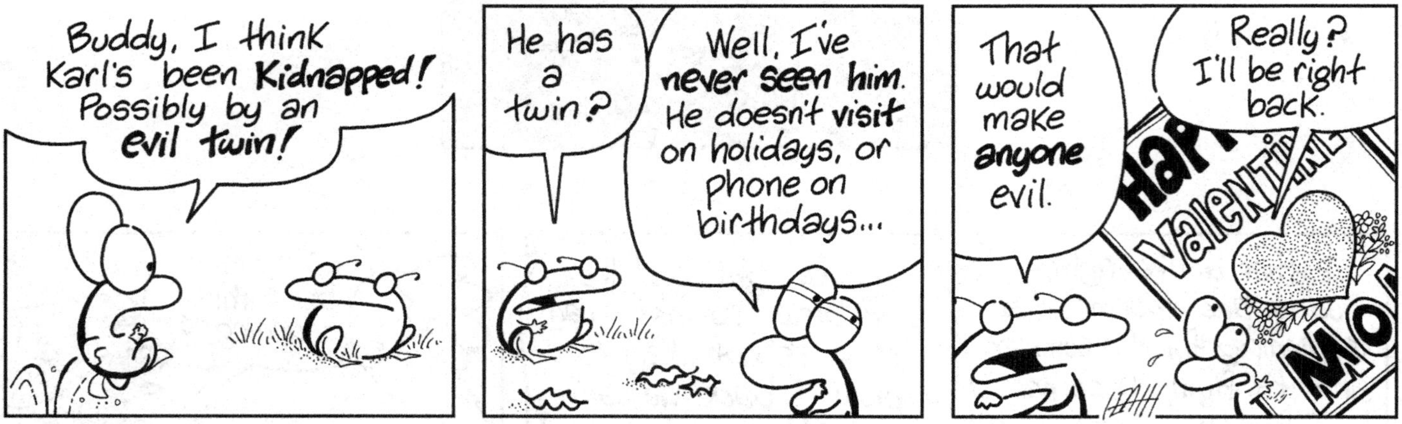
Buddy, I think Karl's been Kidnapped! Possibly by an evil twin!
He has a twin?
Well, I've never seen him. He doesn't visit on holidays, or phone on birthdays...
That would make anyone evil.
Really? I'll be right back.

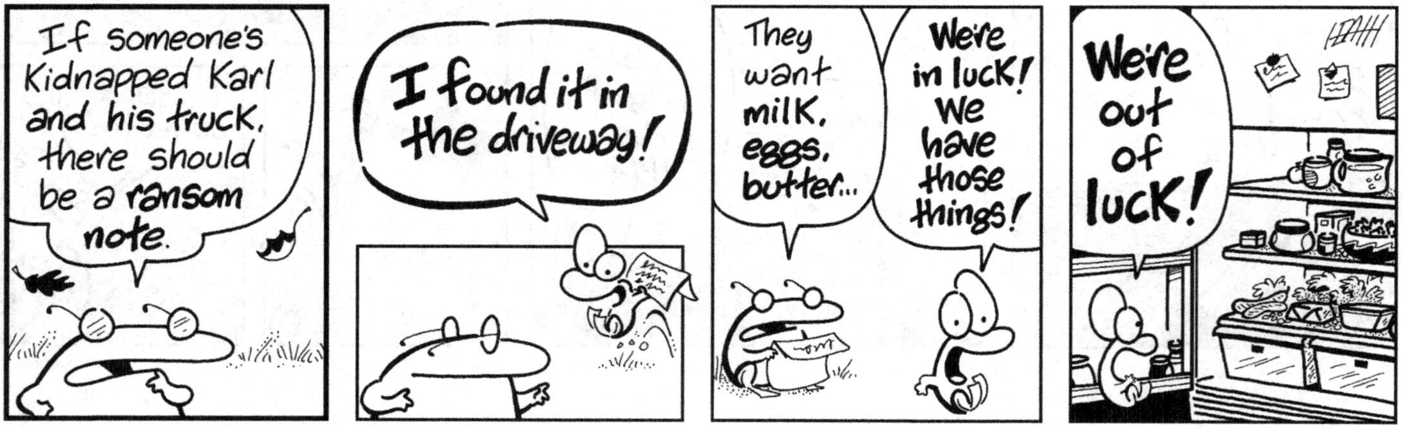
If someone's Kidnapped Karl and his truck, there should be a ransom note.
I found it in the driveway!
They want milk, eggs, butter...
We're in luck! We have those things!
We're out of luck!

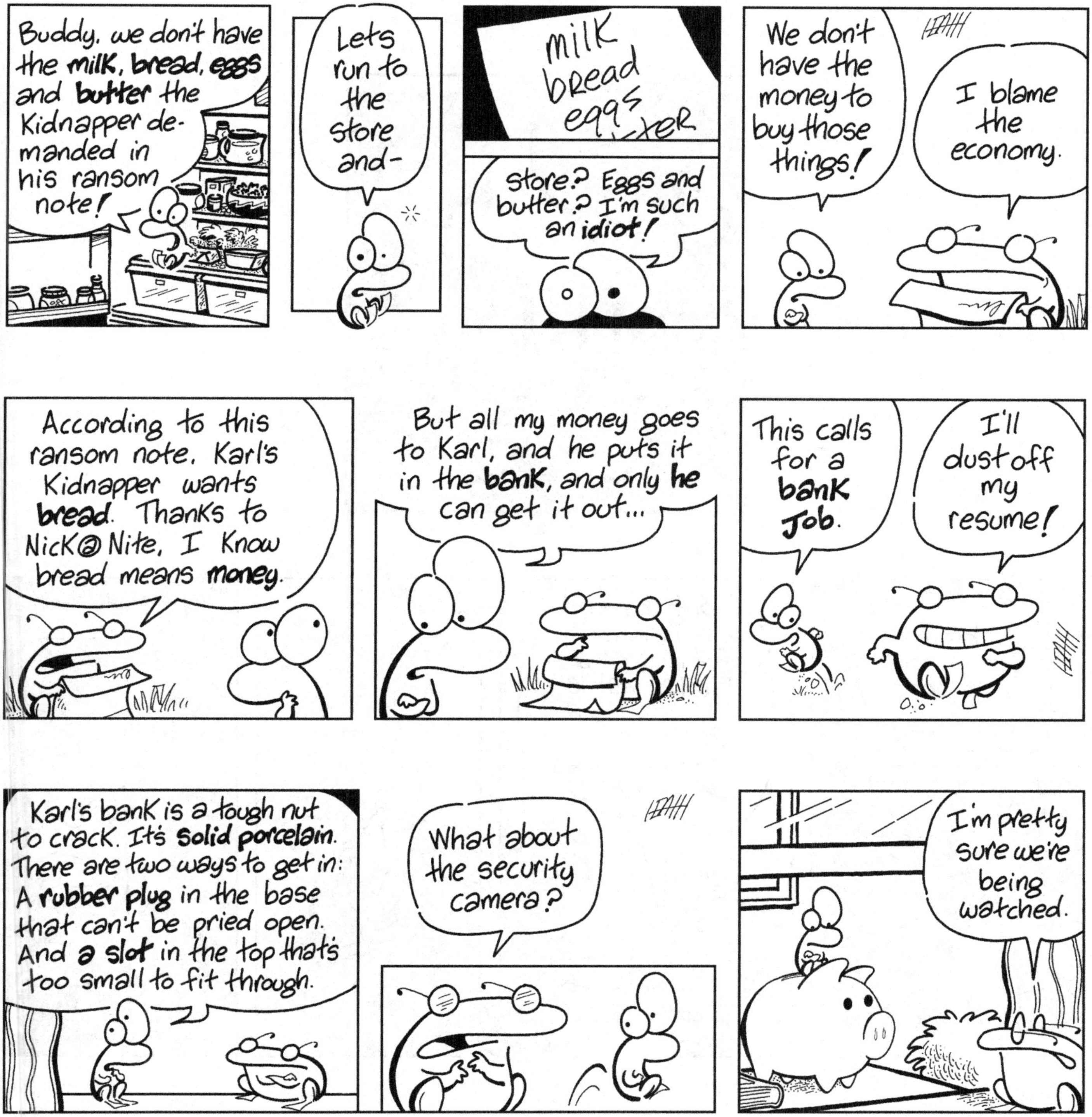

Buddy, we don't have the **milk**, **bread**, **eggs** and **butter** the Kidnapper demanded in his ransom note!
Lets run to the store and-
milk bread eggs
Store? Eggs and butter? I'm such an **idiot**!
We don't have the money to buy those things!
I blame the economy.
According to this ransom note, Karl's Kidnapper wants **bread**. Thanks to NicK@Nite, I Know bread means **money**.
But all my money goes to Karl, and he puts it in the **bank**, and only **he** can get it out...
This calls for a **bank Job**.
I'll dust off my resume!
Karl's bank is a tough nut to crack. It's **solid porcelain**. There are two ways to get in: A **rubber plug** in the base that can't be pried open. And **a slot** in the top that's too small to fit through.
What about the security camera?
I'm pretty sure we're being watched.

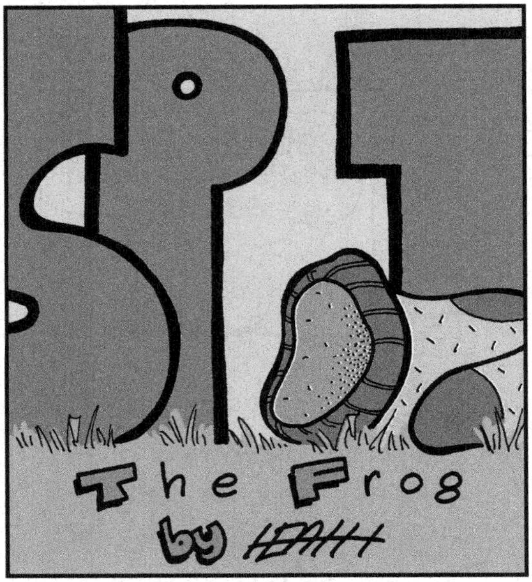
The Frog
by

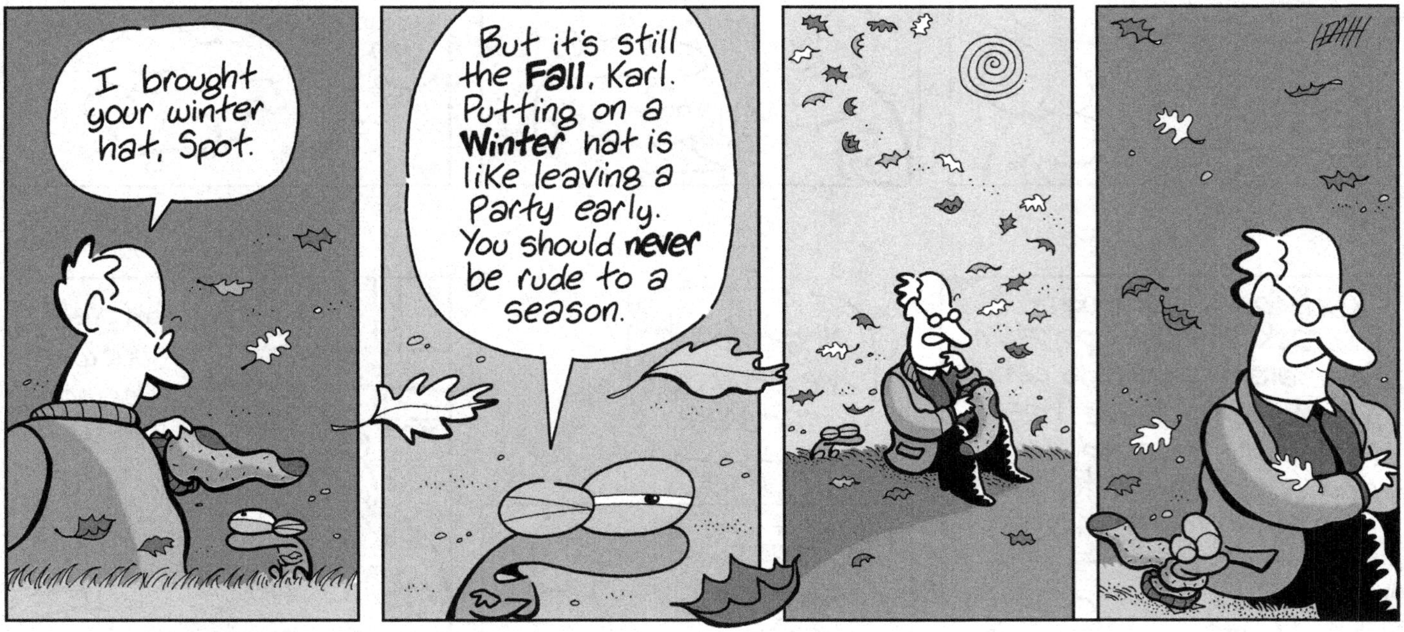
I brought your winter hat, Spot.
But it's still the Fall, Karl. Putting on a Winter hat is like leaving a party early. You should never be rude to a season.

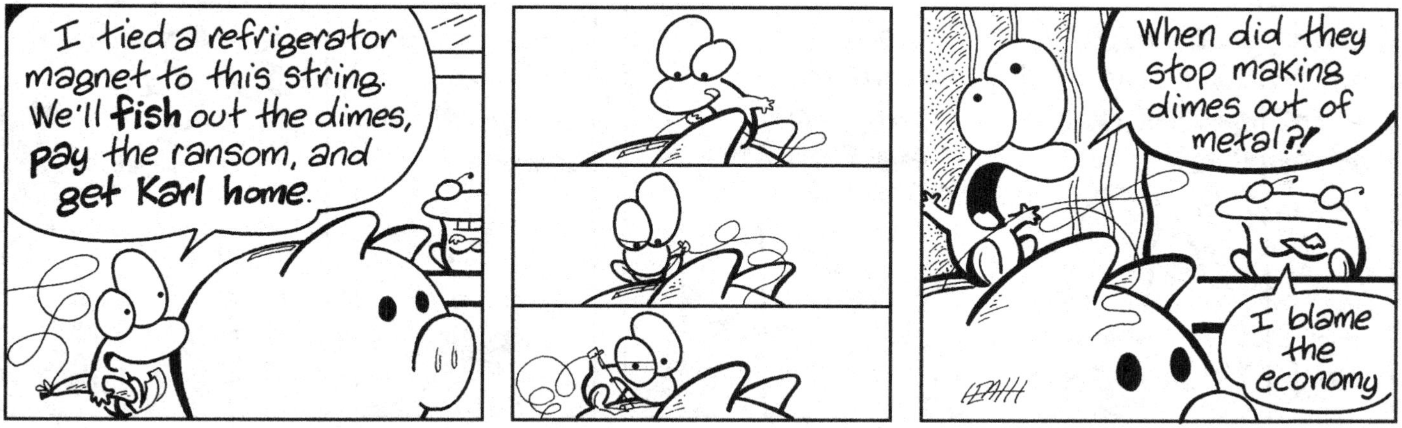

I tied a refrigerator magnet to this string. We'll **fish** out the dimes, **pay** the ransom, and **get Karl home**.
When did they stop making dimes out of metal?!
I blame the economy

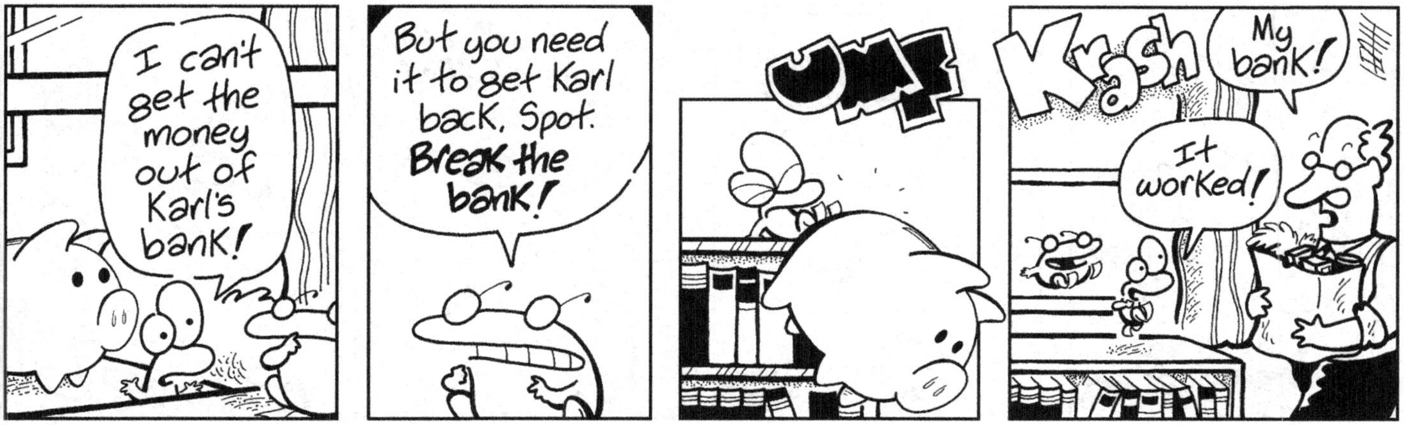

I can't get the money out of Karl's bank!
But you need it to get Karl back, Spot. **Break the bank!**
UMF
Krash
My bank!
It worked!

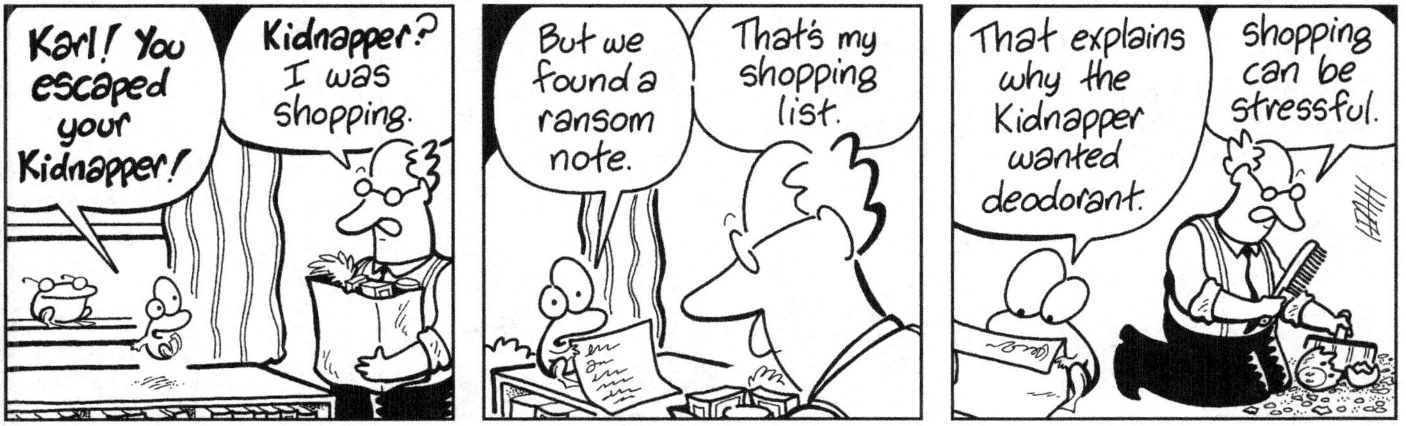

Karl! You escaped your kidnapper!
Kidnapper? I was shopping.
But we found a ransom note.
That's my shopping list.
That explains why the kidnapper wanted deodorant.
Shopping can be stressful.

Grab your weapons! Fortify your homes! A **stampeding herd of rogue cats** is heading this way!

Actually, Lumpy, we're taking a break from wacky adventures this week.

Oh. OK. No problem.

This is why I hate to make plans.

Any plans to go home for Thanksgiving?

My family doesn't celebrate it.

They're too busy **eating** as much as they can before hibernating.

Come Thanksgiving, they're **stuffed**, **sluggish** and **sleepy**.

Thanksgiving's redundant.

We call that seconds.

Refresh my memory. Why don't you guys hibernate in the Winter?

It's the environment, Karl. We're increasing the biodiversity of our species...

By expanding into other niches.

We're doing it for the children.

But mostly, we like the hats.

I'm waiting for mine to fly home.

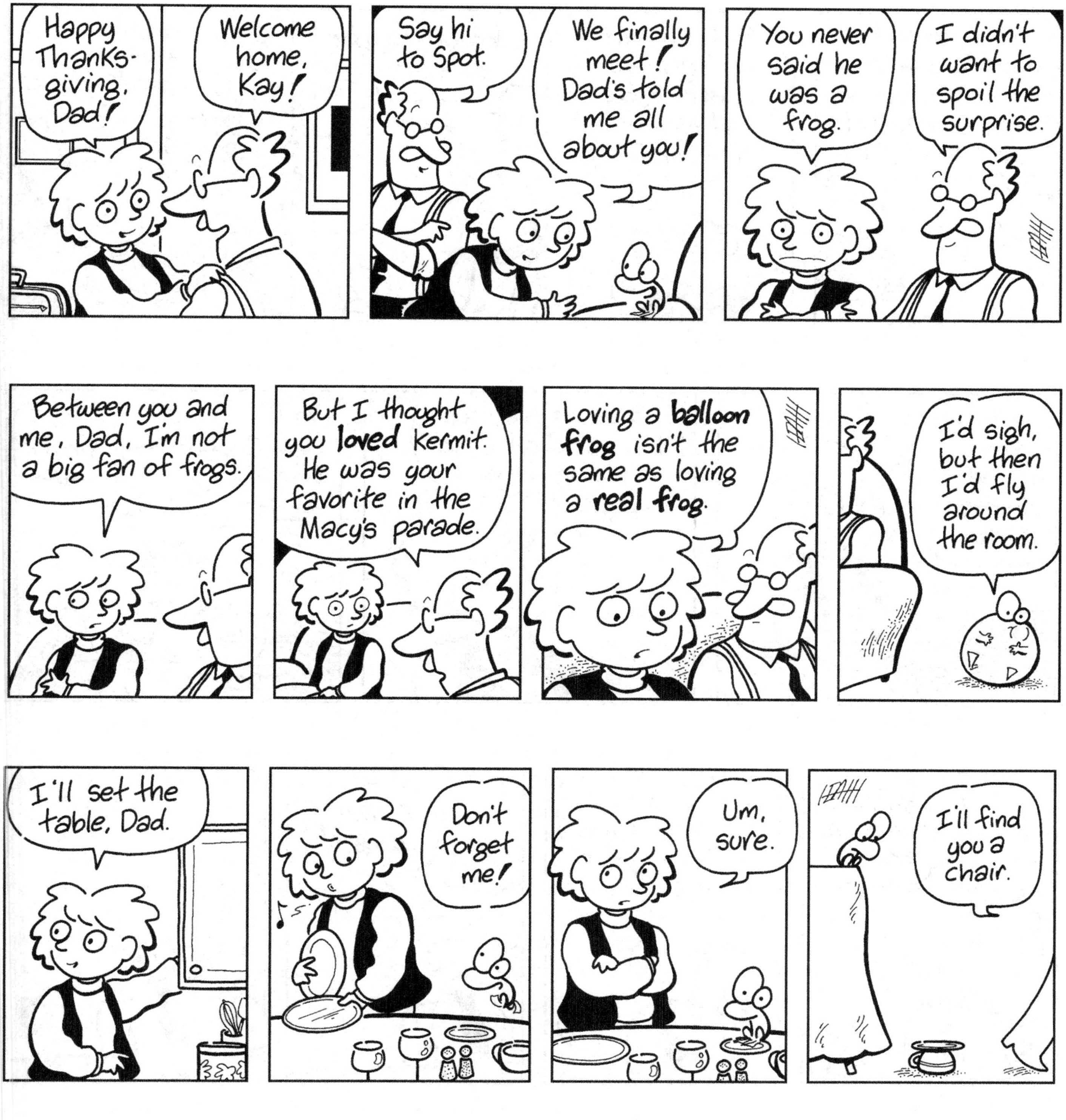
Happy Thanks-giving, Dad!
Welcome home, Kay!
Say hi to Spot.
We finally meet! Dad's told me all about you!
You never said he was a frog.
I didn't want to spoil the surprise.
Between you and me, Dad, I'm not a big fan of frogs.
But I thought you **loved** Kermit. He was your favorite in the Macy's parade.
Loving a **balloon frog** isn't the same as loving a **real frog**.
I'd sigh, but then I'd fly around the room.
I'll set the table, Dad.
Don't forget me!
Um, sure.
I'll find you a chair.

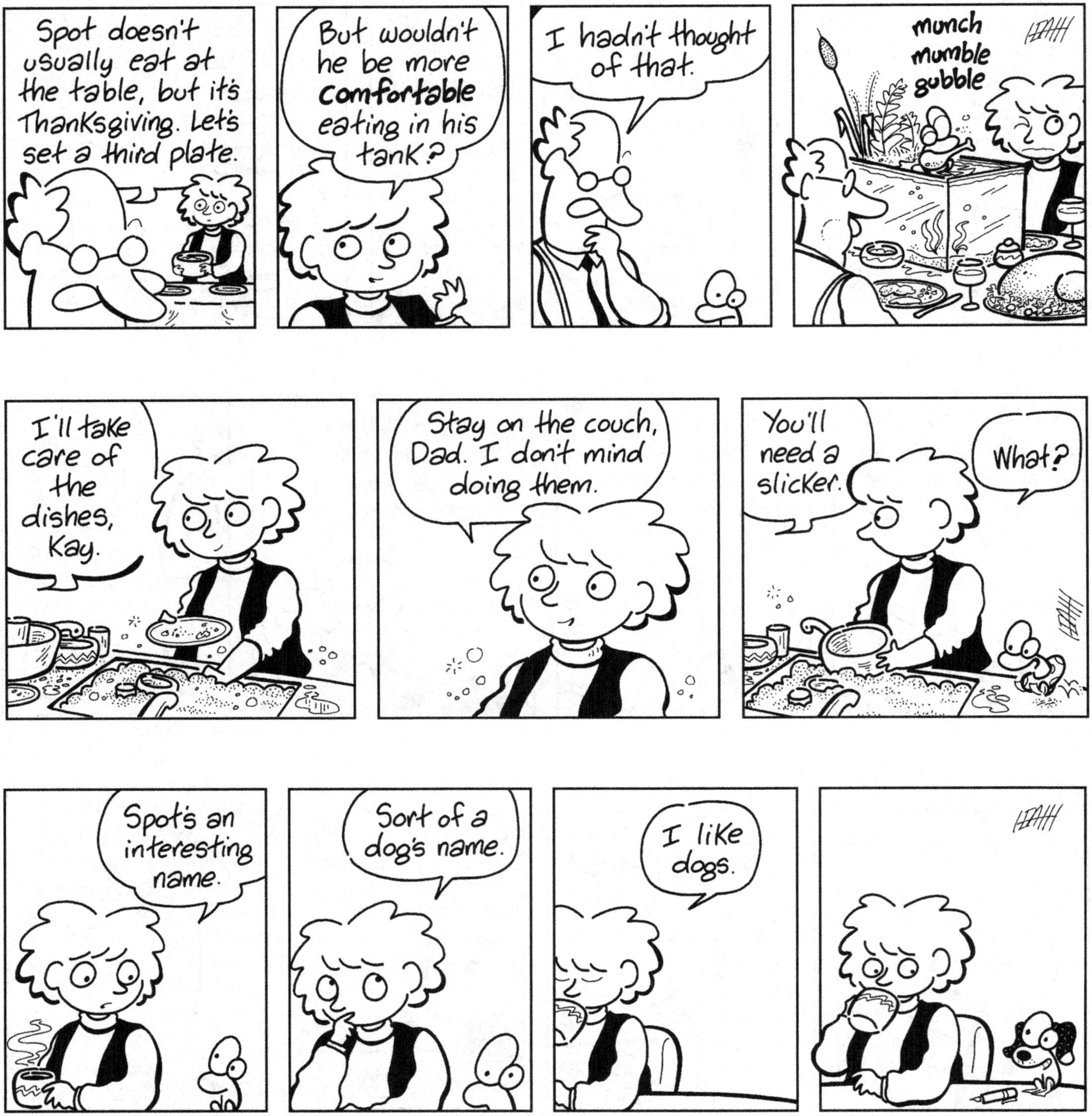

Spot doesn't usually eat at the table, but it's Thanksgiving. Let's set a third plate.
But wouldn't he be more **comfortable** eating in his tank?
I hadn't thought of that.
munch mumble gubble
I'll take care of the dishes, Kay.
Stay on the couch, Dad. I don't mind doing them.
You'll need a slicker.
What?
Spot's an interesting name.
Sort of a dog's name.
I like dogs.

SPOT
The Frog
by HEATH

rattle
bump
rattle
bump
Pull!
ba-da BAM
When it snows, we won't need the logs or rope.
Let's Keep the rope.

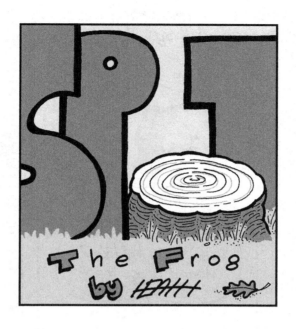

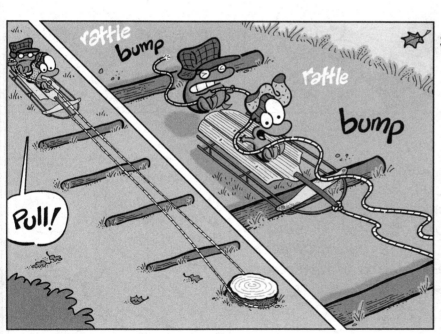

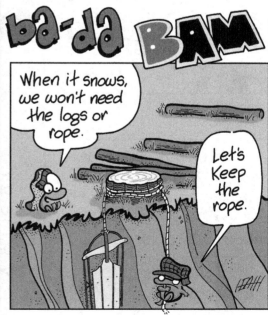

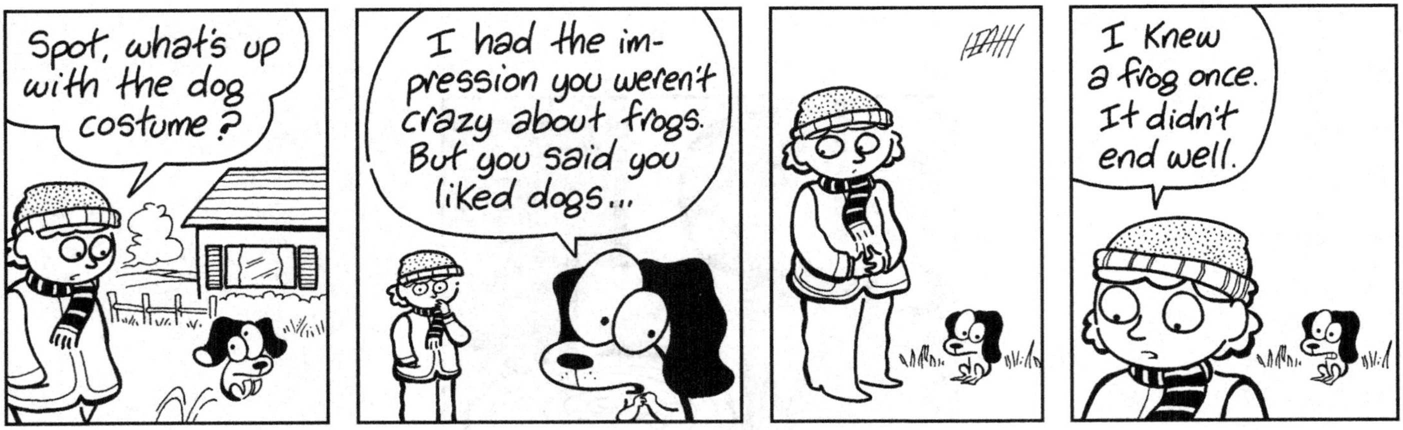
Spot, what's up with the dog costume?
I had the impression you weren't crazy about frogs. But you said you liked dogs...
I Knew a frog once. It didn't end well.

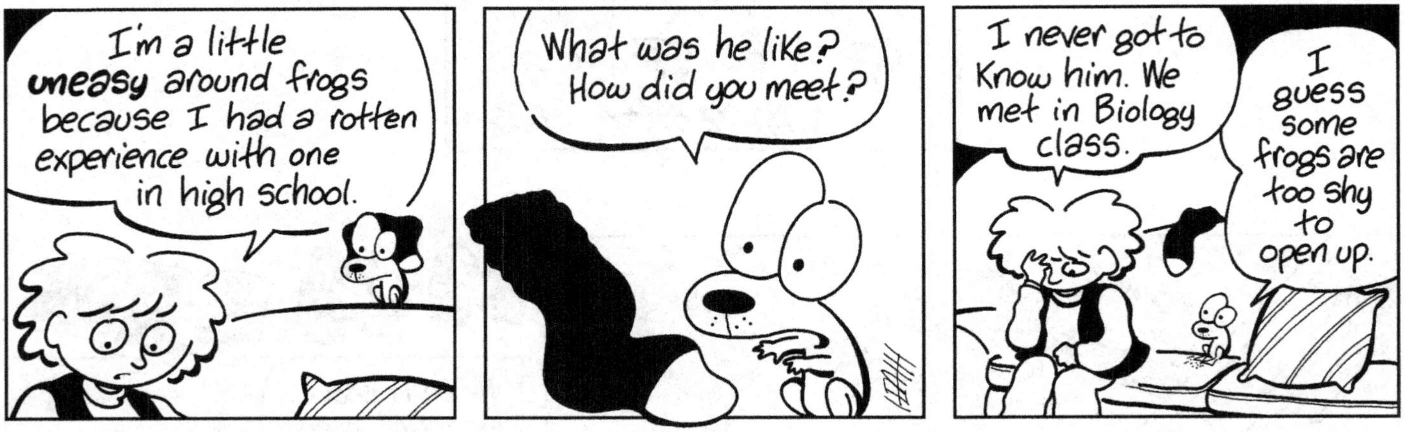
I'm a little **uneasy** around frogs because I had a rotten experience with one in high school.
What was he like? How did you meet?
I never got to Know him. We met in Biology class.
I guess some frogs are too shy to open up.

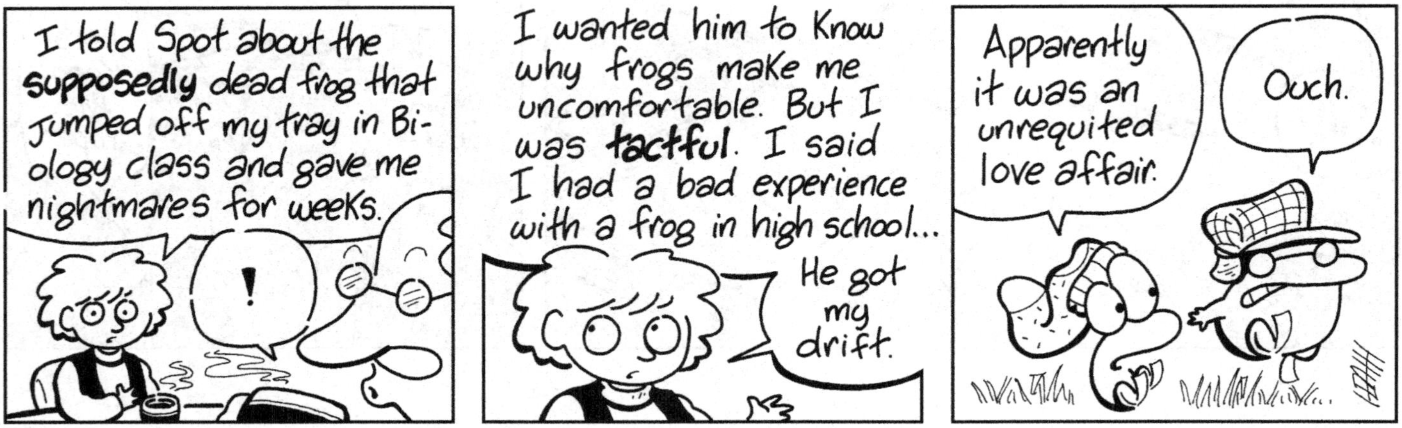
I told Spot about the **supposedly** dead frog that jumped off my tray in Biology class and gave me nightmares for weeks.
!
I wanted him to Know why frogs make me uncomfortable. But I was **tactful**. I said I had a bad experience with a frog in high school...
He got my drift.
Apparently it was an unrequited love affair.
Ouch.

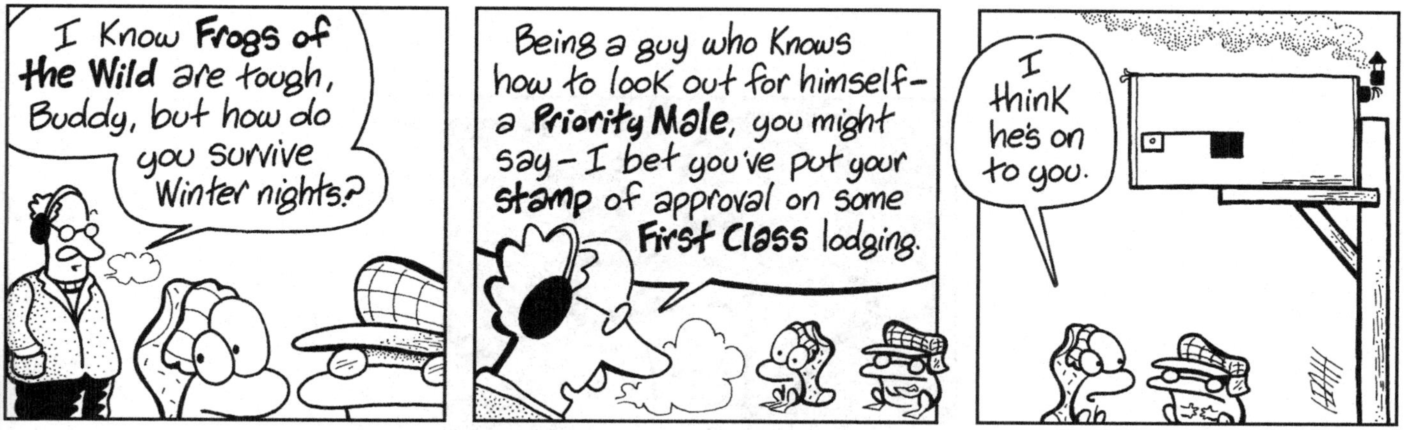
I Know Frogs of the Wild are tough, Buddy, but how do you survive Winter nights?
Being a guy who Knows how to look out for himself- a Priority Male, you might say - I bet you've put your stamp of approval on some First Class lodging.
I think he's on to you.

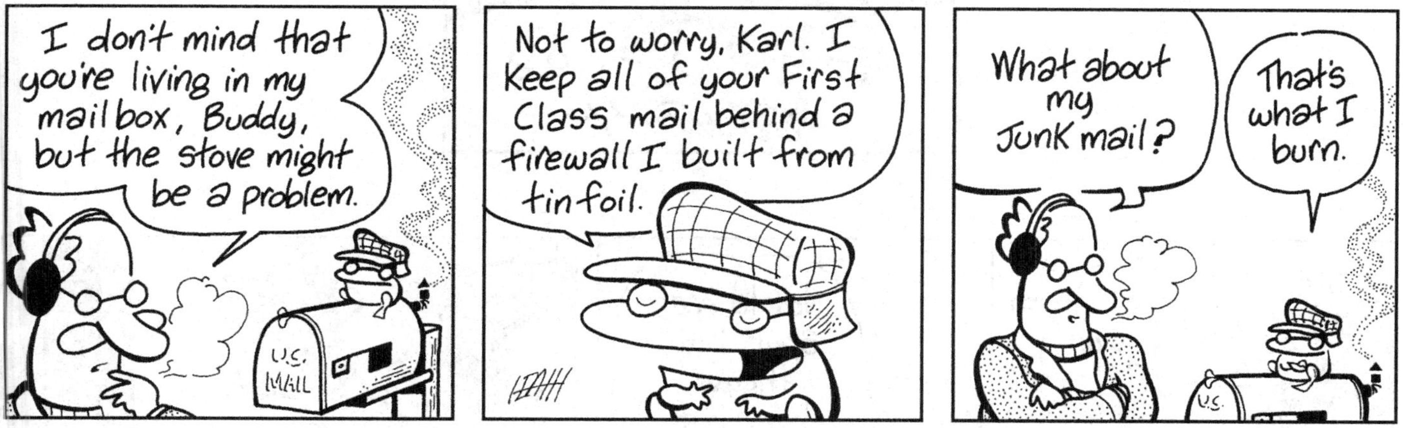
I don't mind that you're living in my mail box, Buddy, but the stove might be a problem.
U.S. MAIL
Not to worry, Karl. I Keep all of your First Class mail behind a firewall I built from tin foil.
What about my Junk mail?
That's what I burn.

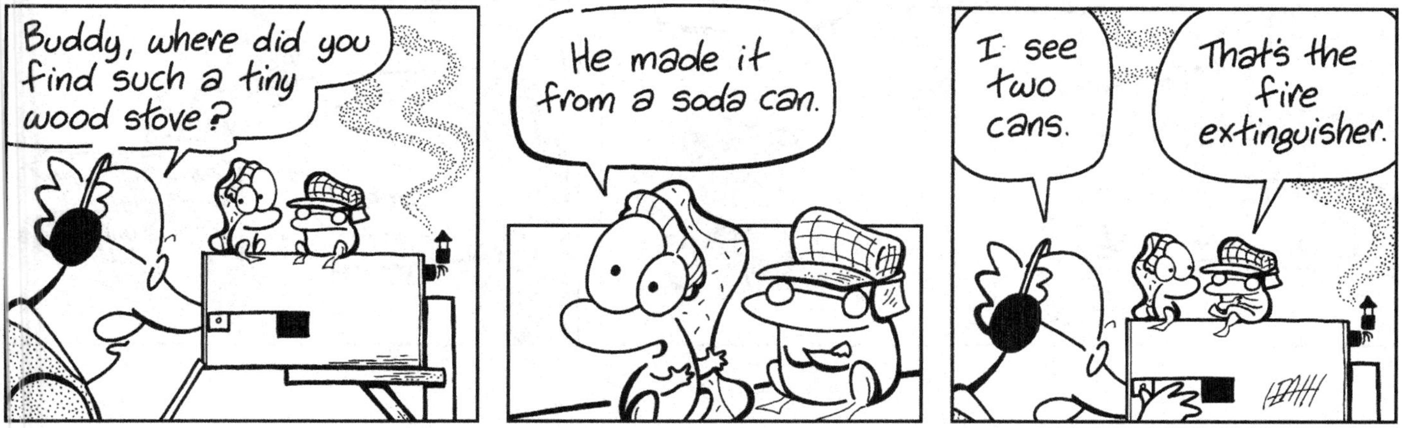
Buddy, where did you find such a tiny wood stove?
He made it from a soda can.
I see two cans.
That's the fire extinguisher.

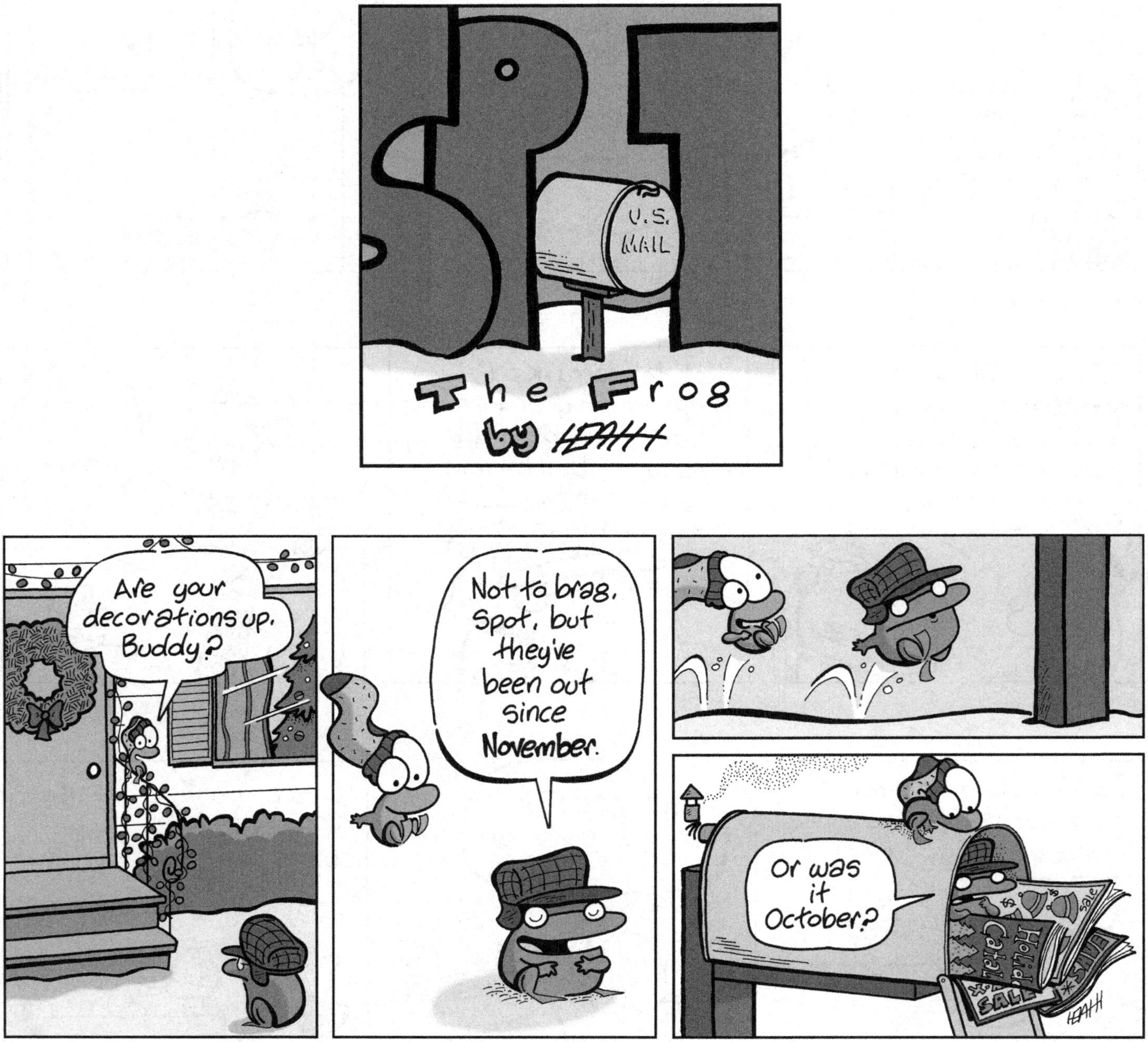
U.S. MAIL
The Frog
by
Are your decorations up, Buddy?
Not to brag, Spot, but they've been out since **November**.
Or was it October?
SALE
SAVE

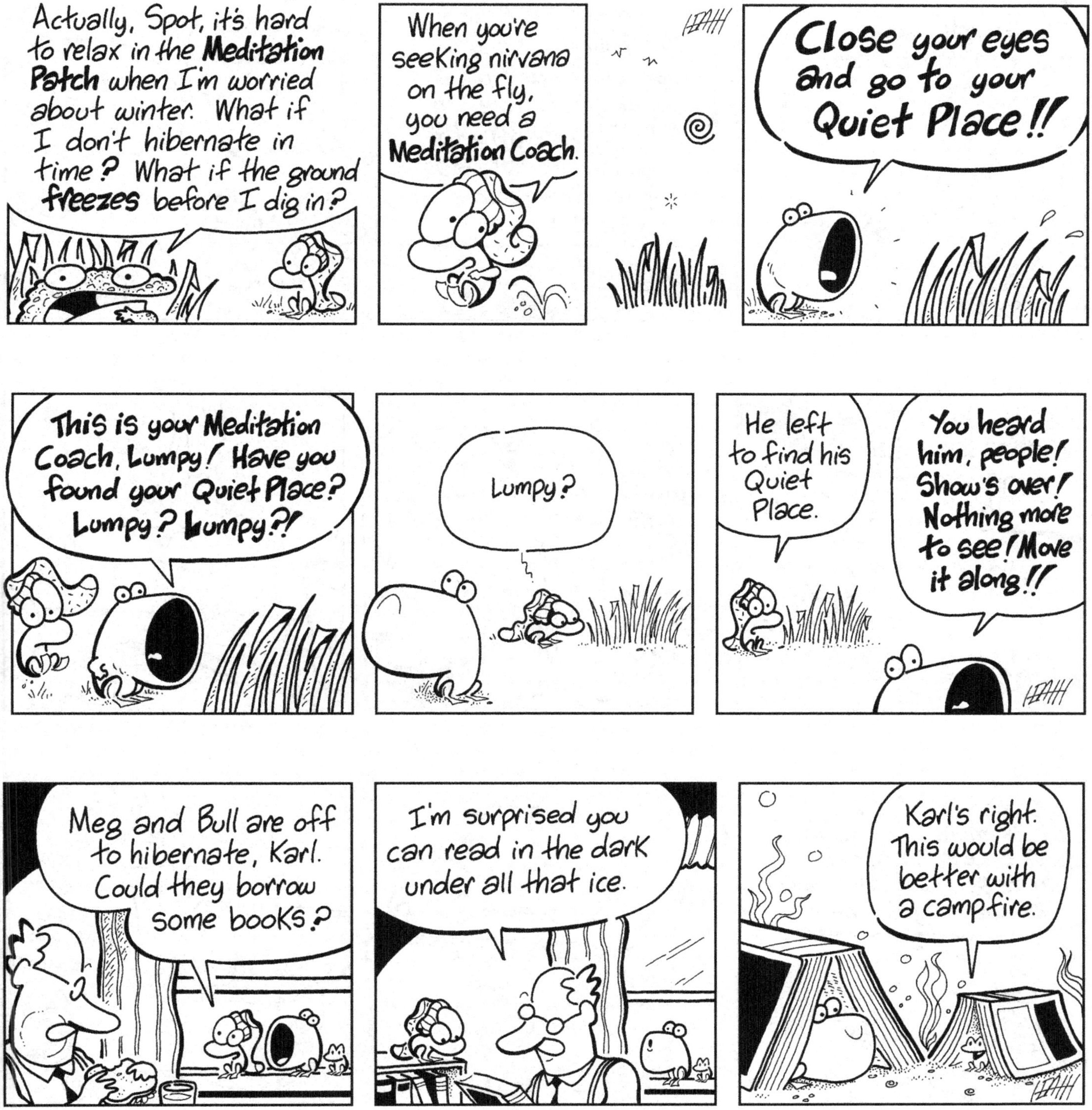
Actually, Spot, it's hard to relax in the **Meditation Patch** when I'm worried about winter. What if I don't hibernate in time? What if the ground **freezes** before I dig in?
When you're seeking nirvana on the fly, you need a **Meditation Coach**.
Close your eyes and go to your Quiet Place!!
This is your Meditation Coach, Lumpy! Have you found your Quiet Place? Lumpy? Lumpy?!
Lumpy?
He left to find his Quiet Place.
You heard him, people! Show's over! Nothing more to see! Move it along!!
Meg and Bull are off to hibernate, Karl. Could they borrow some books?
I'm surprised you can read in the dark under all that ice.
Karl's right. This would be better with a campfire.

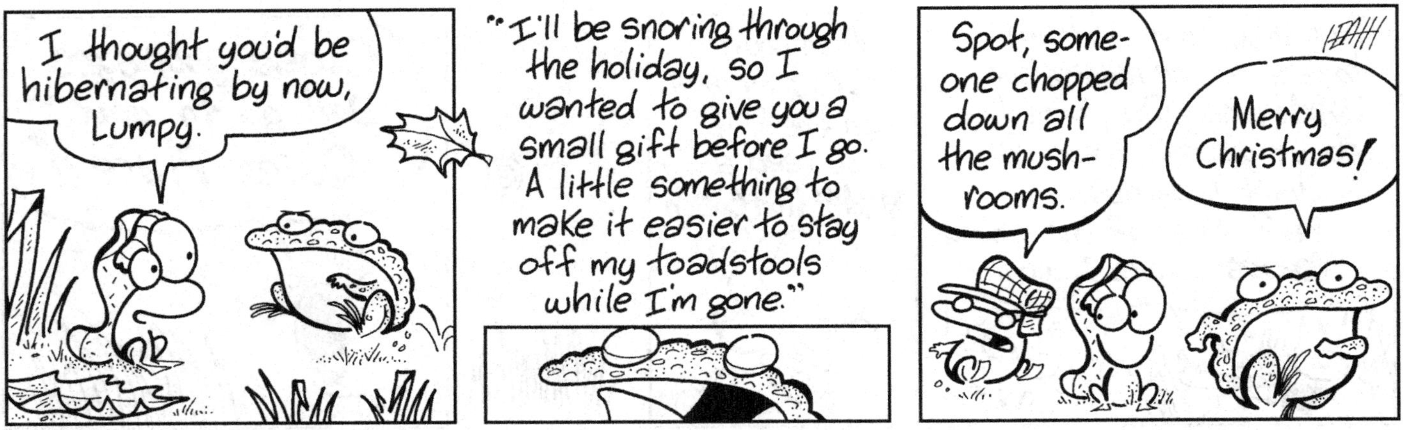
I thought you'd be hibernating by now, Lumpy.
"I'll be snoring through the holiday, so I wanted to give you a small gift before I go. A little something to make it easier to stay off my toadstools while I'm gone."
Spot, someone chopped down all the mushrooms.
Merry Christmas!

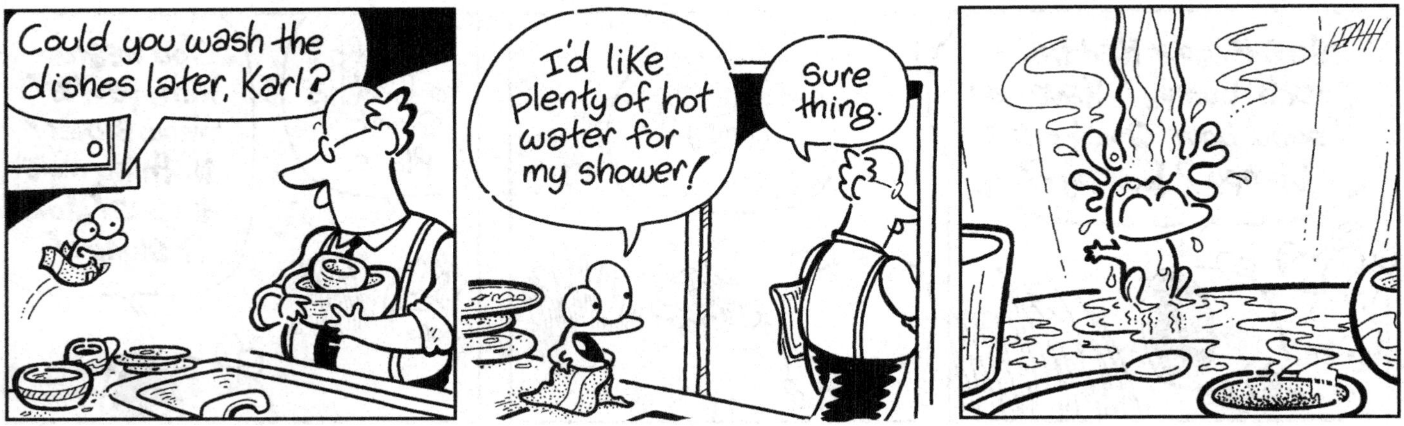
Could you wash the dishes later, Karl?
I'd like plenty of hot water for my shower!
Sure thing.

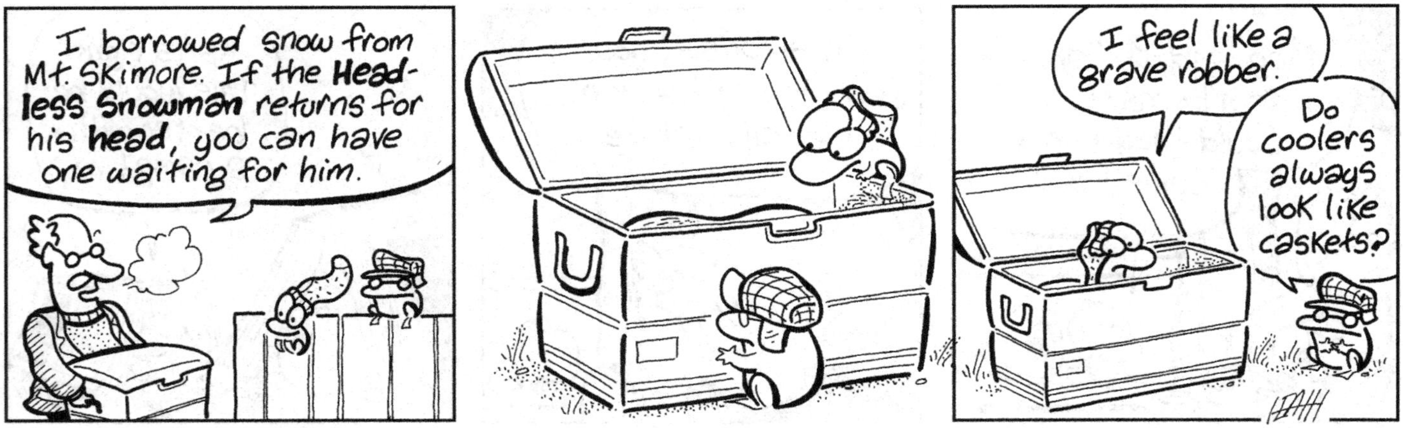
I borrowed snow from Mt. Skimore. If the Headless Snowman returns for his head, you can have one waiting for him.
I feel like a grave robber.
Do coolers always look like caskets?

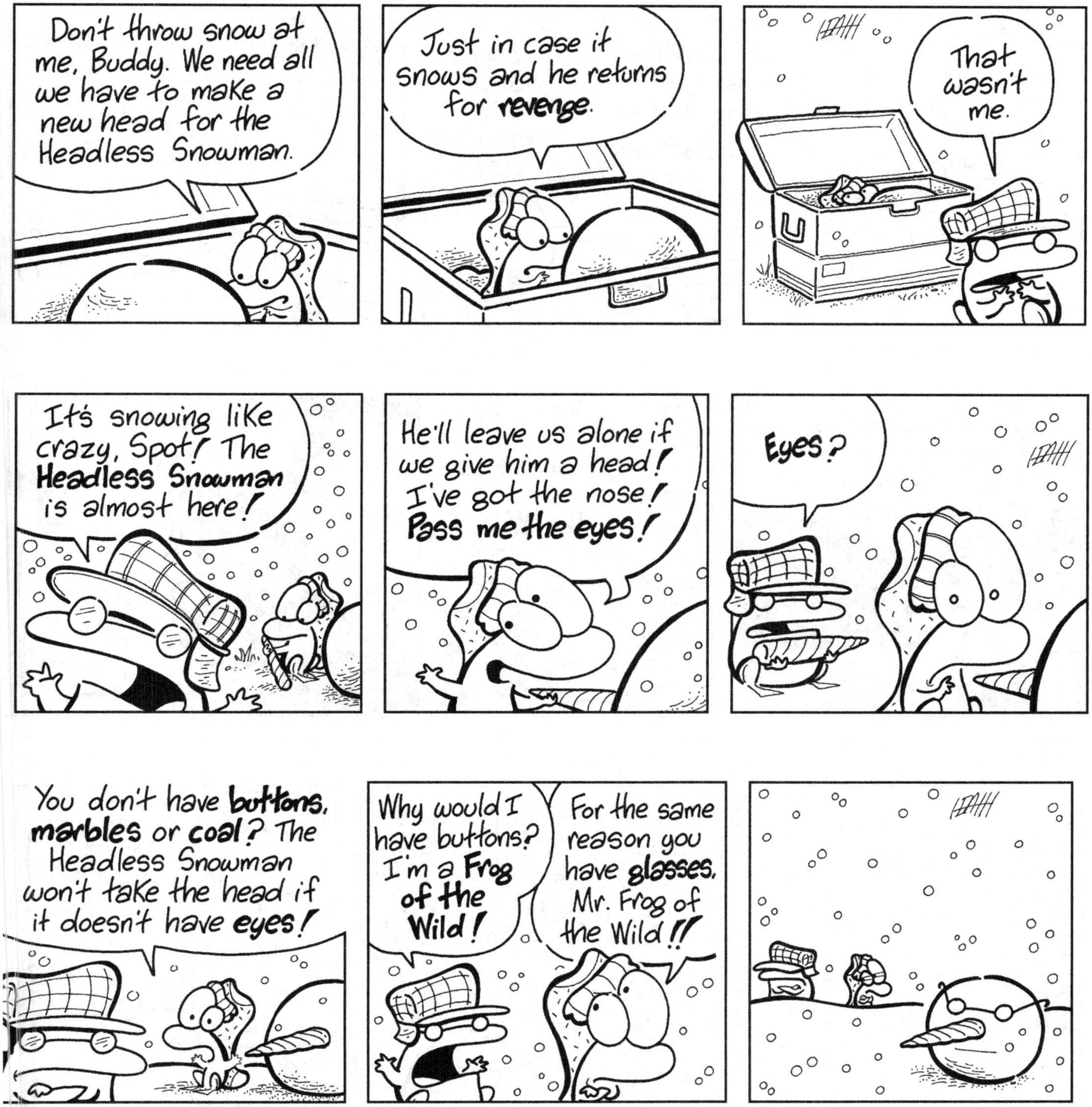

Don't throw snow at me, Buddy. We need all we have to make a new head for the Headless Snowman.
Just in case it snows and he returns for **revenge**.
That wasn't me.
It's snowing like crazy, Spot! The **Headless Snowman** is almost here!
He'll leave us alone if we give him a head! I've got the nose! **Pass me the eyes!**
Eyes?
You don't have **buttons, marbles** or **coal?** The Headless Snowman won't take the head if it doesn't have **eyes!**
Why would I have buttons? I'm a **Frog of the Wild!**
For the same reason you have **glasses**, Mr. Frog of the Wild!!

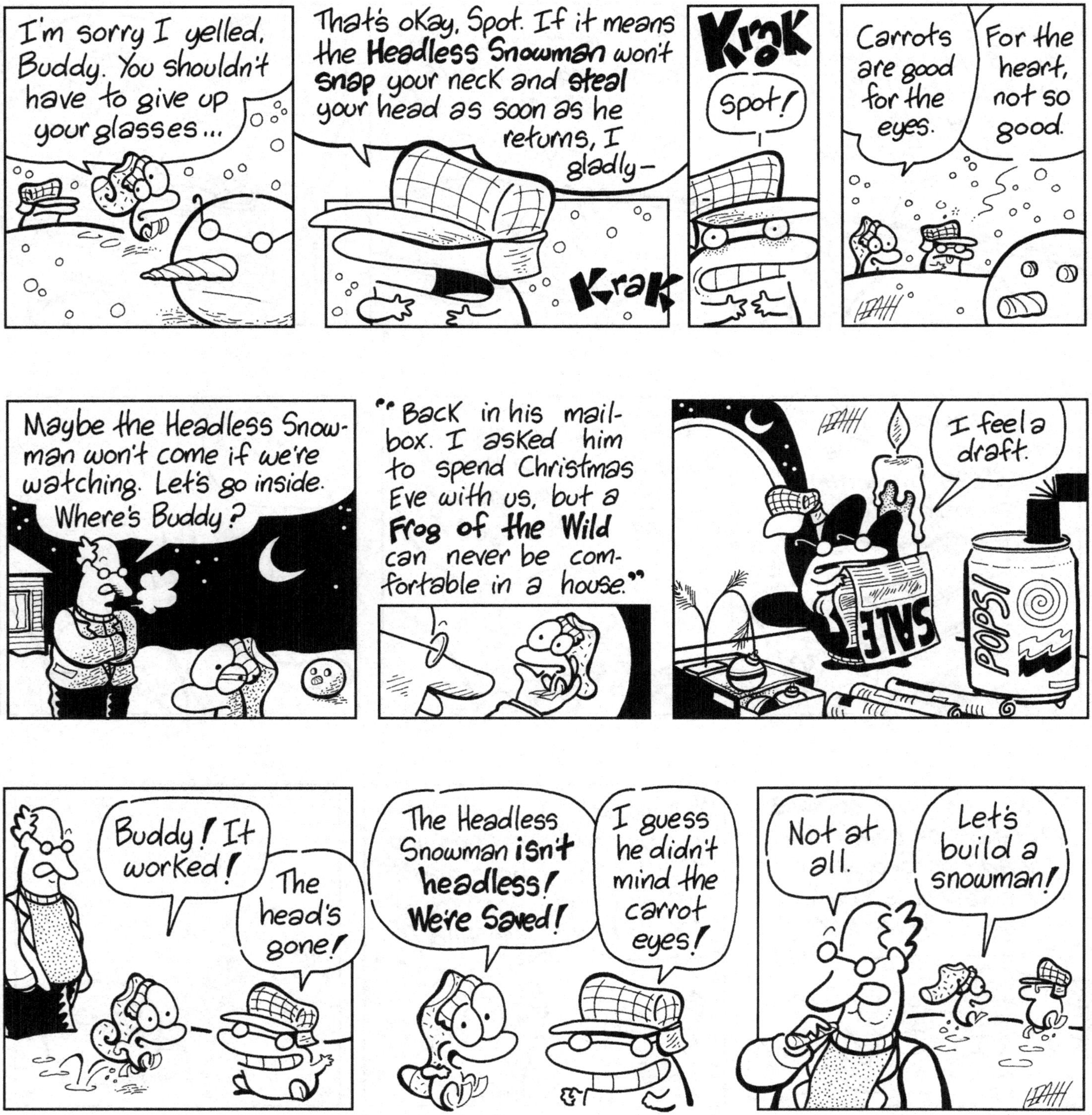

I'm sorry I yelled, Buddy. You shouldn't have to give up your glasses...
That's oKay, Spot. If it means the **Headless Snowman** won't **snap** your neck and **steal** your head as soon as he returns, I gladly–
Krak
Krak
Spot!
Carrots are good for the eyes.
For the heart, not so good.
Maybe the Headless Snowman won't come if we're watching. Let's go inside. Where's Buddy?
"Back in his mailbox. I asked him to spend Christmas Eve with us, but a **Frog of the Wild** can never be comfortable in a house."
I feel a draft.
SALE
POPS!
Buddy! It worked!
The head's gone!
The Headless Snowman **isn't headless! We're Saved!**
I guess he didn't mind the carrot eyes!
Not at all.
Let's build a snowman!

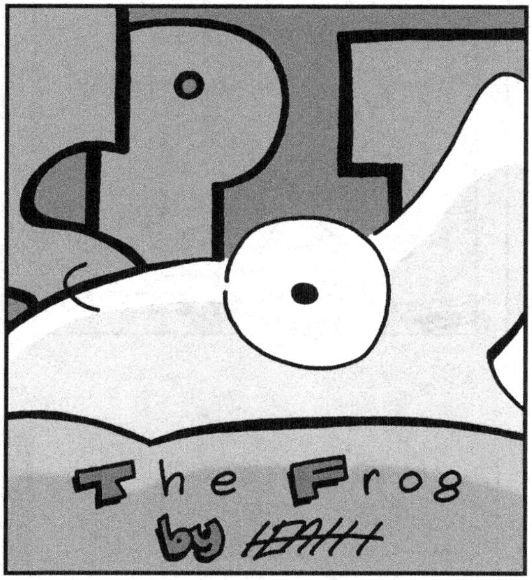
The Frog
by HEATH

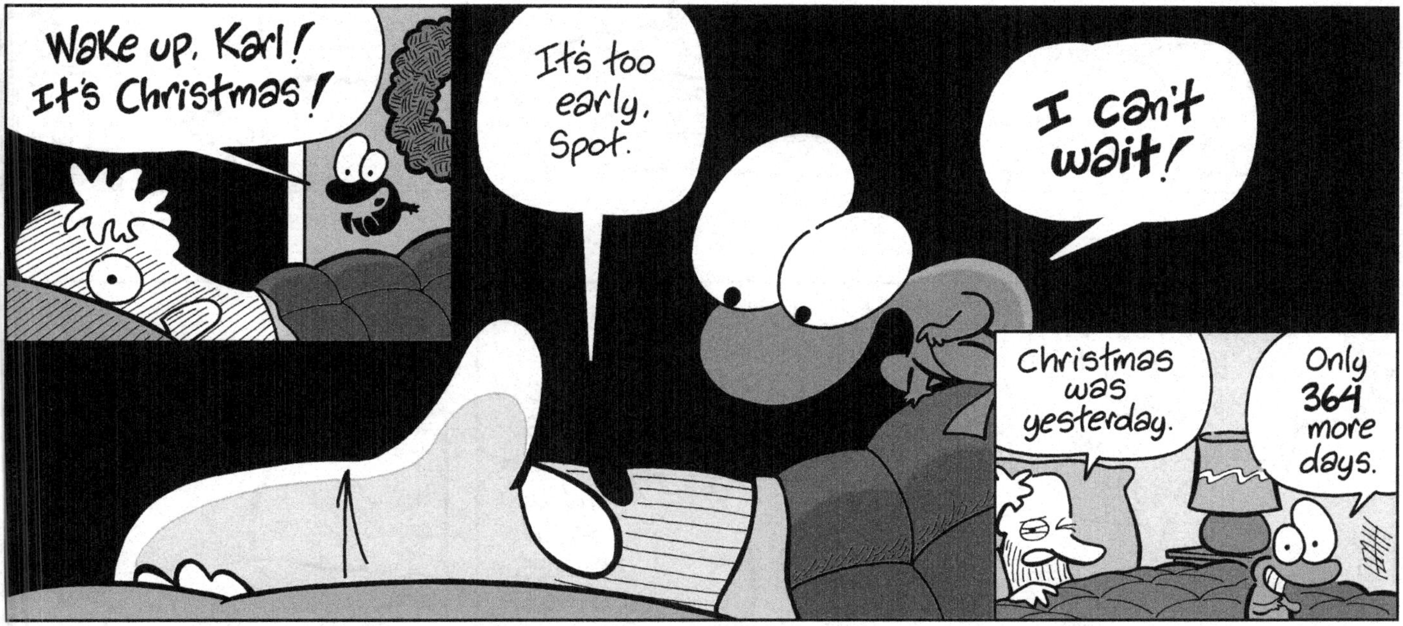
Wake up, Karl! It's Christmas!
It's too early, Spot.
I can't wait!
Christmas was yesterday.
Only 364 more days.

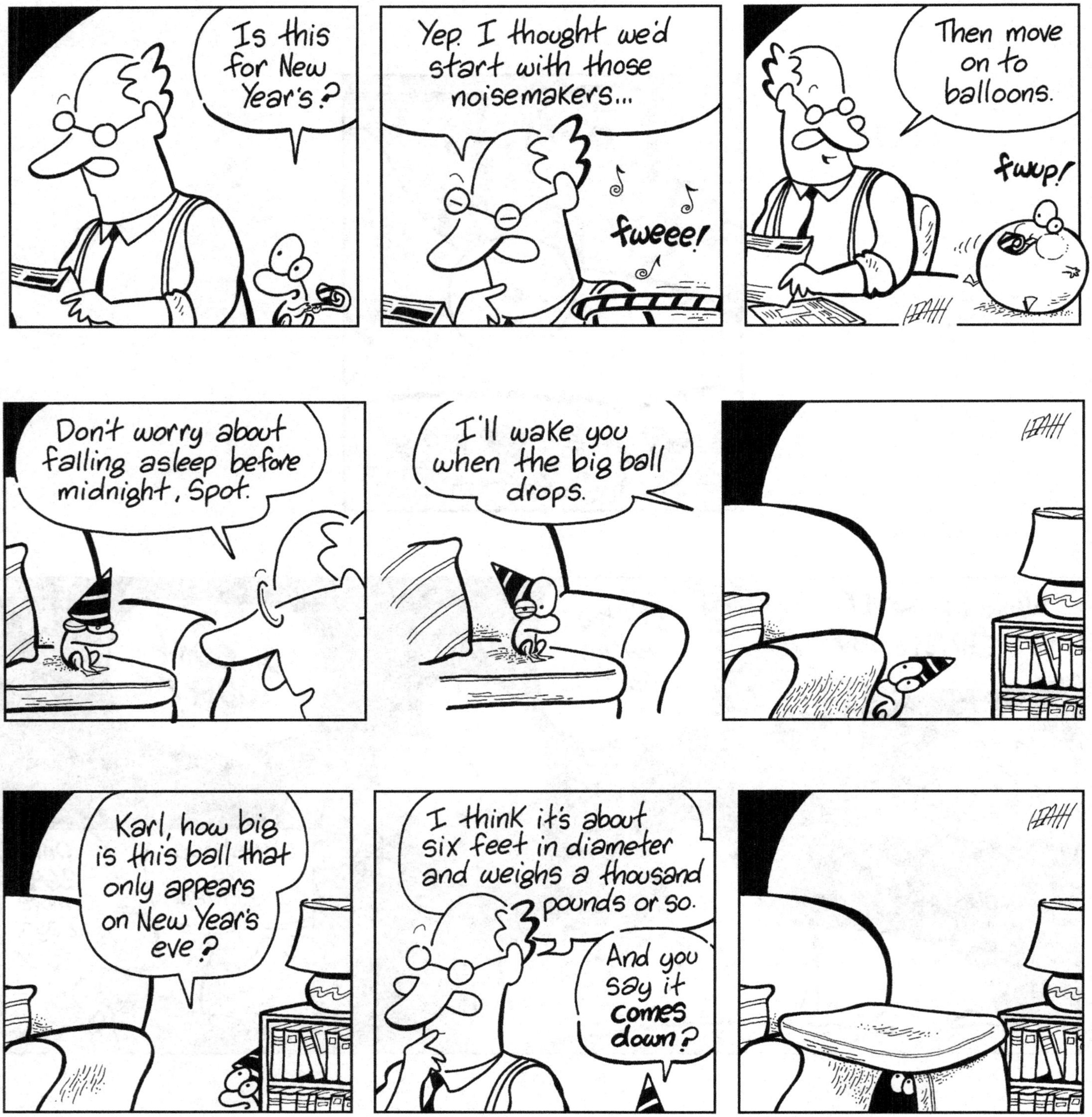

Is this for New Year's?
Yep. I thought we'd start with those noisemakers...
fweee!
Then move on to balloons.
fwup!
Don't worry about falling asleep before midnight, Spot.
I'll wake you when the big ball drops.
Karl, how big is this ball that only appears on New Year's eve?
I think it's about six feet in diameter and weighs a thousand pounds or so.
And you say it **comes down**?

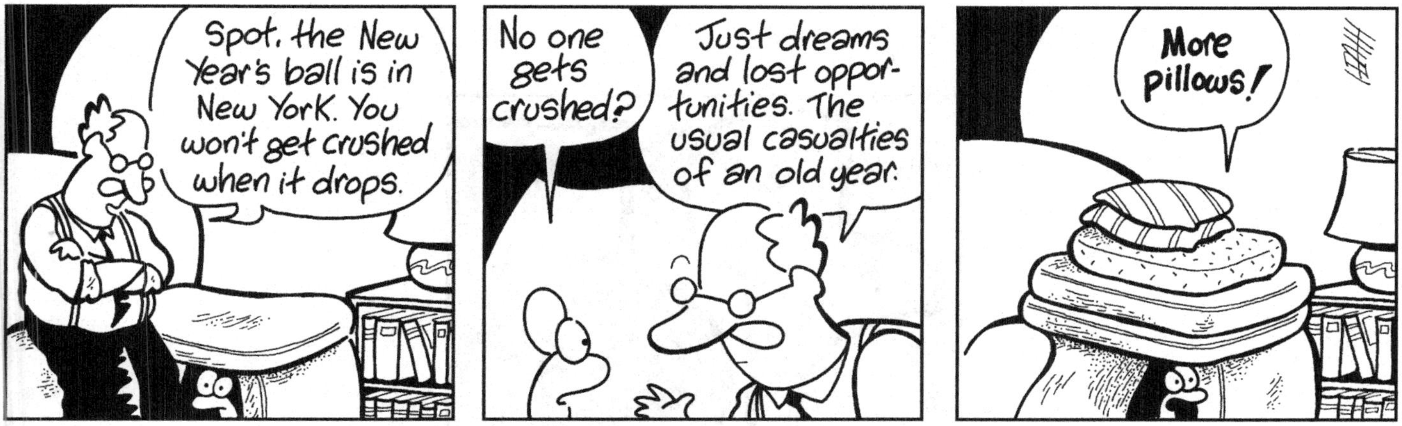
Spot, the New Year's ball is in New York. You won't get crushed when it drops.
No one gets crushed?
Just dreams and lost opportunities. The usual casualties of an old year.
More pillows!

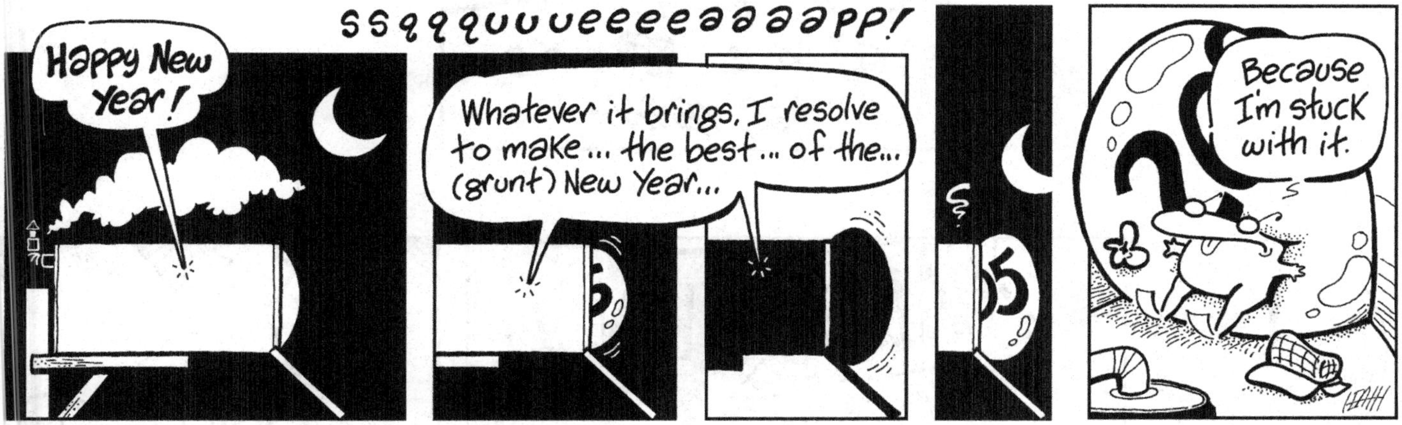
Happy New Year!
Whatever it brings, I resolve to make ... the best ... of the... (grunt) New Year...
SSQQQUUUEEEEAAAAPP!
Because I'm stuck with it.

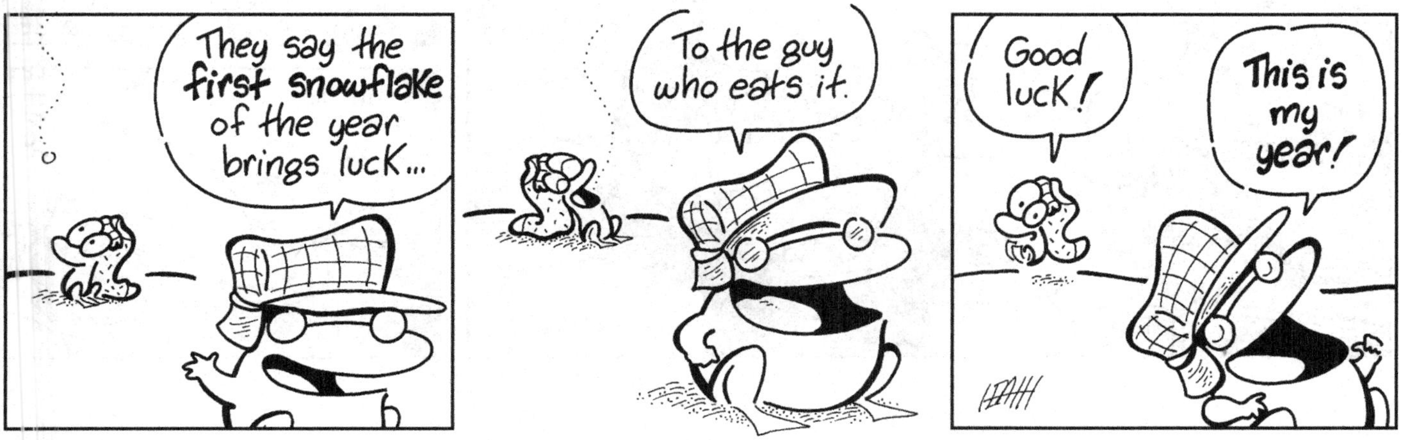
They say the **first snowflake** of the year brings luck...
To the guy who eats it.
Good luck!
This is my year!

Spot
The Frog
by HEATH

3... 2... 1...
HAPPY NEW YE
HEATH
TK TK TK TK

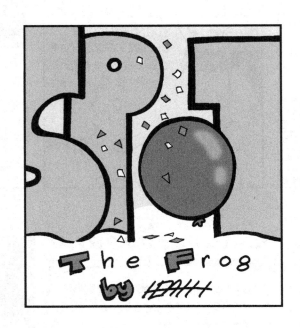

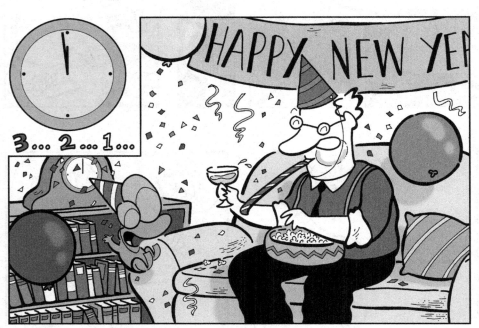

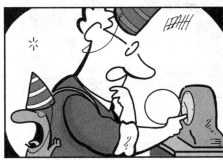

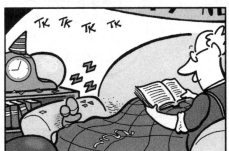

CPSIA information can be obtained
at www.ICGtesting.com
Printed in the USA
FSOW04n2016271116
27885FS